research on deviance

EDITED BY Jack D. Douglas UNIVERSITY OF CALIFORNIA AT SAN DIEGO

Random House, New York

research on deviance

ISBN: 0–394–31154–x

Library of Congress Catalog Card Number: 74–162703

Manufactured in the United States of America by Cherry Hill Composition
and printed and bound by Halliday Lithograph, Inc., West Hanover, Mass.

Typography and cover design by Hermann Strohbach
Cover photo by Charles Gatewood

First Edition

987654321

The editor wishes to thank all of those people
who read and offered valuable criticisms
of the essays in this volume

Preface

The sociology of deviance, crime, and social control has been undergoing a rapid transformation in recent years both in theory and methods of research. For the first century of its development this broad area of sociological theory and research was dominated by official definitions of deviance and by the desire of sociologists to help officials eliminate or control that deviance as officially defined. Sociologists relied predominantly on official information, especially official statistics, to construct and test their theories. Though some objections to this method were raised, they were lonely voices that had little effect on the mainstream of professional research and theory. Only in the past few decades have these objections increased vastly and turned the mainstream in wholly new directions. Most sociologists studying deviance today would agree that such a transformation has taken place and that it constitutes important progress for sociology.

Sociologists now realize that they must collect their own information if they are to construct valid theories of deviance. Only information subject to their own scientific controls over the methods of observation will provide such valid information. More specifically, the transformation has consisted of replacing statistical information with information gotten through participation in the everyday lives of the deviants that sociologists wish to study. This change has come about not because of any disregard for the importance of numbers, but simply because we do not yet have any means of getting statistical information that is reliable and valid. We believe firmly that we must concentrate our efforts on getting highly reliable and valid information about deviance through intensive case studies involving the use of participant-observation. Only when we have solved the problems involved in doing this can we hope to get comparable studies that will justify extensive quantification of our data.

There are now a large number of participant-observation studies of deviance that many sociologists have been using to construct theories of deviance in American society.* In view of this, it is remarkable that there has been so little effort to systematically describe and analyze the participant-observer methods used to do these studies. Since any method involves fundamental problems that must be analyzed and solved, one of the crucial aspects of progress in the field of the sociology of deviance will surely be that of describing and analyzing the

* Some of the outstanding participant-observer studies of deviance have been published in a companion volume, Jack D. Douglas (ed.), *Observations of Deviance* (New York: Random House, 1970).

methods of participant-observation used to do these important studies. This volume is intended to be a beginning of the serious effort to advance these methods.

As a first step in the development of systematic efforts, this work should be of major interest to all sociologists. But, in part because it is such an early stage of our efforts, this work will also be easily understood and appreciated by all students of sociology. And to make sure of this we have insisted on a clear and readable style in all the essays. In addition, the essays have been arranged so that the volume as a whole moves from the more general considerations of the nature of these methods to the problems involved and then to the best solutions to those problems. Because of these elements, this volume should serve, for all students, as a basic introduction to the methods of studying deviance, crime, social control, and many other social problems in American society today.

It is obvious that no work of this size can cover all the major forms of study in this broad area today, but I believe we have succeeded in covering the most important forms. Very importantly, I think that we have also succeeded in giving systematic, comparative consideration to all the problems and possible solutions that now seem to be the most important in the study of deviance.

While the volume as a whole goes from the more general to the more specific, and in part from the early stages of research to the later stages, each essay necessarily covers some of the same basic topics, such as the problem of establishing trust and managing fronts. This comparative approach is crucial in providing students and professionals with the information to determine what is essential in such studies and what is merely contingent on the peculiar circumstances of a given study.

It will undoubtedly take many years of efforts similar to those described in this book before we can feel very confident that we have unearthed all the basic questions concerning participant-observation studies of deviance or of any other form of social action; and, indeed, we may never be able to answer all the questions. But I believe the essays in this volume will contribute greatly to initiating the kind of systematic analyses of these studies that will eventually show us what the basic questions are and provide us with the best answers we can hope to obtain.

La Jolla, California   *Jack D. Douglas*

Contents

research on deviance

Observing Deviance

Jack D. Douglas

Until recently, sociologists have relied almost exclusively on official information on devlance to develop and test their theories of deviance. They have done so both because of the prevailing structural perspective on deviance and because they have found it personally difficult, or even distressing, to attempt to get information on deviance in any other way. Sociologists have only two obvious alternatives to making use of official information or to studying those subjects provided by officials. They are: (1) sociologists can claim omniscience, then take the common-sense stance and impose those meanings on deviance that they find most useful for the practical purpose at hand[1] (which until recent times was to denounce sin and to help officials to "control" it, but which lately has been to "show sympathy for the underdog"); or (2) sociologists can take a firsthand look at deviance, certainly commonsensical and long the standard practice of journalists. Sociologists have always been quite aware of both possibilities, but when committing themselves to an alternative to official information, they have almost always chosen to assume sociological omniscience.[2]

There are some practical reasons why sociologists have chosen commitment to official information and armchair omniscience over learning through participation. Participation is very time-consuming and arduous, especially when one must keep the offbeat hours of many deviants, as is evident from John Irwin's study of criminals. It is far quicker and easier to use previously constructed official information. Indeed, it is easier still to *impose* meanings on deviance rather than to have to beg, wheedle, inveigle, browbeat, threaten, or buy the information from individuals so "ignorant" as to distrust the intentions of the social scientist.

It is also safer, since it protects the sociologist from both deviants and law enforcement agents. And, finally, it is more respectable than keeping strange hours with odd people, which seems to be the crux of the matter.

As Ned Polsky has said, ". . . most sociologists find it too difficult or distasteful to get near adult criminals except in jails or other official settings, such as the courts and probation and parole systems."[3] Most of the "practical" reasons given for what we shall see is the very impractical surrender of the one reliable form of information on deviance have probably been rationalizations for what Polsky has rightly called the "sociologists' cop-out."

This situation is crucial to contemporary sociology, especially to that part of it concerned with the study of the fundamental aspects of moral meanings and moral actions in society—that is, with the study of deviance. We now know quite clearly that official information is not only an unreliable source for studying deviance but is systematically biased in line with the needs and desires of officials and important segments of the public, so that it provides a systematically distorted picture of deviance. We are equally convinced that we cannot do worthwhile scientific studies of deviance by assuming sociological omniscience, but must, rather, see the social meanings of the actions of members of society as fundamentally problematic to them and to ourselves as sociological observers.[4] In short, *the only alternative is to use almost exclusively some form of participation in order to observe deviance in its natural setting.*

We also know that we must become involved in the everyday lives of the individuals we wish to study so that we can come to share enough of the commonsense meanings of those activities to the individuals doing them to be able to understand what those meanings are. Only through such involvement can we "observe" the all-important social meanings of actions, since human beings are very subtle in controlling the impressions they give off about themselves. This is especially true of those groups considered deviant by important other groups in our society.[5] As we shall see, the necessity to become involved in the everyday lives of those labeled deviant entails some basic problems, including the danger that "hip sociologists" will *go native* and become "sympathetic" spokesmen for *moral interest groups* rather than seek objective knowledge of those groups. But these dangers simply must be met and overcome.

While almost all sociologists of deviance now recognize the necessity of using participant-observer methods to study deviance, there has been remarkably little attempt to analyze the general and special properties of such methods. Yet, because those considered deviant in our society are commonly so distrustful and so concerned with managing their own self-presentations, including hiding their identities,[6] there is great need to analyze and solve the special methodological problems involved. The purpose of this article and the others in this volume is to analyze these basic problems and to propose what now seem to be the best solutions to them.

The Research Bargain: The Sociologist's Risks and Gains in Overt and Covert Research

All problems of participant-observation involve the nature of the researcher's interaction with the people to be studied. As Martin S. Weinberg and Colin J. Williams have argued in the article entitled "Fieldwork Among Deviants," there are many phases in fieldwork interaction, but, from the researcher's point of view, the first question is: Why do these people agree to be studied? What do they get from allowing themselves to be studied at all? From the point of view of the people to be studied, the question is: Why be studied at all? And this immediately becomes the question: Why is this outsider studying us? Why does he want to talk with us? Why does he want to know things? What is he up to? Rarely does this problem not arise in participant-observer research. (One example of research in which there were no problems of this kind is Charles Fisher's study of protest demonstrations.)

From the very beginning of contact, the researcher has to decide upon the nature of his own involvement, which is of crucial importance in determining whether he can reach a successful research bargain with the group he wants to study. And most important, he must decide at the beginning whether he is going to try to do his research covertly (secretly) or overtly and try to provide some explicit reason for doing it that will both communicate the idea of research to the group and be seen as justified by them.

As one would expect, there has been considerable argument, both among sociologists and those outside the field, over the whole issue of *secret research*. Two fundamental questions are involved in this issue: (1) the question of *effectiveness*—Which provides the more reliable evidence, secret or nonsecret involvement? and (2) the question of *morality*—Is secret research immoral and, if so, should it therefore be rejected by sociologists?

The tradition of field research developed by the Chicago sociologists, which is the only highly developed tradition of field research in sociology, generally involves the assumption that secret methods are both ineffective and immoral. Effectiveness is really the primary issue, since one must first decide that secrecy is somehow effective before he cares whether it is moral. Invalid information, whether morally or immorally obtained, is worthless.

The Chicago field researchers argue that the definition of oneself as a sociological researcher does not bias the observations. They believe that individuals under study may at first find the idea strange and that this may affect their observable behavior, but that they quickly get used to the idea and often forget about it. They believe the sociologist becomes a taken-for-granted presence—that is, *if* he establishes trust and *rapport,* which are, in any case, necessary to his being accepted at all or gaining *entrée* to the group. Moreover, the Chicago researchers generally argue that defining oneself as a member and trying to do secret research actually make many things unobservable to a researcher. There are things that members would be willing to expose to a trusted individual who is not a member because he will not use the information against members to advance himself in the organization, as ordinary members might do.

But how is one to know that these answers are correct? Howard Becker, probably the best-known member of the Chicago school of the study of deviance, argues that it is generally best to define yourself as a researcher to the group being studied, but at the same time he notes the disagreement that exists over this and has suggested that there may well be situations in which the researcher on deviance must "pass" as one of the deviants. He also notes the lack of good evidence to test the point:

Supposing you have found your observation post, what role will you play once you are there? The major choices are to disguise yourself as one of the deviants . . . , to be one of the service personnel associated with the location (a waitress in a homosexual bar, for example), or to make yourself known as a researcher. The latter choice gives you great freedom to pursue your scientific interests, for you need not tailor what you do and ask to what would be appropriate to an occupant of either of the other roles, but can instead ask and do a great variety of things, offering science as the justification. Furthermore, you can avoid incriminating or distasteful participation in deviant activities on the reasonable grounds that, while perhaps sympathetic, you are not really "one" yourself. Many researchers feel, however, that to be known as an outsider will severely limit the amount of information one can get. I do not believe the problem that severe, but know of no evidence on the point.[7]

Neither the Chicago sociologists nor anyone else has ever systematically sought to determine the truth of such assumptions by subjecting them to systematic comparisons—that is, by doing research with one method and comparing the results with those obtained by using other methods. Indeed, the whole Chicago tradition has remained very largely an oral tradition that is unexplicated and certainly undemonstrated. Their argument seems to be that their long experience in the field has shown them that the definition of oneself as a researcher does not significantly affect the findings and it may lead to more useful information. This would seem to imply that they have tried it both ways, but this does not appear to have been the case, since they also generally have such strong moral rules against secrecy. They could quite legitimately argue, however, that in some few instances they have studied groups, in which they had previously been involved as members, by explicitly defining themselves as researchers. To some extent, for example, this could be argued for Becker's study of marijuana use among jazz musicians.[8] The researcher had been a member of the same or similar groups for long periods and then did explicitly defined research on them. Presumably, he found no basic differences between his *member knowledge* and his *researcher knowledge.* But there is a problem involved here. For this argument, were it made, would not only imply that one *should* have comparisons with secret research, but that, in fact, in these cases the researchers did *what amounted to secret research,* though without raising a moral issue.

An evaluation of the effectiveness of covert versus overt participant-observer methods is not yet possible, for we know too little about the actual effects of the different methods on the individuals being observed. It will take more systematic comparisons of alternative methods to determine the effectiveness of the methods. Even then there will be some irreducible element of uncertainty, since in order to check the validity of any findings we would have to compare them with what we know to be "true" from some other method, which, in turn, would presuppose that we already know what is a more valid method.

Strictly from the standpoint of effectiveness, it seems apparent that we should remain flexible in our methods.[9] Since some deviant groups are loath to be "revealed" to anyone, it is probable that some forms of information can be gotten only through using secret research. This would necessitate an individual's having a high degree of member knowledge, which he would presumably get only from long involvement with the group *as a member,* either from previous membership or from a carefully controlled entrance for purposes of research. This approach has serious potential problems; for example, exposure of one's research identity, or "blowing one's cover," could prove dangerous in some cases. But for some purposes researchers may decide that the possible information gained through such risks outweighs the problems. In fact, some sociologists studying deviance have long accepted the risks. Both Howard Becker's study of marijuana use among jazz musicians and Ned Polsky's study of poolroom hustlers were based largely on their member knowledge gained from years as members of those groups. Laud Humphreys' study of public restroom homosexuality involved the acceptance of the far greater risk of arrest and stigmatization entailed by his becoming a "lookout" for the homosexuals.[10]

Although some of the moral objections to secret research undoubtedly involve considerable academic posing and "priggishness," there are serious moral questions involved that any sociologist considering such methods must certainly face. In a pluralistic society such as ours—but one in which there is nonetheless a strong emphasis on public conformity to the absolute public morality—privacy becomes a highly valued thing.[11] This is especially so today because of the development of technical devices that can secretly circumvent the traditional measures taken to protect privacy. In addition, it is precisely such invasions of privacy that could facilitate the establishment of *technological tyrannies*;[12] and few of us wish to make a contribution toward creating a *1984.*

But, while I believe we must take the moral issues seriously and move cautiously to keep from contributing to the forces of technological tyranny, I do concur with James Henslin that we must avoid any form of *methodological puritanism.* Most members of our society believe that the search for truth, while never wholly devoid of personal interests and moral dangers, is justified in itself, but we are all dimly aware of the early doctors who were suspected of ghastly crimes because of their perseverance in exploring the mysteries of the human body. And today, many people still find this secularization—and "desecration"—of our physical being morally repulsive; they cannot appreciate the common medical cast of mind in which gynecological examinations of young girls and autopsies are seen as necessary forms of medical bookkeeping and are assumed to be devoid of all moral significance for the people involved. On the other hand, most of us can also appreciate the moral courage of those early doctors which supported their "immoral" invasions of the body's mysteries, and, while we condemn the scientistic mechanism that makes some doctors blind to our human sensibilities, most of us do support the *moral exceptions* to our usual moral feelings that allow their work to continue.

There is a danger, then, that the use of secret research will encourage a moral blindness and a willingness to *use* people among sociologists, especially among those who already have the scientistic stance. Like all human action, research on deviance involves the possibility of abuse, of going too far. We must specifically guard against such abuse by recognizing it as a danger and instituting measures against it.

As doctors, lawyers, and other professionals have done over the centuries, sociologists must work purposefully to carve out a special *moral niche*, or to construct a *situational morality*, for their research activities. Exceptions to important social rules, such as those concerning privacy and intimacy, must be made only when the research need is clear and the potential contributions of the findings to general human welfare are believed to be great enough to counterbalance the risks. If we can agree that these factors are present (so that we do not run the risk of unleashing "mad social scientists" upon the world to fulfill their own Frankenstein fantasies), then we should have the courage to try to change the morals of our society and to do the research with as little invasion of privacy as possible.

As is obvious from the legal risks taken during James Carey's research, we must try to extend to social scientists the legal protection lawyers and doctors have from prosecution for being accessories to crimes. As Polsky so rightly argues, until we are able to do this, sociologists cannot avoid violating laws against being accessories:

If one is effectively to study adult criminals in their natural settings, he must make the moral decision that in some ways he will break the law himself. He need not be a "participant" observer and commit the criminal acts under study, yet he has to witness such acts or be taken into confidence about them and not blow the whistle. That is, the investigator has to decide that when necessary he will "obstruct justice" or have "guilty knowledge" or be an "accessory" before or after the fact, in the full legal sense of those terms. He will not be enabled to discern some vital aspects of criminal life-styles and subcultures unless he (1) makes such a moral decision, (2) makes the criminals believe him, and (3) convinces them of his ability to act in accord with his decision. That third point can sometimes be neglected with juvenile delinquents, for they know that a professional studying them is almost always exempt from police pressure to inform; but adult criminals have no such assurance, and hence are concerned to assess not merely the investigator's intentions but his ability to remain a "stand-up guy" under police questioning.[13]

While it is probable that legal exclusion from prosecution for such "research offenses" will eventually be given, there will be some small risks involved for a long time to come, which will have to be accepted if truthful information is to be gotten.

The case for purposeful involvement in the crimes themselves is very different. Though refusal to at least "go along" to observe the on-site action *might* jeopardize one's research relations and will certainly prevent our knowing what really happens at the scene of a crime, legal defense of such participation does not at present seem possible. In addition, this participation is generally unnecessary and can itself endanger research relations. William Foote Whyte, who took part in the illegal actions of multiple voting with his gang boys, recognized this long ago:

That was my performance on election day. What did I gain from it? I had seen through firsthand personal experience how repeating was accomplished. But this was really of very little value, for I had been observing these activities at quite close range before, and I could have had all the data without taking any risk. Actually, I learned nothing of research value from the experience, and I took a chance of jeopardizing my whole study. While I escaped arrest, these things are not always fixed as firmly as the politician's henchmen think they are. A year later, when I was out of town at election time, somebody was actually arrested for voting in *my* name.

Even apart from the risk of arrest, I faced other possible losses. While repeating was fairly common in our ward, there were only relatively few people who engaged in it, and they were generally looked down upon as the fellows who did the dirty work. Had the word got around about me, my own standing in the district would have suffered considerable damage.[14]

The Research Bargain: The Member's Risks and Gains in the Research Situation

Whether the researcher uses a *research cover* or explicitly defines his research purposes for the group, once he has answered the group members' first crucial question—What is he up to?—he will be asked the second—What's in it for me? While the economic exchange model of human behavior is a gross distortion of social interaction, nonetheless a primary concern when we first encounter a stranger who seeks to make our acquaintance is the potential value, help, bother, burden, fun, and so on, of this relationship to us: What's in it for me? What good? What harm?

Rosalie Wax has given an excellent outline to this exchange model of the research encounter:

"Why should anybody in this group bother to talk to me? Why should this man take time out from his work, gambling, or pleasant loafing to answer my questions?" I suggest that as the field worker discovers the correct answers he will improve not only his technique in obtaining information but also his ability to evaluate it. I suggest moreover, that the correct answers to these questions will tend to show that whether an informant likes, hates, or just doesn't give a hoot about the field worker, he will talk because he and the field worker are making an exchange, are consciously or unconsciously giving each other something they both desire or need.

The gifts with which a field worker repays the efforts of his informants will, of course, vary with each investigational situation. Some will be simple gifts like relieving boredom or loneliness. Others will be on a more complicated psychological level, like giving an informant who thinks himself wronged an opportunity to express his grievances. And, not infrequently, the field worker who comes to understand why an informant talks to him will not be particularly flattered by this knowledge.

The fact that many informants talk freely because they are lonely or bored is perhaps not sufficiently appreciated by young field workers. Notebooks full of data may be acquired from an elderly person or from an individual who does not get along well in his community. The skill of the interviewer often plays a minor part in the accumulation of these data. The lonely informant has simply found someone who will listen to him.[15]

In general, the specific situation in which any human communication takes place becomes the contextual determinant of the meaning of that communication for the individuals involved. The sociologist seeking information on a group must, therefore, understand the meaningful properties of the situation in which communication occurs for the people with whom he is communicating. This is necessary so that he can analyze the ways in which the situation is determining the meanings of the communications. He must know the properties of the situation not only to determine how "true" the information is but to be able to even determine the meanings of the communications.

Specifically, in studying deviance we must be concerned with determining the meaningful properties of the encounter situation with deviants, especially the *initial encounter situation*—the *entrée situation* in which the sociologist is trying to specify his intentions in such a way that the deviants will find them acceptable and will be willing to give him truthful information. (There will, of course, be a fundamental difference between those situations in which the sociologist is trying to join the group for purposes of secret research and those in which he is trying to define himself for the group as a researcher. There is probably little that can be said of the secret research situation that would be of much help to any researcher. There are, of course, certain obvious things, such as the risk involved in disclosure or the possible problems involved in getting information from someone who simply sees you as another member of the group. Much more can be said about the encounter situation involving an explicit definition of oneself as a social researcher and, since the great mass of social research on deviants will probably continue to be of this sort, this more important situation will concern us here.)

In any situation, there are the inevitable contingencies of human interaction that can in no way be anticipated; for example, the invitations by homosexuals to Weinberg and Williams to "slow dance." The researcher must use common sense in such a situation to accurately manage it. These are, in fact, the most important aspects of any research encounter and, other than such general commentary as this, we necessarily leave them unexplicated. What we must seek in any analysis of the research situation is not specific details on how to handle the situation but general understandings or *research recipes* that the individual can use in constructing effective situational strategies for managing the situation.

As Carol A. B. Warren found during her research into the gay community, *trust* is the crucial factor involved in establishing a research relationship. This is true of the situation of deviance in general. In the deviant encounter situation, the most important factor related to trust is probably the suspicions that deviants might have about the relationship existing between the researcher and the deviants' enemies, especially official control agents. It is, therefore, essential that the researcher in some way convince the people he wants to study that he does not represent the officials and that his future statements about the group will in no way be of value to officials in controlling that group. He accomplishes this partly by his *personal style*—that is, by showing that he is not the kind of person who is apt to cooperate with officials. Although overconcern with the issue would probably be self-defeating by arousing suspicion that, perhaps, the researcher does in fact have something to hide, in most situations of overt research it is important to inform the individuals about his relations to the official world and something about his motives. Taking into consideration the obvious reasons for the deviants' suspicions, it seems likely that the researcher will at various times be subjected to testing, or "sounding," to determine his degree of loyalty to their way of life as opposed to the official way.

Ultimately, of course, actions speak louder than words, and the researcher will have to demonstrate by his actions that he is on the side of the deviants or, at least, not on the side of the officials. Today this generally means showing not only that he won't blow the whistle, but also that he shares the *way of life* of his group. Most importantly, most groups that today would in any way be considered deviant by important segments of our society make a fundamental distinction between the *hip* and the *square* (though the terms vary greatly). The hip are those who know and share, or sympathize with, the way of life of the "deviant" group; the square are those who oppose that way of life, who categorize it as "deviant" by opposing it to their own. The hip way of life includes not only external signs but also the beliefs and feelings of the group that such signs represent. Given the fact that so many deviants assume that they are under siege by the squares, it is highly unlikely that any sociologist would be able to study them without appearing to share to at least some minimal degree their way of life and without appearing to be quite independent of the square world. To most deviants anything else will seem too risky, if not because of potential disclosure to the officials, then because of the implied attack on them that involvement in the square world constitutes.

Our discussion of establishing trust and gaining entrée thus far would seem to fall into the usual mode of treating these subjects in fieldwork analyses, but we must not conclude that this is all there is to trust and maintaining one's research relations. In the traditional treatments of these subjects, once the researcher has established trust and gained entrée, that's all there is to it; he then can spend all his time observing the truth. In fact, as John Johnson has shown in his own studies, field research is a *developmental process,* always changing and fluid.[16] The person who trusts you today may see you as his enemy tomorrow. The person who appears to trust you may be doing so to be better able to hide things from you. Actually, this should not be so surprising, since the same is true of most human relationships. Marriage partners of 25 years, for example, may suddenly find reason to suspect each other and to hide things from each other. There are no easy paths to observing deviant groups, no guarantees that relations once established will not be destroyed or used against the researcher. The researcher must continually deal with the problems of building trust and maintaining his lines of information.

On balance, there might appear to be little reason why deviants would choose to be studied. But there is a crucial aspect to the situation of deviance in our society that makes it very likely that most deviants will in fact want to be studied. And if the researcher can in some way point it out, it seems likely that the deviants will be more willing to participate with him. Like most people, deviants are interested in themselves and see themselves as people whom others would find interesting; as such, they prize publicity highly. But, unlike people defined as "normal," deviants experience a profound public relations problem and are often anxious to have somebody "study them," especially if such study will result in a book. In addition to their desire for the world to see what they are like, they also often want to justify themselves to the world or to show that they are superior to those who consider them "deviants." Even though professional criminals are among the *least* concerned with public relations, Edwin Sutherland, David Mauer, Ned Polsky, and a few others who have successfully studied them have found that they too are very interested in being studied and in being written about.[17] In fact, many professional criminals (or exprofessionals) have written their own books.

The nonprofessional deviants are often even more anxious to be studied. A basic reason for their becoming "deviants," for joining the group and accepting the social categorization of themselves as "deviants," is often the desire to show that they are different from the rest of the world, especially the square world. This is especially true today of some young people, such as those who use marijuana or hard drugs. In many cases, the deviance becomes a symbolic device by which they dramatize their rejection of the square (middle-class) world, and by being studied they can communicate their rejection of this world. It becomes a stimulus to self-dramatization and can be extremely valuable to them. This is, presumably, the basic reason why such young deviants today are often very open about their deviance and are willing, even anxious, to be studied—and even, sometimes, to have their names used.

By utilizing this desire on the part of deviants to be studied, to have their way of life openly communicated "like it is" to the rest of society, the sociologist, if he is trusted and respected, can generally get cooperation in his research. As Polsky has shown from his own experience, the barrier against everyday-life studies of deviants has been created almost entirely by sociologists as a result of their own fears of the deviants rather than as a result of deviants' reluctance to be studied.[18]

However, for the researchers, the willingness of deviants to be studied can produce the same kind of difficulties as their fear of exposure. One of the not uncommon problems is the desire of deviants to be paid by the researcher for the information they give when they suspect that the researcher will be writing a book or that the researcher himself is paid for this kind of research. In one instance, a student doing a study of call girls immediately encountered a demand for payment. In such a case, paying for information would defeat the purpose of the research, for it would probably call forth on the part of the deviant extreme dramatizations and fronts common to that form of deviance. Call girls are aware that there are many highly successful and profitable books written about their occupation—books that are successful because they constitute a kind of publicly acceptable pornography. Thus they assume that anyone writing such a book would be interested primarily in lurid descriptions rather than in mundane everyday details, and they would be very apt to strain to find lurid details for a researcher willing to pay. To avoid such presentations of the lives of deviants, the sociologist must avoid paying them or intimating in any way that the research he is doing may prove remunerative. When the student studying call girls told them firmly that he had no money for the research and did not expect to get any (which was in fact the case), he did not face any further problem. They were then willing for him to do the research and were anxious in many ways to tell him about their lives.

The fundamental problem here, however, is the danger that the anxious concern of the deviant to present himself to the rest of the world through the work of the researcher will result in self-dramatizations. Research involving explicit definition of the researcher will always face this problem to some degree, and it can only be solved by comparing the results of such research with those of secret research.

But we have little reason at this time to believe that this *uncertainty effect*—that is, the effect of the method of observation on the resulting observations—or, in this case, the more specific *dramatization effect*, cannot be minimized over the long run by the researcher's simply becoming a taken-for-granted part of the deviant's everyday life. While deviants may never forget that they are more on stage when the researcher is around than otherwise, if the researcher ceases to emphasize his research role and the possible publicity resulting from his research, he can probably recede into the background. The effective solution to this problem of self-dramatization involves the whole question of the degree to which the sociologist participates in the everyday lives of the deviants.

Managing Fronts and Establishing Trust

The deviants' fear of exposure coupled with their desire to be studied can produce a fundamental problem for any sociologist trying to become involved in deviant groups in order to study them. As Dorothy Douglas found, both motives can cause the deviants to use their many *fronts* to lead the sociologist astray, so that the unsuspecting sociologist may get a consistently false idea of what the deviants' lives are like.

As with all individuals, important groups in our society have both friends and enemies. Thus, since a deviant group is one considered by some significant other groups to be deviant, by definition it has enemies who would often be willing to take strong measures against it. Groups legally defined as deviant are in a particularly dangerous situation because they often face real possibilities of official action being taken against them. Even if they are not violating laws, officials may still exercise paralegal controls over them. (For example, most students today appear to agree that police see young people, especially students, as almost all potentially deviant. The young thus feel that even when they are not doing anything the police might legally construe as deviant, the police will investigate and threaten them anyway.)

Because deviant groups face great problems of this sort, they have become especially adept at constructing *fronts* behind which they can carry on their activities. They have become particularly clever at managing what Lofland has very appropriately called "insider information" and "outsider information."[19] Indeed, some deviant groups, such as professional criminals and prostitutes, have developed "lines" for those outsiders who are potentially dangerous to them and have passed these lines down over the centuries. The effectiveness of such lines is shown by the fact that so many outsiders still take them to be truths.

Such ageless fronts can probably be spotted and managed effectively, but most fronts are not so easily managed. Most fronts are created by specific groups to meet specific social situations so that they change rapidly as the social situations change. A kind of *cultural wisdom* can probably be learned about such groups so that one does suspect when he is being given a line, or "put on." But only prolonged association with any particular group can make the sociologist aware of *situational fronts* and allow him to develop effective strategies for dealing with them. Situational fronts are created by individuals out of bits and pieces of old fronts, and out of their own creative thoughts, to deal with the situation-at-hand. These are *idiosyncratic fronts*—or fronts peculiar to an individual or a situation—that can only be spotted if the researcher knows enough about the specific group and, perhaps, even about the specific individual, so that he already knows a good deal of the truth about the group and the individual. Only such specific knowledge of the situation and of the group in-the-situation will allow the student of deviance to *check out* what he is told by individuals in specific situations.

But, unless he is able to gain *initial acceptance* by the group, the researcher could not even participate sufficiently to be able to gain this minimal degree of necessary understanding. Deviant groups appear willing to allow outsiders to observe them in *some* of their activities long before they are willing to let outsiders see *all* of the kinds of things the group is involved in. This constitutes a kind of *limbo membership,* in which an individual is granted tentative acceptance by the group—that is, one sufficient to allow them to evaluate his trustworthiness. No clear line is drawn between insider and outsider information, but tentative acceptance usually means granting the individual the right to exist somewhere between the two. Thus he can observe the group in their everyday lives and can talk with them and be tested by them without gaining so much information as to constitute a real danger to them. An example of a group today that would act this way would be marijuana users, who will discuss at length their use of marijuana without allowing an individual to witness them in possession of it, without naming the other people involved, and, most especially, without telling from whom they buy marijuana or to whom they sell it.

As we have seen earlier, *trust* is the crucial factor in determining if an individual is granted such limbo membership, let alone allowed to participate with the group. *Trust is the basic consideration of any individuals or any group in determining whether they will allow an individual to pierce their public fronts and observe their private behavior.* For those who are deviant, this is an *overriding* concern. They are very conscious of it, and in many cases develop explicit strategies for testing the trustworthiness of individuals.

Deviants also develop many diffuse and specific ideas about personal *styles* and believe that one's style is an adequate *symbolization of one's social purposes.* Personal style thus becomes a crucial determinate for them of whether one can be trusted. Police, for example, are commonly thought to have personal styles that they are unable to hide and that give them away, and any individual showing such personal style is not to be trusted. (This idea seems less important today because police more frequently use undercover agents, who are often former members of deviant groups and who know how to make use of deviant personal styles.) Such personal styles must be effectively managed by the sociologist before he comes into contact with the deviant group, for changes in one's personal style, like changes in one's ideas, will give an impression of inconsistency, which will arouse suspicion among members of the group. (This principle of consistency of personal behavior results primarily from the commonsense assumption that an individual has a *substantial self* that must be the same at all times. When an individual appears to behave inconsistently, then our immediate conclusion is that our former ideas about his substantial self must have been wrong. We then must consider whether he was trying to manipulate our beliefs about him—that is, whether he was putting up a front in our initial encounter with him. Inconsistency gives rise to suspicion, which can only be overcome by moving to a greater synthesis—that is, moving to an idea of his substantial self that would plausibly include both of the previous impressions we had received of him.)

Once one has managed such problems of initial encounters and has, presumably, established some kind of limbo membership so that he is at least able to observe the group of deviants in their daily lives, the problems of establishing and maintaining trust become more a matter of personal beliefs and personality types than of general symbolic style. Attention to language, hand motions, and so on, could be important. Polsky, however, from his own experience with hustlers and professional criminals, argues that it is ineffective for a sociologist to try to fit in with the group of deviants by using their styles of language. Indeed, this can have exactly the opposite effects from what one intends; a sociologist with little previous involvement with the group he is trying to study and who assumes the linguistic and behavioral styles of that group may be detected and may be seen as attempting to deceive them into believing that he is one of them. Polsky argues convincingly that such dishonesty will destroy the whole relationship. Certainly it is true that any seemingly dishonest use of the deviants' language or life styles will destroy trust and, thus, prevent the sociologists' getting valid information about the group. But there are a great many research situations in which the sociologist has become enough of a member to honestly use the same language and life styles. The use of such language and life styles is part of the fundamental issue of the degrees and kinds of researcher participation in the deviants' lives.

The Degrees and Kinds of Participation

The sociologist's observations of social action involve varying degrees of participation in the action, ranging from no participation to total immersion. Differences in the degree of participation are significant in determining what can be observed and how "objective" the observations are likely to be.

At one extreme would be observation with absolutely no participation. This situation, which Fred Davis has aptly called the "Martian situation,"[20] has never actually been used by sociologists because they always have vast commonsense knowledge of our society before they begin any study, and some of this knowledge will be shared by any subculture. Many sociologists, however, have held it up as an ideal method toward which we should strive. The early form of this minimal-participation method was that adopted by the mechanistic social analysts who sought to study and explain social behavior without any reference to social meanings or to the analyst's commonsensically derived understandings of those meanings. While this particular form of this method is rarely used today, except in some of the atypical mathematical models of social actions, it has been replaced by a modified version, which seeks, ideally, to determine social meanings completely from outside the commonsense understandings of those meanings. The most serious presentation of this ideal is found in the plea for a "presuppositionless" method—that is, a method of observing and analyzing phenomena that would in no way presuppose any basic properties of thought or any ideas about the phenomena. There are some good philosophical critiques of the fundamental weaknesses of this "method" as a philosophical ideal;[21] and these critiques seem to hold for the linguistic analyses that constitute the only Martian method much used in the social sciences today.

At the opposite extreme from the Martian method is the total immersion of the self in the group being studied, an immersion that, at least for its duration, abrogates study *of* the group for experience *in* the group. This is the experience that Kurt Wolff has called *surrender* and that he has described so well for his own experience in a community study:

It was years before I understood what had happened to me: I had fallen through the web of "culture patterns" and assorted conceptual meshes into the chaos of *love*; I was looking everywhere, famished, with a "ruthless glance." Despite admonitions to be selective and form hypotheses that would tell me what to select, I was not and did not. Another thing I sensed was that I was not content with the probable but wanted to *know*; and I thought I might *know* if, instead of looking for culture patterns, for instance, I looked directly—not through the lens of *any* received notion but the adequate lens that would come out of my being in Loma. "Culture pattern," indeed any conceptual scheme, had come to strike me as something learned *outside* Loma that I would import, impose, and that has been imposed on me. Instead, I was busy, even panicky at times, observing, ruminating, and recording as best I could. Everything, I felt, was important, although the ways in which it was important would yet have to become clear.[22]

"Surrender" has a number of basic meanings for Wolff:

Its seminal meaning is cognitive love, in the sense in which this is redundant for love. "Surrender" has a military connotation, as well as the sound of passivity, of "giving up." I have therefore thought of other words, such as "abandonment," but this suggests a dissoluteness alien to it; "exposure," but this had a gratuitous ring of exhibitionism; "devotion" or "dedication," but these envisage only an attitude and inappropriately introduce a moral note; "laying oneself open" or "laying the cards on the table," but these, too, convey only part of the meaning—unconditionality or honesty. Thus I have stuck to "surrender." Its meaning of "cognitive love" is seminal because all the other meanings follow from it. Major among them are: total involvement, suspension of received notions, pertinence of everything, identification, and risk of being hurt.[23]

Minimal participation might provide the sociologist with information on deviance. For example, some kinds of ecological information concerning habits of "hanging out," which involve little more than counting appearances at certain spots at certain times, might prove to be of value. But even such observations of events are rarely of interest to us unless we can see the relations between these patterns of events and social meanings. And *social meanings can only be "observed" by using participation, because this is the one way by which we can learn how to relate the perceivable states of communication* (linguistic statements, facial expressions, hand signs, utterances, and so on) *to the internal states of mind and feeling that are the meanings of the external states.*

In order to understand the necessity of such participation, let us consider a version of the Martian method that one might try to use to determine "meanings" without using participation. In this method one tries to get at the observable relations between linguistic statements, body signs, situations, and actions without making use of any direct participation with the individuals involved.

In its ideal manifestation, the first step of this external method would include the exact recording of all verbal and nonverbal communication found in any situation (perhaps by using sound films). The next step would be the preliminary analysis of the patterns of invariant *linguistic items*—that is, words, phrases, sentences, facial expressions, and so forth. Following this, one would analyze such communications to determine the *varying structures* in which these linguistic items appear—that is, one would determine the *usages* (or *constructions*) made with these linguistic items. One would then attempt to determine the relations between the constructions and the general *situations,* or contexts, of the social actors, as defined by the actors. And finally, one would be ready to venture a more general theory relating "meanings" to each other and to actions.

Presumably, such an externalistic approach would have to define "meaning" not in terms of internal states, which is what we mean commonsensically by the term, but in terms of the associations or relations between linguistic and other expressions of the individuals involved, the other kinds of activities they perform (walking, hitting, and so on), and the situations in which these expressions and actions occur. There would be two crucial problems for this would-be Martian researcher. First, the number of possible relations between the various external activities would be infinite because of the great freedom individuals have—and must have because of the infinite complexity of the world we live in—in constructing their activities and because of the openness of the world for each individual. If this infinite complexity is so, it would not be possible to realize the ideal meaning, even with the finest computers. One would have to have prior knowledge of these unspoken devices before he could understand how the individuals construct meaning in their everyday situations.

Second, the Martian researcher would not be able to determine from his exact and total recording of externally perceivable events what the *situations for the participants* are, because the situation is almost always meaningful to the participants only in terms of unspoken, taken-for-granted meanings. The Martian researcher, therefore, would have to know the meanings of the situations to the participants before he could adequately determine the meanings of the events he has witnessed. He could probably only break this chain by asking the participants, and, although this would involve a minimal form of participation, it would still be participation. (We might also add that, *even if* one could approximate this ideal Martian method, the expenditure of human effort would not be worth it, for it is doubtful that one would achieve anything unique by this method.)

Member participation, or previous involvement in the everyday lives of a group of deviants as a member, can be a great help in studying deviants. First of all, it can be an aid in gaining some insight into one of the most crucial problems faced by sociology—the relation between the commonsense experience of everyday social life and the experience of an individual who has received a formalized education in sociology or one of the other social sciences. Formalized education, the academic world, sociological theory, and so on are all basic to the preconceptions with which a social researcher approaches fieldwork. After many years of such training, much of it using technical jargon greatly removed from everyday life, these formalized preconceptions can become so taken for granted that they form an unconscious frame around everyday experience. These preconceptions may prevent the researcher from grasping the meanings that the members may be taking for granted; and the researcher may find that he can "make sense" out of his observations in terms of his own preconceptions rather than in terms of theirs.

Secondly, previous experience with a group of deviants can be extremely important in providing an individual with a "natural" understanding of the deviants' style of life. Such an understanding is of special importance in establishing trust with the deviants. As we have noted, there are a number of useful studies of deviants done by sociologists that have made primary use of earlier *member participation*, though in most instances the sociologists using such insider information have not reported their methods. For example, Marvin Scott's highly interesting interpretation of the deviance of jockeys was based on his long-standing insider experience at race tracks, which occurred well before he thought of becoming a sociologist.[24] Although Scott has not provided us with enough information on the exact ways in which he inferred the existence of jockey strategies, it should be apparent from the work that he could only have gotten at such strategies, and could only have been very sure that they existed—that is, that they are "going through the minds of jockeys" and determining their behavior— through very long and intimate association with people at race tracks.

Regardless of whether the sociologist has had such previous insider experience in the deviant subculture he is studying, he has at least had extensive insider experience in our culture. Since almost all groups of deviants in our culture have only subcultural differences from the general culture, he will already share many understandings with them. The sociologist will necessarily be making primary use of this insider experience in our culture to participate with deviants and to understand the meanings of things to them. His knowledge of the language, American English, is the most obvious and important form of insider information he will be using. But his general understanding of the values of American society, of subcultural styles, of subcultural attitudes toward other subcultures, and so on will also be used extensively. While these understandings are absolutely essential, they may also be the basis for the formation of dangerous preconceptions unless the sociologist is always very careful to assume that the meanings to the members of the subculture must be treated by him as being problematic—that is, he must always be trying to determine how *adequately* these understandings meet the *practicality test*: How effectively can he interact with the members of the group in a given situation?

Any sociological research on deviants requires a great degree of involvement with the deviants, since trust, the important factor, can be established only in this way. Thus, the sociologist studying deviants must live with them much of the time, even if he does not intend to do the research secretly. If, for example, one is to do a valid study of delinquents, then one must participate with the boys, as Carl Werthman did in his study of gang boys;[25] and, if one is going to study the hippies in the Haight-Ashbury, one must live much of the time in the Haight, as Sherri Cavan did.[26] If one cannot live with them or run with them, then one must make use of the next best thing, which is "commuting" or "hanging out" with the deviants. This has, in fact, been the most widely used form of participation with deviants, as we can see in the article "Problems of Access and Risk in Observing Drug Scenes," by James T. Carey.

This emphasis on "intimacy" and "living with" the deviants does not mean that the sociologist must "surrender," "go native," or become "one of the blood" in order to get at what the meanings of things are to them. Becoming "one of the blood" can be extremely useful to sociologists in gaining insight into those kinds of things that members of any group take completely for granted. Even more significantly, it can provide insight into those kinds of things that are really secrets within the group itself—things that are understood by the members of the group but that are so intimate or so deviant from their own standpoint that they must not be talked about. While this form of "surrender" affords one the easiest source of insight, it does create some of its own problems, especially those of being objective and of being able to observe what the members take for granted—that is, if the sociologist becomes extremely involved as a member it can be difficult for him to see those things which the members themselves find hard to see. While I believe the sociologist can overcome these problems by using *retro-*

spective analysis of his experience after he is no longer involved and has returned to his identity as sociologist, and while I believe surrender should, consequently, be encouraged as long as his primary identification remains with sociology, it does create its own problems. Moreover, it is probably not necessary for getting at most of the kinds of meanings that concern us.

While most sociologists of deviance in recent years have not believed in surrendering to the deviant groups, many have felt it essential that sociologists *take the side of* or *sympathize with* the deviants. It is precisely because of the fundamentally important distinction between empathy and sympathy, and their often opposite relations to gaining reliable understandings of social meanings, that sociologists must be extremely careful about committing themselves to political interest groups if they want to keep the search for truth about human beings as their primary goal.[27] It is the commitment to narrow political interest groups that makes so many sociologists believe that sympathy is necessary and desirable. If a sociologist has a broader perspective and has a truthful understanding of human actors as his primary goal, such sympathetic concerns for (narrow) moral or political interest groups can be a fundamental failing.

There has always been a very important and influential minority of American sociologists who, primarily because of their liberal and leftist political stances, have tried to take the side of deviants.[28] For example, these sociologists have taken a definite sympathetic attitude toward the lower-class black culture that middle-class people would commonly see as deviant. On the other hand, there have been some areas in which there has been little evidence of this sympathetic stance. For example, sociologists, as one might expect from any middle-class group, have shown little sympathy toward prisoners and "hardened criminals."

It is crucial to realize that this sympathetic stance is very different from participating in a deviant group for purposes of gaining an objective understanding of it. The aim of objective understanding can be defeated by taking the sympathetic stance, especially when it is done primarily for political or ideological reasons. The sympathy that sociologists in our society have shown for various groups of deviants and lower-class people has raised grave dangers of just this sort. Some of the most recent and highly touted studies of the poor, especially of the black poor, have come close to being *romantic justifications of the ways of the poor* to the educated and the middle class. For example, a large portion of *Tally's Corner*,[29] one of the most popular works of social science in many years, consists primarily of trying to justify the activities of the lower-class blacks Elliot Liebow had gotten to know so intimately through his long participation in their everyday lives. Indeed, much of the work is written from the perspective of trying to "tell it like it is" to the middle-class white world. While such writing is a political activity in our society today, it must be seen, too, as a suspect report of actual occurrences in the everyday lives of these people, for it seems unlikely that they spend such a large portion of their lives seeking to justify themselves to the middle-class world. If they did so when Liebow was present, then we must suspect that his being a member of the white middle-class group must have biased the contact situation and must have resulted in the blacks spending much of their time justifying themselves to him as a representative of that group. In that case, the work could not be taken as a valuable scientific study of the everyday lives of these people.

The kind of bias resulting from taking the sympathetic stance is in no way a consequence of using the participant-observer method. There is no evidence to suggest that participation in deviant or lower-class groups necessarily causes one to take the sympathetic stance or that there is more bias in the participant-observer method than in any other. On the contrary, greater bias is more likely to be found when a method other than participant-observation is used. An excellent example of this is Chapter 1 of Kenneth Clark's *Dark Ghetto*,[30] in which an attempt is made to depict the lives of the people of Harlem in New York City. This chapter, entitled "The Cry of the Ghetto," is based on an interview study of members of the Harlem community done by social scientists. The interviews were done in the setting of a social-problems oriented (community action) organization called Haryou, presumably because the social scientists doing the study were primarily concerned with the problematic, or "suffering," aspects of the everyday lives of the residents of Harlem and with ways of getting social and financial support for solving these problems and ending this suffering. The overall effect of the dialogue in the chapter is a dismal picture of everyday life in Harlem. From these selected excerpts, which Clark presumably took from the interviews in order to give some "objective picture" of everyday life, it would seem that the members of the Harlem community spend all their time suffering. They have no ordinary joys, such as having fun with friends, joking with acquaintances, playing with children, making love, drinking with comrades, and so on, which all of us with direct experience with lower-class groups have in the past found to be the dominant aspects of everyday life among these groups.

It seems apparent that the social scientists doing this study were primarily concerned with eliciting support for the particular political programs intended to solve what they defined as social problems. They focus, through the use of the interview method, on the information they expect to use to justify their appeals for these programs. And the interview method, especially when its results are combined with excerpted illustrative material, is extremely amenable to such purposes. The participant-observer study is less amenable, since it has to take into consideration a far wider range of life and is less capable of structuring the situation so that the individuals to be observed respond primarily in terms of those aspects of their lives relevant to suffering.

Taking a sympathetic stance toward deviants is by no means a necessary or even a major cause of bias in studies of deviants, though many sociologists have in recent years come to assume that this is the case. I would suggest that the actual circumstances are the complete opposite of this. Instead of becoming sympathetic toward the group being studied, and thence having great problems of objective reporting, sociologists facing situations in which bias is involved seem *to have already been sympathetic (and often biased) toward the group.* Because of this they have gone out *to "study" the group in order to show that the deviants are "more right" than their attackers,* whom such sociologists often see as *their own attackers as well.* One kind of evidence for this is that the same sociologists can do "studies" showing how "bad" the officials are, even though they do the studies by participating with them. If participation were the biasing factor, rather than previous political and ideological commitments, then these sociologists would, presumably, wind up doing reports on the officials that are quite favorable to them. There are definitely instances of this happening, but it also goes the other way.[31] There are also reports on deviant groups, based on long participation, that are in no way sympathetic; obvious examples would be most of the early ethnographic studies of deviants done in Chicago in the 1920s. Works such as *The Gang* and *Taxi Cab Dance Hall Girls* appear to be neither sympathetic nor unsympathetic. They are a real mixture, probably in the style of much of social-work reporting. But one of the best examples of a work involving high participation without sympathy is the recent work done by Hunter Thompson on *Hell's Angels.* Though not a professional sociologist, Thompson spent a good part of a year or more riding with the Hell's Angels, so that he did far more fieldwork on them than all but a few sociologists have done on any deviant group. The work is in no way a sympathetic report on the Angels. Though he argues that most of the newspaper and political pictures painted of the Angels are completely false, and that the members are certainly not inhuman, his final commentary on the Angels—which came after a stomping they gave him for a minor mistake—is a malediction:

On Labor Day 1966, I pushed my luck a little too far and got badly stomped by four or five Angels who seemed to feel I was taking advantage of them. A minor disagreement suddenly became very serious.

None of those who did me were among the group I considered my friends—

but they were Angels, and that was enough to cause many of the others to participate after one of the brethren teed off on me. The first blow was launched with no hint of warning and I thought for a moment that it was just one of those drunken accidents that a man has to live with in this league. But within seconds I was clubbed from behind by the Angel I'd been talking to just a moment earlier. Then I was swarmed in a general flail. . . .

My next stop was the hospital in Santa Rosa, nearly fifty miles south of the Angel encampment. The emergency-ward waiting room was full of wounded Gypsy Jokers. The most serious case was a broken jaw, the result of a clash earlier that evening with a pipe-wielding Hell's Angel.

The Jokers told me they were on their way north to wipe the Angels out. "It'll be a goddamn slaughter," said one.

I agreed, and wished them luck. I wanted no part of it—not even with a shotgun. I was tired, swollen and whipped. My face looked like it had been jammed into the spokes of a speeding Harley, and the only thing keeping me awake was the spastic pain of a broken rib.

It had been a bad trip . . . fast and wild in some moments, slow and dirty in others, but on balance it looked like a bummer. On my way back to San Francisco, I tried to compose a fitting epitaph. I wanted something original, but there was no escaping the echo of Mistah Kurtz' final words from the heart of darkness: "The horror! The horror! . . . Exterminate all the brutes!"[32]

Even prolonged participation involving considerable personal involvement can lead to antipathy and negatively biased reporting against the group. It seems likely that the nature of one's initial commitment to studying the group and one's initial sympathies and antipathies toward its way of life become the primary determinants of whether one takes the side of the deviants or the side of their enemies.

Surrender, sympathy, and other forms of identification with the deviants and with their (self-defined) best interests do not seem to be necessary in the way in which some sociologists of deviance have assumed them to be. These various forms of identification are quite different from what earlier sociologists called "empathy." I believe *empathy* is what is needed, rather than sympathy. Empathy is an ability *to feel with,* to see things from the standpoint or perspective of the individual being studied rather than to identify with or act from this standpoint. There is no reason whatsoever to believe that to understand is to sympathize with or to agree with, although this may be necessary for certain individuals because of their own feelings, identifications, and so on. But there is no reason to believe it is true of all individuals. On the contrary, many individuals are able to take the standpoint of others for purposes of understanding it without surrendering to or getting inside it. It is even quite possible for some individuals to empathize with their enemies. Indeed, one would suspect that all great military commanders have had precisely this ability and have tried to train their subordinates to have it so that they could better destroy their enemies. In a way, empathy is a hard-headed stance, while sympathy is an analogous but soft-hearted stance. We must recognize that reliable understanding demands a hard heart but a supple mind.

Participation and Objectivity

Sociologists must be involved as participants in the everyday lives of deviant groups if they wish to observe the social meanings of things to those deviants. This is the only way to get valid information on social meanings, especially those shared by deviants. The need for participation outweighs the problems produced by becoming involved, as long as one believes that such participation does, in fact, provide him with valid information on the meanings.

Only two serious arguments have been put forward against the conclusion that participant-observation studies provide us with valid information. The first argument is that based on depth psychology. Depth psychologists have argued in many different works on crime and deviance that the individuals doing these things are themselves not aware of their "real reasons" for doing them. Alexander and Staub, in *The Criminal, the Judge, and the Public*, for example, argue that in most crimes there is a "basic neurotic process."[33] They maintain that criminals really feel quite ambivalent about their actions, that they want to express their aggressive feelings, to get revenge, and so on, but that at the same time they feel guilty about their activities, so they want to be punished for them. Alexander and Staub argue that this is the basic reason why most criminals continue to commit crimes after punishment and thus become recidivists—that is, they return to be punished further for things for which they have already been punished. They argue that this also explains the obvious "irrationality" involved in criminal actions. They believe that most individuals doing these things are unconscious of their "real reasons" for doing them. To the depth psychologists, criminal and deviant actions are "pathological." Being "irrational," these actions are not subject to the conscious understanding of the individuals involved. It would seem then that there is no value to becoming involved with the members of the group in order to get at the meanings of things to them, because the meanings would simply be the conscious meanings, and these meanings are quite misleading.

The depth psychology argument is wrong on four counts. First, there is no reason to believe that deviant behavior, including criminal behavior, is like the neurotic behavior psychologists might study in a clinical setting. The argument that deviant behavior is neurotic or "pathological" is the result of uncritically assuming an absolutist stance[34] toward such behavior—that is, one assumes that things must in an absolute sense have the same potential meanings for deviants as for nondeviants, that there is only one conception of motives, of values, of rationality, and so on. This assertion is not based on any kind of evidence. Depth psychologists have assumed this absolutist stance and have then chosen a small number of examples from the mass of complex everyday behavior of criminals and deviants to justify their assertion that such behavior is irrational. Although there are criminals and deviants who try to advertise their acts and who may even give hints to officials on how to capture them, most criminals go to great extremes to avoid detection or apprehension.

Second, to determine whether deviants are thinking irrationally, and not simply acting "irrationally" from the standpoint of a psychologist assuming an absolutist stance, one must become involved enough in deviants' activities to see things from their standpoint. If psychologists were to do this, they might have a completely different idea about the causes of crime.

Third, the psychological argument regarding unconscious motivations has never been demonstrated to have significant value for explaining everyday behavior. It has consisted of little more than the assertions by the psychologists that ordinary people do not know why they are doing something, that they are not aware of their "real motives," that only psychologists can know why they are "really" doing something. This is unfounded and contrary both to our commonsense experience and to the experience of sociologists involved in studying people in their everyday lives.

Fourth, and most important, there is no reason to believe that participant-observation would not provide valid information on the meanings to participants even if it were true that the participants were not aware of their "real reasons" for doing something. Serious participant-observers of everyday life in general do not assume that the members of society will know the "real reasons" for their behavior. In fact, those who have been most involved in using this method argue that members are very often unaware of the important meanings of their actions at any given time. As participant-observers have argued, we should concentrate on asking "how" the members do something, rather than on asking "why" they do it. Members come to take certain meanings so much for granted that they no longer have to think about them, and, indeed, in many cases are unable to give a very clear account of them; but these participants are not "unconscious" of the meanings. These are the *background meanings* that provide much of the meanings, for the members, of things being said or done in the group, but they are not immediately accessible to the members. If questioned in the right way, members can probably provide an account in accord with one given by a participant-observer researcher who had studied the group long enough to see what meanings must be in the background to make "adequate sense" out of what is said and done in the group. But even this *agreement with member accounts* is not a necessary part of participant-observer studies.[35]

The second serious argument against the validity of information gotten by participant-observer methods assumes that any external observation of the group so alters its everyday behavior that what is studied is an artifact of the research method and in no way the same as the group's everyday activities. This argument is far more serious for any participant-observer than the one based on depth psychology and must be carefully considered. This argument makes it very important for us to try to compare research using an *explicit definition of the researcher* with that using a *research cover* that allows an individual to become a *normal member* of the group who can observe the group's behavior. Until we have extensive comparative information of this kind, we can never feel very certain of our conclusions. But at the present time the *uncertainty effect* of the participant-observer method (involving explicit definition of the researcher) does not seem that overwhelming, although it is there and certainly must be taken into consideration in evaluating one's findings.

The participant-observers' reports of deviant groups have normally been found to agree with the commonsense understandings of those groups held by former members or even by individuals who were members when the group was being studied. Unfortunately, there has rarely been any systematic test of the fit between researcher and member accounts. This *member test,* or the plausible fit between the *researcher understanding* and the *insider, commonsense understandings,* is itself a significant indication of the validity of the findings, though not definitive.[36] In addition, the researcher's commonsense understandings of secrecy, reluctance to give information, front management, and so on allow him to have some sense of when these mechanisms are being used, especially because he gets to know the members of the group so well. It is precisely this kind of commonsense understanding that the participant-observer can bring to bear on his evaluation of the truthfulness of statements by his group that is possible in no other research method.

In general, then, the participant-observer method does provide reliable information on the social meanings of things to the deviant group being studied. But there remains one serious question concerning the objectivity of participant-observer findings on deviants. Sociologists have normally assumed, and with some very significant commonsense justification, that involvement and objectivity vary inversely—that is, the more involvement, the less objectivity. This simple formula points to a crucial problem, which lies in the direction indicated by the formula. The problem has at least two important aspects: (1) observability and (2) interpretation and reportability.

The problem of observability concerns the tendency of the researcher to begin to take for granted the fundamental meanings, or background meanings, of the group. Just as the members come to take things, especially meanings, for granted and, therefore, find it difficult to clearly express those meanings or to see their importance in determining the specific meanings of things for them, so the researcher who becomes a member, even a *limbo member,* may have increasing difficulty in observing those background meanings or in observing their significance in determining more specific meanings. This problem is especially difficult since the background meanings are hard to observe before one has had a large degree of participation with the group. We are faced with a situation in which we must make use of participation in order to observe the background meanings, and, yet, the more we have of that participation, the harder it becomes to observe them.

Fortunately, the relationship is broken by the sociologist's primary involvement in other identities and other groups. The sociologist doing a participant-observer study of deviant groups remains, first and foremost, a sociologist studying the group. While this is an identity he may wish to play down in his involvement with the group, it is an identity of which he himself remains quite aware. (There are, of course, some individuals who quite literally "go native" and never return to sociology or anthropology, but they do not concern us, since they infrequently write reports on their experiences.) The sociologist usually makes many trips back to the world of sociology and to his more middle-class surroundings, eventually returning and largely giving up his "identity" in the deviant group.

Continually confronted with contrasting perspectives and experiences, the sociologist is made conscious of those background meanings of deviant groups that are different from those of the other groups in which he is involved. This *tension between his different involvements and between his different perspectives of meanings* is, in fact, a crucial element in the participant-observer method and makes it possible for the sociologist to provide much worthwhile information on the deviant group. It is this *epistemological tension,* this tension between different ways of interpreting the world, that makes the sociologist constantly seek to better understand the background meanings of things to the deviants. And because of this tension, he experiences many conflicts of meanings in his everyday interaction with the members and must constantly search for that understanding which will allow him to avoid such conflicts. Only by achieving a greater synthesis of meaning, which allows him to translate and, thus, communicate between one group or identity and another, can he resolve this tension.

The essence of participatory action, then, is a tension-inspired search for a clearer, more explicit truth about the meanings of things to the people involved. It is this tension that drives a sociologist to formulate for himself a more explicit understanding of the meanings of things to this group and to make use of this more explicit understanding in his interaction with them (using the *practicality test of meanings*). This interaction involving the use of initial understandings leads to a further tension, which leads to a reformulation of one's understandings, then to further interaction, and so on. The ideal of the participant-observer method is to reach the best approximation of the truth of the meanings of things to the members through this tension-inspired dialectical process. It should be clear, then, that the researcher can manage the observability problem and can actually benefit from its nature. He can alternate involvements of differing depths in order to maintain and optimize the tension that inspires the dialectical process leading to ever greater understanding.

The problem of interpretation and reportability is probably the one that most commonly occurs to people when they think of the methodological problems involved in participant-observation. It is the idea of this problem that lies at the root of such commonsense beliefs as "one looks at the loved one through rose-colored glasses." This is the problem involved in the considerations of sympathy and empathy examined above. Part of the solution to the problem, as we have already seen, consists in the emphasis upon empathy, rather than sympathy. But there is more to it than this.

Gouldner has rightly argued that a fundamental aspect of the whole problem of objectivity is the moral one: there is a very real question of honesty involved here.[37] When an individual becomes committed to the interests of a specific group, he is especially apt to approach understanding of and, even more, public reporting of that group as political activities—that is, he is likely to *want* to present the group favorably, so he will think about it and report on it primarily in terms of his understanding of what he wants the audience to think about "his group." Individuals undoubtedly sometimes do this very cynically, especially when they feel they are doing politics, advertising, or public relations. But it is normally more subtle than this.

The researcher's honesty with himself and his honesty in reporting are especially acute in an area such as deviance in which there can be so few restudies of groups. Often we must rely on a single report or, at most, a few reports on a given type of deviant group, and rarely do we have reports on the same group in the same or very similar situations. Because of this it becomes harder to check on the honesty of individuals by comparing their findings with others. An internal analysis of a report will sometimes provide a crucial clue that something is wrong. But more importantly, sometimes we can see that the report does not fit our understandings of members of our culture or members of a similar subculture that we have known firsthand—that is, it simply isn't *plausible.* (For example, from my general understanding of members of this society and of the black subculture, I am convinced that Kenneth Clark's picture of everyday life in *Dark Ghetto* is quite mistaken, presumably because of the political goals of the work rather than any personal lack of understanding on his part. No major groups in our society continually bewail their fate in their everyday lives. They may rail and rant in political situations, and, in fact, almost all groups, including the very rich, do this; but they do not do this in their everyday lives, which are never that politicized.) Sometimes we are able to spot internal inconsistencies in a report—that is, it doesn't *check out.* But very importantly, we must also be able to rely on the general professional integrity of the people doing the studies.

Fundamental training in professional standards can and does take care of this problem in part. Sociologists place a tremendous emphasis upon professional integrity, which consists, above all, in trying to honestly understand and communicate the phenomena being studied. Keeping high standards for field notes, maintaining field notes so that they can be read by others if necessary, and reporting on case studies are important checks on professional honesty.

The usual checks on the objectivity of scientific findings and reportings—that is, the use of public and reproducible methods of observation —while done from a very different perspective, apply also to the study of deviance. In the natural sciences this takes the form of using experimental situations that are precisely reproducible. This is irrelevant to the field of deviance research, but we could place a greater emphasis on restudies and on *team studies* of any given type of group, as has recently been done in team studies of the police by David Bordua and Albert Reiss. This would give us a far better idea of the objectivity of the studies.

In participant-observer studies of deviance, however, we must rely heavily on two other methods of achieving objectivity. First, each study must present far more evidence on the *actual* methods used to produce the resulting observations. Second, essays on methods, such as the classical one by William Foote Whyte concerning his methods of observation that led to *Street Corner Society,* must become far more detailed and far more integral to the reporting of the study. Only in these ways will we be able to adequately judge the validity of the observations and to attempt to *reproduce* studies to see if similar methods of studying similar groups produce similar findings.

Notes

1. The sociologists' use of the commonsense stance to infer social meanings is examined in Jack D. Douglas, *American Social Order* (New York: Free Press, 1971), especially Chaps. 3 and 4.
2. For a discussion of the assumption of sociological omniscience see *ibid.*, Chap. 2.
3. Ned Polsky, *Hustlers, Beats, and Others* (paperback ed.; Garden City, N.Y.: Anchor Books, 1969), pp. 109–143.
4. The sociological literature on official information on deviance is too extensive to analyze here. For complete analyses of the facts and the literature see Jack D. Douglas, *The Social Meanings of Suicide* (Princeton, N.J.: Princeton University Press, 1967); *American Social Order;* and *Youth in Turmoil* (Washington, D.C.: Government Printing Office, 1970).
5. See Erving Goffman, *The Presentation of Self in Everyday Life* (Garden City, N.Y.: Anchor Books, 1959).
6. The problems involved in managing these self-presentations and fronts are discussed in most of the essays in this volume. See, especially, Dorothy J. Douglas, "Managing Fronts in Observing Deviance."
7. Howard S. Becker, "Practitioners of Vice and Crime," in Robert Habenstein (ed.), *Pathways to Data* (Chicago: Aldine, 1970).
8. Howard S. Becker, *Outsiders: Studies in the Sociology of Deviance* (New York: Free Press, 1963).
9. Becker, in Habenstein, *op. cit.*, calls for a similar strategy.
10. Laud Humphreys, *The Tearoom Trade: Impersonal Sex in Public Places* (Chicago: Aldine, 1970).
11. See the discussion of public and private situations in Douglas, *American Social Order.*
12. Technological tyranny is discussed in Jack D. Douglas (ed.), *Freedom and Tyranny* (New York: Random House, 1970).
13. Polsky, *op. cit.*, pp. 133–134.
14. William Foote Whyte, *Street Corner Society* (Chicago: University of Chicago Press, 1955).
15. Rosalie Hankey Wax, "Reciprocity as a Field Technique," *Human Organization,* 11 (1952), pp. 34–37.
16. See John Johnson, "Field Research" (unpublished paper).
17. See, especially, Edwin Sutherland, *The Professional Thief* (Chicago: University of Chicago Press, 1937).
18. Polsky, *op. cit.* Also, see the article in this volume by John Irwin, "Participant-Observation of Criminals."

19. See John F. Lofland, *Doomsday Cult* (Englewood Cliffs, N.J.: Prentice-Hall, 1966).
20. This was in private communication from Fred Davis.
21. See the discussion of this in Jack D. Douglas, *Understanding Everyday Life* (Chicago: Aldine, 1970).
22. Kurt Wolff, "Surrender and Community Study," in Arthur J. Vidich, Joseph Bensman, and Maurice R. Stein (eds.), *Reflections on Community Studies* (New York: Wiley, 1964), pp. 233–263.
23. *Ibid.*
24. Marvin Scott, *The Racing Game* (Chicago: Aldine, 1968).
25. Carl Werthman, "The Function of Social Definitions in the Development of Delinquent Careers," in *Juvenile Delinquency and Youth Crime,* Task Force Report of the President's Commission on Law Enforcement and Administration of Justice (Washington, D.C.: Government Printing Office, 1967).
26. Most of this study has not been published, but part of it appears in Sherri Cavan, "The Hippie Ethic and the Spirit of Drug Use," in Jack D. Douglas (ed.), *Observations of Deviance* (New York: Random House, 1970).
27. I have discussed this crucial point in Jack D. Douglas (ed.), *The Relevance of Sociology* (New York: Appleton-Century-Crofts, 1970).
28. See Howard Becker, "Whose Side Are We On?" *Social Problems*, 14 (Winter 1967), 239–247.
29. Elliot Liebow, *Tally's Corner* (Boston: Little, Brown, 1967).
30. Kenneth Clark, *Dark Ghetto* (New York: Harper & Row, 1965).
31. This is especially obvious from journalistic "exposés" and police investigations that involve undercover work.
32. Hunter S. Thompson, *Hell's Angels* (New York: Random House, 1966), pp. 277–278.
33. Franz Alexander and Hugo Staub, *The Criminal, the Judge, and the Public* (New York: Collier, 1956).
34. Absolutist sociology is discussed in Douglas, *American Social Order.*
35. See Douglas, *"Understanding Everyday Life,"* in *Understanding Everyday Life, op. cit.*
36. *Ibid.*
37. Alvin W. Gouldner, "The Sociologist as Partisan: Sociology and the Welfare State," *American Sociologist,* 3 (May 1968), 103–116.

Studying Deviance in Four Settings: Research Experiences with Cabbies, Suicides, Drug Users, and Abortionees

James M. Henslin

We would say then that the sociologist (that is, the one we would really like to invite to our game) is a person intensively, endlessly, shamelessly interested in the doings of men. His natural habitat is all the human gathering places of the world, wherever men come together. . . . And since he is interested in men, nothing that men do can be altogether tedious for him. . . . The sociologist, in his quest for understanding, moves through the world of men without respect for the usual lines of demarcation. Nobility and degradation, power and obscurity, intelligence and folly—these are equally *interesting* to him, however unequal they may be in his personal values or tastes. Thus his questions may lead him to all possible levels of society, the best and the least known places, the most respected and the most despised. . . . We could say that the sociologist, but for the grace of his academic title, is the man who must listen to gossip despite himself, who is tempted to look through keyholes, to read other people's mail, to open closed cabinets. . . . Perhaps some little boys consumed with curiosity to watch their maiden aunts in the bathroom later become inveterate sociologists. . . . What interests us is the curiosity that grips any sociologist in front of a closed door behind which there are human voices. If he is a good sociologist, he will want to open that door, to understand these voices. Behind each closed door he will anticipate some new facet of human life not yet perceived and understood. The sociologist will occupy himself with matters that others regard as too sacred or as too distasteful for dispassionate investigation. He will find rewarding the company of priests or of prostitutes. . . . **Peter L. Berger (1963:18–19)**

I don't ever remember watching any maiden aunts in the bathroom when I was a child! Before some psychiatrist says that I have probably repressed this guilty aspect of my past, let me quickly add that I did not even have a maiden aunt. But Berger does pose an interesting question, that of motivation for sociological research. As a sociologist, he of course denies a psychological or psychiatric basis for sociological research. I would also join his defense of "sociological keyhole watching," agreeing that a sociologist has license to be a Professional Peeping Tom without having to launch into a defense against accusations of sublimated voyeurism. Fortunately, the sociologist does not have to "psychologize" underlying motivations for his research activities and interests, and he is permitted to give a more straightforward (read "superficial," if you are inclined that way) account for his involvement. However, the question can still legitimately be asked why some of us are more interested in prostitutes than in priests.

The first research setting I entered was that of cab-driving. At the time I was (1) a very broke first-year graduate student without an assistantship but with a family, and (2) in need of gathering original data for a term paper for a class in "Social Interaction." I had no special interest in cab drivers; I did not know any cab drivers personally; I did not have any theories that I wanted to prove or disprove, nor did I have any "drums that I wanted to beat" regarding either the working class in general or cab drivers in particular. My total experience with cab drivers at that time had consisted of riding in a cab as passenger about three times. However, since I had already planned on working during the Christmas vacation in order to supplement our meager family income and I was too late to apply for a post office job, I thought that cab-driving might be suitable for fulfilling both needs: money and data. Consequently, I chose for the topic of my term paper the simple subject: "An Analysis of Greetings That Passengers Give Cab Drivers as They Enter Cabs," and I took a job as cabbie for Metro Cab Company of St. Louis (a pseudonym).

This turned out to be a fortuitous choice that greatly affected both my professional and personal lives. I found myself "in the midst of data," suddenly immersed in a world that I really hadn't known existed, and so overwhelmed by data that I began taking extensive field notes of my experiences with passengers, dispatchers, and cab drivers. I became so involved in this "world of data" that I never did write the simple paper that had been the partial purpose for my entering this setting. This initial entrance into the world of cabbies established a frame for both my general interests in deviance as a major subject of sociological analysis and for my general methodological orientation in sociology, that of participant-observation. And I am happy to share with readers of this volume the experiences and methodological insights that I have gained through my studies of deviance.[1]

It might be asked what is deviant about doing research on cab drivers. In the first place, the methodology that I happened onto because of the job that I took—that is, participant-observation—does not fit in with the "hard," "scientific," mathematical, hypotheses-testing research that is so prevalent in current sociology and that seems to have been elevated to a sacred or even semidivine status. The methodology of participant-observation, although traditional and still popular in sociology, is, at best, considered second-rate and, at worst, thought to be an irrelevant, archaic, obsolete, and even obstructionist nonscientific approach to the study of human behavior. Given the current orientation of sociology, the approach of participant-observation is in itself a deviant approach to the study of man. In many areas of sociology participant-observers are not accepted but are merely "tolerated" as sort of curious reminders of prescientific sociology. They are treated as sort of aged relatives who overstay their visit, remnants of the musty past-that-was and that somehow should no longer be; they are sometimes venerable because of their previous position, but ordinarily it is embarrassing that they are still present because they are so out-of-step with the way things are, mere relics of a former world that no longer seems to apply.

Being relegated to this definitely secondary, sometimes questionable, and perhaps deviant position forces participant-observers themselves into doing something they frequently observe among the deviants they study doing—defending their deviant orientation in sociology, using "deviance disavowal" (Davis 1964). This results in the peculiar situation of specialists in the study of deviance having to take up the cudgel of rhetoric in defense of the deviant position in which they find themselves (e.g., Lofland 1969, Matza 1969, and Polsky 1967). Although this defense is usually made without the motivation behind it being spelled out, it seems to me that the lowly status of participant-observation in sociology can account for much of the "deviance disavowal" on the part of participant-observers. I am quite happy to join this "chorus of defense" in behalf of the method that I also find so amenable to sociological research.

In the second place, my cabbie research was deviant because of the particular type of participant-observation I chose—covert participant-observation. Because of its seeming threat to a privacy about which we seem to be more and more concerned in our society, covert participant-observation is the deviant form of a deviant method. Perhaps simply listening to and observing persons who did not know that I was gathering data on what they were doing would have been sufficient to call my approach deviant, but I chose to go one step further and do what some consider to be indefensible—use a hidden tape recorder in order to investigate the comments and actions of passengers and fellow cab drivers, with neither their awareness nor their permission.

Putting it as baldly as this, which I am purposely doing, almost offends my own moral propriety and makes me quake at such thoughtless and insensitive invasion of the person and intimacies of others. It appears to me, however, that one of the best defenses for my approach is the stance of antimethodological puritanism taken by Jack Douglas in his article "Observing Deviance." Very convincing is his analogy between sociological research techniques that are looked on by the establishment with suspicion and our now highly esteemed medical practitioners, who at one time were held in disrepute because they illegally secularized and desecrated the dead, but who now not only honorably do so, but in addition secularize and desecrate our living physical being as well—for example, by taking intimacies with our daughters, wives, and mothers in their probing gynecological examinations (cf. Henslin and Biggs 1971). How moral attitudes do change! Perhaps, as Douglas suggests, such an attitudinal inversion will also take place regarding covert participant-observation.

In a third sense, this cabbie research was deviant not, as above, in the choice of methodology, but in the selection of occupation itself. While cab-driving is not a deviant occupation in the same sense that prostitution is, it is "offbeat," and cabbies themselves certainly cannot be described as a conventional group of men in our society. Cab drivers are just "not respectable." While they may not be as "disreputable" as are criminals or even pool hustlers (Polsky 1967), they are certainly not as "respectable" as teachers, ministers, businessmen, or *today's* medical men.

Although cab drivers are not deviant in and of themselves, they do have certain things in common with some types of deviants, for example, the hours they keep. Many of them drive from 3:00 P.M. to 3:00 A.M. They also frequently engage in off-duty activities with fellow cabbies until 6:00 or 7:00 A.M. before going home to sleep for a few hours, after which they get up for another shift, and so on, in an ever-recurring cycle.

Furthermore, the occupation of cab-driving itself leads to an inevitable association of cab drivers and deviance. Apart from any particular predilections that the cab driver might have, he is inevitably exposed to deviance because of his occupation. Because of his job, he is often called on to take drunks home, deliver and pick up call girls, and deliver lovers to their meeting places, as well as on rarer occasions being called on to search out a trysting husband for an enraged wife or to drop off and pick up burglars at their "places of work."[2]

But there is an additional reason why I put the deviant label on cab drivers, and that is because of the deviant activities that cab drivers themselves engage in. I am here referring not to cab drivers serving as middlemen for deviance, as above, where they provide the vehicular transportation for call girls, but rather to such common activities of cab drivers as shooting craps, rolling drunks, overcharging in various forms, and, in some cases, extortion and pimping, as well as to the ways in which they communicate the techniques of such practices to the novice cab driver.

The Benefits of a Subjective Perspective: Studying Cabbies

The major advantage of using participant-observation to study a group such as cab drivers is that the sociological researcher is able to gain the *subjective perspective.* Participant-observation allows the researcher to understand deviance from the viewpoint of the deviant himself. By experiencing the life style of the cab driver, sharing his occupational problems and compensations, and coming into direct contact with the social forces that impinge upon him, the researcher is able to understand forces that cause deviance to be a "normal" or logical outcome of the cab driver's experience. Participant-observation gives the researcher the insight that *not to be deviant in such a situation would be deviant.*

Because of the *pressures* to which the cab driver is subjected (e.g., the goals of economic success that he has been socialized into believing he must reach, the pressures that his family correspondingly places on him to achieve these goals, the everyday occupational tensions and pressures he is subject to, and the unfavorable economic situation in which he finds himself), the *opportunities* for deviance to which he is continually exposed, and the *sharing with fellow occupational members of a common outlook* that is accepting toward certain deviances, deviance becomes normal. It is this subjective perspective that the researcher engaged in participant-observation can grasp, a perspective that I am firmly convinced would be impossible to achieve outside this particular method (cf. Matza 1969).

Participant-observation also allows one to understand such things as why craps is such a common game among cab drivers. Through this method the researcher is able to understand the relationship between the *structure* of the occupation and craps, to see that cab-driving provides the opportunity for crapshooting, that it produces both financial and personal needs on the part of cab drivers to shoot craps, and that it also recruits workers who find craps to be need-satisfying. By experiencing the game himself and seeing that it makes financial goals

appear accessible, provides feelings of both control over and escape
from their life situation, and also provides much needed primary relations, the participant-observer is able to understand why craps can
become so meaningful to cab drivers. As a sociologist, he is also able
to see that cab drivers have a propensity to shoot craps because of
craps' simplicity, its speed, the mobility and availability of its equipment, its opportunity for expressivity, and its similarity to the world
of cab-driving (Henslin 1967, 1970a). Without actually experiencing the
occupational problems of cab drivers and the situation in which they
shoot craps, it is extremely unlikely that a sociological researcher
would gain much insight into or understanding of the reasons why crapshooting is so attractive to cab drivers.

In sociological research the participant-observation method is more
advantageous for gaining meaningful information about the subjects
than official statistics or someone's omniscient ideas about what those
persons are like. If one were to use either official statistics or the
sociological omniscience approach to the study of cab drivers, for
example, how much could be learned about cab drivers? Official statistics might yield certain information concerning their arrest rate, if
it were available, and one would be able to obtain certain economic
information about cab drivers across the nation. But given this information, how much would one actually know about the world of the cab
driver? Official statistics simply do not talk about his world, and
economic and demographic data appear to me to be typically devoid of
meaning unless they are related to the realities of everyday life.
Although sociological omniscience, like official statistics, can provide
some insight into situations that cab drivers face, it, too, is unable to
reproduce the meaning of those events for the cab driver himself, does
not allow us to accurately picture the cab driver's world as he sees it,
and does not allow us to grasp the cab driver's motivations as he interacts within the world that is so peculiarly his. Only by actually getting
out with cabbies themselves, preferably by driving a cab and experiencing cab-driving life, with its attendant problems and satisfactions,
or by hanging around cab drivers, or at least by interviewing cabbies
in depth, can such information and a view of his world ever be gained.

For example, if one wanted to do research on such a fundamental
element of social interaction as trust (and I here make a plea for more
research by sociologists into basic aspects of "everyday/anyday life-in-
society," whether one calls such research "phenomenology" or whatever), what would official statistics yield? What knowledge? What
understanding? Sociological omniscience, on the other hand, might, in
fact, yield something on this subject, since the sociologist, as a member
of society, could speak from a background of experiences involving

trust. However, it would seem desirable to root such an analysis in some empirical, verifiable situation rather than founding it on generalized experiences. By actually driving a cab, the researcher is able to analyze trust as it operates in the real world, as it provides a basis for decision-making by persons in whose occupational lives it is essential (Henslin 1968). Data that are rooted in the empirical life situation of the cab driver allow the researcher to abstract from the actual experiences of men the essential components of trust, to conceptualize trust in the way that it operates in the cab drivers' everyday world, and to make it applicable to most situations in life. Participant-observation is rather a remarkable method, for it can lead to increased knowledge of aspects of life fundamental to our existence in society.

It would seem that it would be impossible for such knowledge to be gained through any "Martian situation." Even in situations in which a Martian method is supposedly being applied, as in some forms of linguistic analysis, commonsense meanings are being bootlegged into the analysis (see Douglas's "Observing Deviance"). My own experience with componential analysis (Psathas and Henslin 1967) indicates that it is impossible to use the Martian method in such analysis. In order to discover the categories inherent in orders that are dispatched to cab drivers and that are used by dispatchers and cab drivers in the dispatching and picking-up process, I had to know the meaning that the orders had for the cab drivers themselves. In order to gain such knowledge I participated directly in the world of the cab driver. (The only other way in which I could have acquired such knowledge would have been by interviewing cab drivers, and an interview can be a form of participation in someone else's world.) My original categories, sets, and their elements proved to be merely tentative, for they had to be refined, reformulated, and reintegrated as a result of my continued experiences with the world of the cab driver. Again, it was the empirical base—that is, being rooted in participation in the cabbie world—that provided the basis for the development of the initial categories as well as the check for validity and the refinement of these categories. (For more detail regarding "categories," "sets," "elements," and "componential analysis" in general, the reader is directed to [Psathas and Henslin 1967] and to the references cited therein.)

The Benefits of a Subjective Perspective: Studying Suicides, Drug Users, and Abortionees

The need for dealing firsthand with subjects being studied is also borne out by my experiences with a second form of deviance, that of suicide. While there is much official information on the subject of suicide, and while sociological omniscience can perhaps provide some insight into this area (although I find very little of it in sociological writings on suicide), it is only through contact with persons who are suicidal, with those who have attempted suicide, or with those who knew a suicide victim intimately that we are able to reconstruct the meanings of experiences of life for the suicide himself—that is, only by somehow getting into the suicide's world can we picture it and see on what basis the suicide defined certain events in his life and on the basis of those definitions made certain significant decisions, literally life-and-death decisions.

What can official statistics or a sociological approach that does not include speaking to relevant respondents tell us about the world of the suicide or about his family? From the statistics we might learn some data that are interesting or that are "hard" (and ipso facto desirable and desired by some), but beyond such superficial characteristics, what would we know about his world? Would we, for example, understand the reasons why someone committed suicide if our statistics indicate that a certain proportion of suicide victims had lost their jobs, had been demoted, or had separated from their spouses within three months of their committing suicide? But by interviewing or "talking with" persons who express suicidal desires, or with persons who have attempted suicide, or with the families and friends of suicides, we can become familiar in depth with how suicides have reacted to their lives' problems, to their biographical facts, and we can get at or close to their definitions and interpretations of the significant events in their lives. This insight enables us to piece together *motives* for the act of suicide.

The advantage of a sociological method that includes participation of some sort by the researcher, or one that at least includes detailed observation, is that the researcher can understand an actor's own conception of reality—how he sees himself in the context of some life situation—and thereby gain insight into *his* motivation for a particular act. Understanding of this kind is, or should be, a goal for the social sciences. It seems that observation that involves participation of some sort holds the key for the development of a science of human behavior, and such a method is very different from gathering economic and/or biographical statistics.

The benefit of the subjective perspective has also been driven home to me by my research in another area of deviance, that of drug use. In this area official statistics could provide us with some general biographical information and could tell us something about general drug patterns, at least as far as arrest rates reflect differences in geographical, sex, age, residential, occupational, and ethnic distributions. Perhaps something could even be told us by the great sociological "as if," that is, by the sociologist who imagines how it *might* be *if* he were "one of those." But in either case, what would we actually learn about drug users? If one is interested in the *process* by which someone becomes a drug user, one must at least talk to drug users. It is only through some form of association with people who have personally experienced drugs that one is able to understand the significance of such things as different styles of drug use, different patterns of reaction to life's stresses, and the meaning of drugs for the individual in the context of his particular biography. A "talking approach"—that is, interviewing respondents, as I am currently doing with drug users—has the potential, at least, of yielding such information; however, much more "data in depth" and relevant definitions could be gained if I were to participate directly in their life situation and experience the varying problematic situations that confront them.

What, for example, could we possibly determine about such specifics of drug use as the effects of drugs on sexual experience (how perceptions of sexual experiences change while one is under the influence of drugs) unless we at least speak to persons who have had sexual experiences while under the influence of drugs—or unless we take the option of becoming participant-observers in the full sense of the word, and engage in sexual activities while under such influence? Official information is entirely lacking in this area, and sociological omniscience would really have to be omniscient if it were to come up with anything worthwhile on this subject. Even pharmacological characteristics of drugs cannot tell us how the *perceptions* of the user change (Henslin 1970c, 1970d).

A similar situation exists in the study of abortion that I am currently conducting. Statistics on abortion are so inadequate that it is extremely difficult to even approximate with any accuracy the extent of abortion in the United States. And that mythical omniscient sociologist could not be of any help either if he were to try his "as if" approach, if he were to try to imagine what it would be like if he were to undergo an abortion. What experiences could he possibly have that would qualify him for such suppositioning? One must, then, attempt to somehow enter the world of women seeking and undergoing abortions in order to know what is happening within that world. Once one talks to women who are about to have or who have just had an abortion (and, preferably, also watches abortions being performed), one is able to understand something about the dilemma that the woman faces as she unexpectedly finds herself with an unwanted pregnancy. The researcher can gain insight into her attempts to neutralize society's dictates as she begins her lonesome search for the abortionist and can understand something about her feelings as she undergoes the actual abortion and as she relates to her friends and relatives in the postabortion phase of her experience (Henslin 1971).

Through no Martian situation would one be able to reconstruct such social meanings. It takes participation of some sort in the lives of one's subjects in order to understand or to reconstruct the social meanings of their activities. It is only through such participation that we can relate the perceptions of people, their internal states of mind and feelings, with their external actions. The importance of these perceptions and states of mind is that they provide the actor with the meanings by which he interprets his own external behaviors. Such participation requires, at a minimum, that one talk to relevant subjects, but some sort of immersion in the lives of the subjects is required if one is to reconstruct their relevant social meanings. It is sometimes the case that such immersion can take place through detailed or depth interviews, but it is ordinarily more easily obtained through participation in and sharing of life styles with the subjects.

Getting at Background Expectancies

Members of any particular world take certain fundamental assumptions about their world for granted. Day in and day out they live with certain aspects of their world, and these become a part of the background expectancies upon which their everyday interactions are premised (Garfinkle 1967). Because of this, there is much about his world that any subject is unable to verbalize, and it would, accordingly, be futile to ask him questions about certain aspects of his existence. Questionnaires and survey approaches simply cannot get at such aspects of man's "life-in-society." As Malinowski (1922:396) put it:

... We cannot expect to obtain a definite, precise and abstract statement from a philosopher, belonging to the community itself. The native takes his fundamental assumptions for granted, and if he reasons or inquires into matters of belief, it would be always only as regards details and concrete applications. Any attempts on the part of the Ethnographer to induce his informant to formulate such a general statement would have to be in the form of leading questions of the worst type because in these leading questions he would have to introduce words and concepts essentially foreign to the native. Once the informant grasped their meaning, his outlook would be warped by our own ideas having been poured into it. Thus the Ethnographer must draw the generalisation for himself, must formulate the abstract statement without the direct help of a native informant.

Particularly in participant-observation does the sociologist become a part of the world of his subjects. But the sociologist is more than this.

He also remains a trained observer, using his "sociological eye" to study the world that he enters. He asks basic questions about the taken-for-granted background expectancies of his subjects. He does not want to assume; he wants to know. For this reason, he asks questions about the basics of the interaction occurring in that setting. However, in overtly questioning certain background expectancies, the covert participant-observer would surely run the risk of calling into question his bona fide membership in the group and would frequently run the additional risk of being labeled as a "nut." For example, in cab-driving research, a question that I kept in mind as I went about my cabbie duties was "What is a passenger?" For obvious reasons, such a question was too basic to ask any fellow cabbies or the dispatcher or the boss or passengers. Someone who at least ostensibly appears to be a cab driver simply cannot run around asking "What is a passenger?" In this case, such a question could not be asked even if one were an overt participant-observer for at least the reasons indicated by Malinowski. If it were asked, the answer would prove rather unsatisfactory, ordinarily taking the form of "Stick it up your ass." But keeping such basic questions in mind as I participated in the cabbie world sensitized me to what was occurring within that world, and I was then later able to answer such questions from the point of view of the cab driver.

The sociologist, having perceived bits and pieces of the world that he has entered, later puts these pieces together in order to draw a picture of that world. As he puts them together he is acting as a sociologist, utilizing his sociological imagination and his sociological training. The world that he now reconstructs is, however, no longer identical to the world that he observed, because he is now no longer dealing with "behavior-in-process" but, rather, a verbalization of the behavior that he had viewed "in-process." Yet the sociologist attempts to remain as faithful as he possibly can to the world he studied. He tries to reconstruct that world in such a way that if a member of that world were to read his reconstruction he would, hopefully, not only recognize his world but would also better understand it.

Covert Versus Overt Participant-Observation

To get at the meaning of deviance for the members of some group and the relationship of that deviance to other aspects of their lives may require not simply participant-observation but *covert* participant-observation. It is sometimes the case that information can be best obtained by working secretly from the inside (Douglas, "Observing Deviance"). In fact, I would say that this is frequently the case because members of a group share a certain amount of information with one another on the basis of their membership in the same group. They feel that they can confidently share this information not only because they have a "common culture" and therefore share the same perspective on this information, but also because, frequently, revelation of this information outside the group will harm all the members of the group, including the one who revealed it. It is with fellow members of the group that the "front is down." If a researcher who is known to be a researcher steps into such a setting, he will be suspect because he could impart this shared information to others without bringing harm to himself. Now it is at least theoretically possible that this same information could be obtained by other methods; for example, by overt participant-observation. Granted that the members of the group being studied have as much confidence and rapport with the researcher as they do with a fellow member of their group and granted further that they have complete confidence in the trustworthiness of the researcher to hold the anonymity of their information intact, it might be possible to gain access to this same information—that is, it *might* be. But with covert participant-observation, the uncertainty is removed, and once one is fully accepted as a member of the group, one has access to this information.

Persons who belong to a group that is significant to them have a *shared world,* a common culture that tends to cause them to see the world and to interpret their experiences in very similar ways. This common culture provides a frame that surrounds their everyday experiences, yielding a similar interpretation of events that impinge upon that "world-held-in-common." Since this shared world frequently is the very thing that participant-observers are trying to study, it seems that whenever possible those things that can serve as a barrier to information about it should be avoided. It would appear that if one is identified as a researcher, no matter how great the rapport, a gap remains between the identity of known researcher and that of group member, a gap that leads to differential access to information. It is always possible that the overt participant-observer will gain access to this information, and in some cases he will feel confident that he has done so, but he can never know for certain whether this is true or not unless he has actually been a full member of the group. There will always be, at the minimum, an "insider's view" that the overt participant-observer can only *speak about* rather than *speak from,* which he would have been able to do had he actually been a member himself. This qualitative distinction differentiates the data obtained by the research approaches of covert and overt participant-observation.

It is possible, then, to argue that there is both a quantitative and a qualitative difference between the data gathered through covert and overt participant-observation. However, one could attempt to reverse this argument and take the position that there is certain information that can be obtained through overt participant-observation that cannot be obtained through covert participant-observation. And this is true. For example, one problem inherent in covert participant-observation is that there are certain questions that the researcher dare not ask because they do not belong to the member role that he is playing. Asking questions that the researcher role allows but the member role precludes would disrupt the flow of interaction, drawing attention to one's self and possibly causing the researcher to "blow his cover." (Many times, for example, I wanted to ask passengers direct questions, but, as with the question "What is a passenger?" discussed earlier, these questions would have been inappropriate for a cab driver to ask and had to be reluctantly foregone.) This problem can often be overcome by supplementing covert participant-observation with other information-gathering techniques following the cessation of the covert participant-observer role; frequently, however, the stimulus to ask the question is based on some particular interaction situation that will not recur in the same way, and the opportunity is lost for good. Being able to follow such leads is the advantage of the overt participant-observer role, but, as discussed earlier, the information losses inherent in a "less-than-full-member" status make the covert participant-observer role the superior research technique.

Covert Participant-Observation and Ethics

Even if covert participant-observation has the research potential that I have outlined above, what about its ethicality? Kai T. Erikson (1967) has levied a charge against covert participant-observation, arguing that "using masks" in research is unethical because it "compromises both the people who wear them and the people for whom they are worn." Erikson takes the position that it is unethical for a sociologist to deliberately misrepresent his identity for the purpose of entering a private domain to which he could not otherwise gain access or to deliberately misrepresent the character of the research in which he is engaged. (For a similar position, see Barnes 1963.) My particular research on cab drivers would escape Erikson's ethical castigation because my identity was never misrepresented. I represented myself for what I was, a student, and I also gave accurate biographical data to the management of the cab company. Erikson (1967:372) does specify that social settings to which the sociologist can gain legitimate access, access without misrepresentation, are settings in which he can use his "trained eye" to observe without having to reveal himself as an investigator. However, certain sociological research is censured by this ethical stance; for example, that by Caudill (1952); Festinger *et al.* (1956); Sullivan *et al.* (1958); Lofland and Lejeune (1960); and Humphreys (1970).

There is, however, more to the ethical question in sociological research than misrepresentation of identity or purpose. A person who desires to take a strong ethical stance could say, for example, that whenever anyone enters a social setting, he does so as a normal member of that setting, unless he announces a different identity. In other words, he is by his *very act of entering that setting* declaring to other persons there that he has no ulterior research or observational purposes, that he is merely a member like any other. Such an ethical stance means, however, that sociologists would have to constantly reveal their identities *as sociologists* to others in whatever settings they entered or else they would be forbidden from ever utilizing information that they had fortuitously gained from such settings. Additionally, whatever the research design—whether it is experimental, survey, or some other— some form of deceit of purposes appears to always be involved, since revealing exactly what one is looking for would so bias the outcome that the social scientist might as well pack up his research instruments and go home (Roth 1962).

The problem with ethics is that they are not absolute but, rather, are only a matter of definition. And, having undergone differing socialization experiences, different people apply quite different definitions of ethicality to the same situation. This, I assume, is the major reason why the American Sociological Association has been having a difficult time for several years in gaining agreement on a code of professional research ethics for its membership. It would appear that, whatever ethical stance one takes or whatever code of ethics one develops or adopts, exceptions would invariably develop and such a code would face the probability that in a short time definitions of ethicality and unethicality would undergo change. (For a contrary position, see Seeley 1967.) Sometimes this change is even antipodal, as in the case of dissecting cadavers by the medical profession. It appears to me that each researcher must act according to his own system of morality. For example, I would consider any research on my part to be immoral, no matter what method was used, if harm came to my respondents through my findings. However, this stance is based on my own system of morality, and I do not feel that I can impose my system on others, nor do I consider it appropriate for others to force theirs on me. I should emphasize at this point that this position refocuses the ethical question, shifting the emphasis from the ethics inherent in a particular methodology to the ethics of the results of the methodology.

Validity Checks

I want to now turn to other problems connected with research into deviance in general and research done through participant-observation in particular. The first such problem is that of *validity*. Douglas, in his article "Observing Deviance," writes of the need of comparing findings gained through the *role of researcher* with understandings gained from involvement in the activity *as a member* and suggests that such comparisons can serve as a validity check. This appears to me to be an excellent principle to follow, and it was one that was inadvertently applied to my cab-driving research. I had utilized various sorts of checks on my research, for example, the use of a tape recorder to insure the accuracy of quotations, but I had not run any check of validity regarding my interpretations of the world of the cab driver with someone else who knew that world. This validity check, however, was applied to my research in an unanticipated fashion. Dr. Irving Louis Horowitz, one of the senior professors at Washington University at that time, unexpectedly asked to read my dissertation. As a prospective Ph.D. I was filled with trepidation regarding the outcome of this examination by Horowitz, who possessed an intimate knowledge both of the cab-driving world (at one time in his ascent from the New York ghetto, he had driven a cab) and of sociology. Horowitz's reaction to what I had written validated my findings, however—that is, he agreed that the world of the cab driver had been accurately presented.

This brings me to a related problem in sociological research—that of determining whether the researcher's experiences as a member of a group are representative of experiences of members of that group or whether they are representative of the particular background that the researcher brings with him when he enters it. Since the sociological researcher ordinarily has educational and socialization experiences that are atypical of the members of the group he is studying, it is likely that he will react in atypical fashion to what he experiences within that world. In other words, although he is acting as an insider, he might still be perceiving interaction from an outsider's point of view—without even knowing it.

How, then, can the sociological researcher know that his perspective matches that of the members of the group that he is studying? Their life situation, after all, dictates that they shall be members of the group, while the researcher has voluntarily decided to join the group in order to study it; this means that *membership in the group does not have the same meaning for the researcher as it does for the regular members*. Since there is this built-in differential perspective due to differences in the educational, socialization, social-class frame as well as dissimilar motivation for joining the group, some validation of interpretations appears desirable. It is precisely at this point that subjecting one's findings and interpretations to persons who are "bona fide members" of the group can serve as a validity check.

To apply this principle to my own research, my interpretations of and experiences with cab drivers should not be examined only by sociologists who are "former cab drivers." Former-cab-drivers-who-are-now-sociologists are not the same as cab-drivers-who-are-still-cab-drivers. The former have been drastically changed through an exacting, rigorous, and sometimes oppressive socialization process as they learned to be sociologists. They no longer see the world from the perspective of the cab driver, although they are familiar with that perspective and can determine whether or not what is being written rings true. To apply such a validity check, I should, rather, submit my findings to those who currently identify themselves as cabbies, who earn their livelihood as cabbies, and who are "nothing but cabbies."

It appears, then, to be desirable to check out sociologists' findings and their interpretations with members of the group that was studied. On the other hand, there are certain "straight sociological interpretations" of data that become irrelevant to members of the group, for which one needs a sociological background in order to understand them. There are, moreover, cases in which persons who actually share the group's perspective would reject the sociologist's interpretation, not because it is invalid, but because it brings out negative aspects of the group with which they strongly identify. In spite of such drawbacks, however, whenever sociological researchers claim to be presenting their study *from the members' perspective,* some sort of validity check should be run, regardless of the method used to obtain the data.

A validity check was also inadvertently run on my suicide research. A sociologist whom I did not personally know requested a copy of my manuscript on suicide (Henslin 1970b). His reaction was: "Your description of what significant others go through following a suicide makes a lot of sense. And it just isn't academic with me because I have gone through that experience myself."

Although it is flattering to receive such validations, validity checks of this sort could lead to very serious problems for sociologists if they became standard practice. At the very least, they could be threatening. Just as it is threatening to the student to have to submit his work to professors, especially the thesis on which his Ph.D future hangs, so it is also threatening to the professor to have to present his findings to a group of peers who sit in judgment of them, who decide whether his paper will be read at the A. S. A. meetings, whether it will be published in a good journal or not, and so on. If, in addition to this, sociologists also had to submit their findings to persons possessing "inside informa-tion" on the subject they analyzed, this might prove to be too much. What would happen, for example, if one's findings were not validated by members of the group? It would certainly create problems. But such nonvalidation would not conclusively demonstrate that the findings and their interpretations were wrong. It would be possible that the group members had individually undergone different experiences, or even that the groups themselves were not comparable; for example, cab drivers *collectively* undergo disparate experiences depending on the geograph-ical area in which they work, and even those who work for the same company *individually* meet with dissimilar events. Although, because of the nature of their work, their experiences are probably more similar than they are different, it is still possible that such differences could make the cab-driving world presented by the sociologist seem rather unfamiliar to cab drivers. This problem in validation seems insoluble at this time, and so I simply point to the need for further validation of sociological findings.

Blowing One's Cover

Another problem connected with covert participant-observation that overt participant observers do not face is the ever-present potential risk of "blowing one's cover"—that is, exposing one's research identity. As Douglas says in "Observing Deviance," there are certain types of research in which such an eventuality could prove dangerous. In my research with cab drivers there was not much danger to my person if I made a mistake and blew my cover, since I was doing covert participant-observation in an occupation that was open to members of the public. This is drastically different from penetrating the Mafia or, on the other hand, the F.B.I. However, I did get involved in certain aspects of cabbie activities that were deviant, such as crapshooting, which could have possibly led to recriminations for the crapshooters if their activity had become known to the wrong outsiders. My closest brush with blowing my cover occurred one night after shooting craps with the cabbies. I had just finished surreptitiously taping the crap-game, and I was going to give one of the cabbies that had been in the game a ride home. While we were walking to my car, the microphone attached to the patch-cord fell through a hole in the manilla folder in which I had been carrying it. I noticed the microphone dangling in the air at about the level of my knees as we were walking. I quickly glanced at my partner, but he was looking ahead and didn't notice what was happening, and so I shifted the folder to the side opposite him and cautiously worked the dangling microphone back into the folder. I had no cover story for such a contingency, nor do I know how I would have explained my possession at that time of a tape recorder with the sounds of the last hour's game on it.

Blowing my cover would not have had the potentially dangerous consequences that would have resulted had "more criminal" activities been involved. However, it is possible that, having been exposed as a "spy in their midst," I would not have been trusted by the cabbies from that point on. They would have realized that I could utilize this information for their occupational harm, and they certainly would have been suspicious as to whether I might be representing the "fuzz." In the investigation of criminal activities, the potential harm to the subjects is much greater, and the potential retribution for the covert participant-observer who unfortunately blows his cover is, of course, correspondingly greater.

Depth Interviewing

Depth interviewing is a method of sociological research closely related to participant-observation. A depth interview is an interview that follows a general outline of topics to be discussed in which the respondent is encouraged to speak as extensively as he can on the various subtopics of the research. One problem that I have encountered in depth interviewing is that of not being able to anticipate in advance the range of responses to my various probes. This, of course, is the reason why depth interviewing is open-ended. But beyond this, even after a number of respondents have been interviewed, unanticipated areas in the research continue to open up, subtopics that are also worthwhile pursuing. While this is good in terms of yielding data, it means that some areas appear in the later interviews that had not been covered in the earlier ones. The problem then arises when it comes to the analysis of the data of how one should handle incomplete samples for subareas that have proved pertinent to the general research project.

I see two solutions to this problem: (1) "picking up" earlier respondents on the added areas. However, one cannot always re-establish contact with such respondents, and even when one can, they are not always willing to be re-interviewed. (2) Not following up the promising subareas. But since these unanticipated areas are often extremely fruitful for the research, this solution also appears undesirable. The "real" solution would be to anticipate these areas. But this requires either such extensive pretesting and preprobing as to be frequently impractical or else such complete familiarity with the world of the respondents that it presupposes certain knowledge in pursuit of which the research is being conducted in the first place.

Just as there is a problem in covert participant-observation of questions that cannot be asked because they are "out of role," so there is a related problem in depth interviewing of questions that cannot be asked because they are too disturbing or too personal, even for a researcher who feels that he has some sort of professional right to invade privacy. For example, one question that I would like very much to include in the abortion research because it would provoke meaningful responses is: "Do you think abortion is the same as murder?" In the drug research I might also like to ask: "Are you more likely to give blow jobs when you use grass than when you don't use grass?" Asking questions that are either too disturbing or too personal is likely to interfere with the rapport that has been established in the interview setting and endanger further responses in the interview. One way of handling this problem is to include such questions at the very end of the interview, where it is relatively unimportant for the *data-gathering aspect of the research* if the respondent terminates the interview. Another solution is to indirectly approach the general area about which you want information; for example: "How does your sexual behavior differ under the influence of drugs?" "In what ways do you think abortion is wrong?" Such an approach is less threatening to the respondent, and, in my view at least, more ethical. However, if a researcher takes seriously some sort of obligation for the well being of his respondents, he is faced with the fact that there are certain questions that he would like to ask but that, for the sake of the welfare of his respondents, he just cannot.

A related problem concerning questioning in depth interviewing is the opposite of the above—that of questions that must be asked that the researcher really does not want to ask. Either because he knows the area from personal experience or because he has already done considerable interviewing by the time he gets to a particular respondent, the researcher will have a good idea of what the answers to these questions will be, and yet, to reach his goal of subjective understanding, he cannot assume that he knows for certain what the answers are. "Perhaps for this respondent the meaning will be somewhat different" is a possibility that the researcher must always keep in mind. For example, how does the researcher ask the question "What do you mean by 'high'?" and not sound simple-minded to both himself and the interviewee? The answer to the question is one that is well known both to himself and to the respondent, and when the question is asked, it is likely that the respondent might think, "This nut—he's supposed to know a lot about drugs and he doesn't even know what 'high' is. If he doesn't even know this, how can I possibly communicate other things to him? Maybe he is actually straight and can't be trusted."

The solution that I have found to this dilemma is to state before the interview something to the effect of: "I am going to ask you some questions whose answers may seem very obvious, but I have to ask them to

get you to tell me in your own words exactly what they mean to you."
Making a statement like this then sets up a category of thought on the
part of the interviewee in which he can interpret such questions in a
manner neither harmful to the interviewer's own ego nor to the interviewing process itself.

This same dilemma was present in my research on suicide when, in
order to get at subjective meaning, I was forced to ask the question
"What do you mean, 'guilty'?" when a respondent said that he felt
guilty after the death of a significant other. Although the asking of such
questions can frequently make the researcher feel that the respondent
might be perceiving him as a fool, the question is necessary, since he
never knows for certain but that this particular respondent may mean
something entirely different from the expected answer when he says
that he felt guilt. It is also possible that when this respondent elabo-
rates on the meaning of guilt he will give data that have not yet been
touched on by previous respondents or data that will interlock with
earlier data, yielding a fuller picture. Because of these potentials, it
seems to me that it is always better to err on the side of appearing
somewhat naive or foolish than to lose such data.

Another problem in depth interviewing is the "feedback effect." The
researcher must take pains to prevent interviews that he has already
conducted from interfering with interviews that he is yet to conduct.
Depth interviews can very easily change the subject's definition of his
experiences. For example, a respondent will frequently say something
like, "Oh, I hadn't thought of that before. . . . Let's see now." For a
respondent to mentally review an experience and to lay that experience
out before a researcher can often result in his reconceptualizing that
experience. In fact, it would seem unlikely that this would not be the
case. If, then, a person who had already been interviewed were to share
the contents of his interview with a future respondent, he would be
likely to bias the results in a direction similar to the one that his own
reconceptualization took. In such cases one would, in a sense, be un-
knowingly reinterviewing the same respondent! I have handled this problem by impressing upon each respondent at the end of the interview the
importance of the research and the need for secrecy; I then elicit a
commitment from him that he will not talk about the content of the interview with anyone else. One does not have any guarantee that this
promise will be kept. However, it seems that the effort to try and prevent this potential problem in this way has been worth it, because I
have on several occasions asked respondents what they knew about the
research, and have so far never received any indication that such "feedback" has been operating.

Observing Deviance Must Mean Being Deviant

There are certain other problems inherent in doing deviance research. One of these is the assumption, on the part of many "straights" (and sometimes deviants), that someone involved in deviance research has "peculiar" interests, with the implication that the researcher must have something deviant about himself if he wants to do "that sort" of research. This was a frequent reaction that I ran across after I announced my intention to do research into suicide. The assumption seems to be that if one wants to do research into such things as death it is probably because one finds a particular fascination with the subject, a fascination that unwittingly reveals some perhaps hitherto unknown aspect of the researcher's personality makeup. The response that people frequently made when they first found out that I was planning research on suicide was: "Why do you want to do that?" "Who would want to study such a subject?" There was no detached response such as: "Oh, I can see that there is a lot that we don't know about that subject, and it's good that someone is pursuing it." (Actually, neither morbidity nor do-goodism was my motivation. Suicide research was simply a political, or expedient, choice. I had no particular interest in the subject, but a post-doctoral fellowship was available, and I was not ready to cut the umbilical cord with my alma mater.)

People tend to associate the research that a researcher is conducting with the researcher himself. In the case of suicide, they feel that there must be something morbid about the researcher if he is interested in such a morbid topic. In the case of drug research, they assume that the researcher must be a drug user of some sort if he is interested enough in the subject to do research on it. Similarly, if one does research on homosexuality, others tend to attribute homosexuality to the researcher.[3]

Death is a topic not ordinarily freely discussed in our culture. We seem to be culturally unable to face the fact that death will claim all of us, and we regularly utilize a whole host of "escape devices" to prevent us from facing it. These include such things as the common funerary practices of mortician cosmetology in which the corpse is painted so that it appears lifelike and of the decoration of funeral homes with live flowers. It is also implicit in the cultural and religious belief that death is not really death but the beginning of a life to come, that the person will continue in spirit or that he now lives elsewhere in an altered state. Because our cultural emphasis is on escape from the reality of death, anyone deciding to do death research is staking a deviant claim and is going against the prevailing ethos.

Problems of "Front" and Role Conflict

As Douglas says in "Observing Deviance," most sociologists are concerned with the straight world, and they remain protected and somewhat isolated in the environment of academia. However, as part of their identification with the academic community, sociologists frequently wear beards. If a bearded sociologist wishes to do research among certain "straights," his beard, which is part of his ordinarily acceptable front for his university position, can become a disrupting force.

The problem that this presented for my suicide research was whether the beard would hinder the rapport between respondents and researcher that is needed in order to gather data in such a sensitive area. In this case I made the decision to try and do the research with the beard, and this turned out to be a sound decision. The beard did not seem to hinder rapport, but, on the contrary, it seemed to lend an air of legitimacy to my role as researcher. In making appointments, I introduced myself as being from the university, to give the research the academic respectability requisite for gaining entrance into these respondents' lives. The beard appeared to further legitimate this academic respectability, defining me as "one of those people from over there," "one of those professors." It furthermore seemed to legitimate the research itself because, although people with good sense might not be interested in such a morbid topic as death, professors, who are looked on by perhaps most of our citizens as not being usual anyway, might be. There was, however, one woman who was put off by the beard. She associated beards with hippies, and hippies with a rather undesirable type of person. I was never able to fully neutralize the hostility that she expressed during the interview. But this was the only negative case of which I was aware.

The problem of front, the legitimation of presentation of one's self and purpose, is one that all of us continually face, even in our everyday lives. Ordinarily, however, front is not problematic to us because we are so socialized into our roles that we take the props that belong to those roles as being part of our persons; we wear our masks naturally, and we give off cues that match very well the various roles that we are called on to play. It is when either something goes wrong with our ordinary role performances or when we are called on to play a role that we are not familiar with that we must start questioning our whole role behavior, including our response repertoire and our whole front, along with its various props (Goffman 1959).

The *presentation of front* is especially problematic when one is engaged in research into deviance because, as outlined above, certain suspicions attach to a researcher who has chosen an offbeat topic in the first place, and because the legitimation of purpose must be successfully presented to potential respondents in order to create and maintain the requisite rapport. Although my front was for the most part very successful in the suicide research, there was one case where it failed almost entirely. The very first evening appointment I made was with a widow who was about thirty years old. She had become suspicious about the legitimacy of someone doing research on the subject of suicide who wanted to speak to her in her home, and she had checked with her next-door neighbor, a policeman. When I arrived for the appointment, I was greeted in a rather unusual way—fortunately the only one of its kind in the research—I was "cordially" invited to take a ride in a patrol car. The policeman's comment, "Anybody visiting widows at night has to be up to no good," very aptly summarizes my reception that evening. In order to avoid the imputation of sexual motives for the research (and this was extremely problematic since more males commit suicide in our society than females, and a good proportion of widows work during the day and are available for interviewing primarily at night), I hired a female research assistant. The two of us, arriving together, put up a front that appeared to be quite acceptable, since there were no similar incidents during the remainder of the research. This solution had the additional benefit of providing two simultaneous interviews whenever two respondents were present and also made certain that no interviews were conducted in the presence of a third party.

An additional problem existed in the suicide research, one of role conflict. I felt a conflict between my role as researcher and as helper-of-fellow-humans-in-distress—that is, some sort of generalized humane role. When, in the course of my interviewing, I encountered individuals in need of professional guidance or therapy, individuals greatly disturbed by the suicide of someone who had been close to them, and in some instances even individuals extremely suicidal themselves, was I simply to play the role of researcher and not look beyond this? Was I simply to ask my questions, then politely leave and forget these people even though I felt that I held, because of a different life situation, certain keys to their well-being? Should the researcher ever step out of his role as researcher? If the answer to this last question is "no," it certainly legitimates noninvolvement for one's self and reduces the problem considerably. How nice it would be simply to say, "That isn't my role" or "They would have been in the same situation if I hadn't appeared on the scene." However, whether it was the role that I desired or not, I *did* appear on the scene.

The solution that I developed to handle this role conflict was the common one of role segregation (Sarbin 1954:253). I first played the role of researcher and then, where it seemed warranted, that of professional helper. In this way I was able to satisfactorily resolve this conflict. In cases where persons were disturbed about the death, when the interview was finished, I would assure them that the emotions they were experiencing that were so troubling to themselves were normal, that these emotions were ordinarily experienced by others who had had someone close to them commit suicide, and that, therefore, they should not be disturbed about them. Some form of this general statement became almost a part of the standard repertoire of my visits, since most respondents were disturbed in some way and also looked upon me, as a researcher in this area, as someone who knew the answers. In some cases I also stepped beyond this "consoling role" into one in which I directed people to professional help. Others would probably handle this conflict between researcher role and therapist role quite differently, but each person must deal with such moral dilemmas according to the ethics into which he has been socialized.[4]

In drug research, my beard was a natural prop, especially valuable in helping me gain entrance into the drug subculture. The difficulties in gaining rapport with subjects who are engaged in illegal activities, especially activities that carry frightening penalties to anyone apprehended, are well known. One must establish a trust-relationship with potential respondents, and crucial to this establishment is the conviction on the part of the respondent that the researcher does not in some way represent his enemies. In this case respondents had to be convinced that I was not "straight" myself, or that at least my sympathies were with them, or that at a very minimum I definitely did not represent the long arm of any official organization, including the university administration, reaching out for them.

In this case, entree into the drug subculture was gained through a student who had been in one of my classes and who was quite involved in the drug subculture himself. His "okay" then legitimated my presence, but, in addition to this, my "not looking straight," my "personal style," also helped to establish rapport. It was here that my beard and casual clothes became valuable, and as my contacts with the drug subculture continued over time I noticed that I was allowing my hair to grow longer.

Although playing such a role maximizes rapport and contacts with members of the drug subculture, it can also create problems with university administrators. Most university administrators are not exactly known for their radicalism or even their liberality, and the university with which I am affiliated is no exception. Accordingly, when it came time for administrative approval for the research that I had already begun, usually a mere technicality, my front, while positive for purposes of the study, became negative for purposes of securing approval and economic cooperation from the university administration. Thus, another form of role conflict developed because of deviance research—that between the characteristics that facilitate the research and the characteristics that are deemed a mark of university respectability.

The "halo effect" was at work, associating me with the type of research I was doing and creating fear on the part of some members of the committee to which I had submitted my project that the university, by approving research into drug use, was in some way acknowledging or even approving drug use. As a result, my methodology was overtly scrutinized very carefully, and there were questions raised covertly concerning my possible involvement in the drug subculture. Since I was not using drugs, I assume that their suspicions that I might be connected with the drug subculture were based only on my choice of research topic and on my "personal style."

In addition to this "guilt by association," there was the related problem of "doubling deviance."[5] I had chosen not only to do research in an area of deviance involving illegal drug use by students, but also to include gathering data on perceptions of their sexual experiences while under the influence of drugs, most of which involve premarital sex. In my relationship with the committee, I could sense a general feeling, at least on the part of some of the committee members, that such research is better left undone. When it comes to official approval of research into deviance, one of the factors operating is the feeling in regard to some types of deviance that if the deviance is quiet and unnoticeable, it is almost the same as if it did not exist—that is, if it is not brought to anyone's attention, it does not have to be dealt with. By researching such deviance, and by requesting university approval for such research, moreover, the existence of the deviance is brought into the open, where it must be acknowledged. This means that one must officially acknowledge that there is a problem and, if there is a problem, the feeling is that something must be done about it. Thus, if one does not do such research and, thereby, does not raise the deviance to a level where it is visible, administrators and others feel much more secure.

Moral Dilemmas in Deviance Research

In addition to the moral problem already discussed—that of conflict between the researcher role and a helper role—deviance research contains certain moral dilemmas that are ordinarily not discussed in print: the problem of the motivation to experiment with the deviance and the problem of "intimate knowledge." Exposure to deviant activities through secondary contacts such as interviewing can lead the researcher to desire to experience the deviance itself. For example, the researcher may find that he wishes to experiment with drugs, to determine whether drugs will affect him in the same way as they do his respondents or to gain greater insight into the subjective meaning of the respondent's world (cf. Yablonsky 1968). If such motivation for the deviant experience develops, it is also frequently combined with an increased opportunity for such experiences through the contacts the researcher makes in his research and an increased knowledge about the skills that are needed to accomplish the experience. In the case of drugs, for example, not only does he have the opportunity to experiment, but he also learns techniques of administering drugs, information about doses, the right price to pay, and methods of concealment of the purchase. The dilemmas that this poses for the researcher, again, must be solved according to the personal and professional ethics of the particular researcher.

Another moral dilemma facing researchers in the area of deviance is that of "guilty knowledge." Polsky (1967) speaks about the sociologist gaining knowledge of and access to criminal acts, both witnessing them and learning about them secondhand, and his need to make a moral decision regarding his stance concerning these acts and his ability to stand up under police investigation.

There is another form of guilty knowledge, however, that researchers frequently encounter in deviance research, one that we might term "*intimate knowledge*," that is, becoming familiar with the intimate details of a subject's life. Interviews that are conducted in depth, as well as data gathered by participant-observation, can lead to such intimate knowledge. Examples of intimate knowledge that I gained in my suicide research include familiarity with intimate details of familial interaction and conflicts that affect the significant others of a suicide, an awareness of the pressing personal problems that a particular individual is having in his adjustment to the death by suicide of someone who was close to him, the proneness of a respondent to suicide himself and the ways by which he is attempting to handle this potentially lethal desire, as well as knowledge of actions of the respondent toward the deceased that may, in fact, have contributed to his death.

"Intimate knowledge" is perhaps a form of "guilty knowledge," but it does not necessarily involve knowledge about someone's guilt in some matter. It is knowledge that one would ordinarily not possess unless one were a member of the household or a very close friend of the respondent, or unless one were in some official capacity or had been sought out as a counselor. Such intimate knowledge can make the researcher feel rather uncomfortable, but in his research he gains such knowledge. What does he do with it? How is he supposed to react to the respondent? He must react as though this knowledge made no difference, when, in fact, it does. It does make a difference to the researcher because *he knows* that he is aware of intimate aspects of his respondents' lives, and he must find some way of handling or dealing with his awareness.

Frequently the very nature of the research solves the problem of intimate knowledge. Sociologists become familiar with intimate details of their respondents' lives, but usually never see their respondents again. As such, the "uncomfortability" is of short duration, occurring only while they are interviewing a respondent. In some cases such "uncomfortability" does not appear when the respondent is being interviewed, but takes place when some future interaction with the respondent becomes necessary. This delayed reaction can arise particularly if the researcher later interacts with the respondent in a way that is not related to the research.

An example of intimate knowledge that tends to affect interaction in this way, making for a somewhat awkward situation, involves intimate sexual details of a respondent's life, such as those gained from a college girl concerning her perceptions of sexual responses under the influence of drugs. Initially, when the question is asked and the answer given, this can lead to a feeling of "uncomfortability" on the part of both respondent and researcher. If the interaction between the respondent and researcher is limited to the research setting, such "uncomfortability" is of short duration and little consequence. However, If the researcher and researchee are later put into an interactional situation that is outside of the researcher-respondent role, what does the researcher do with his knowledge? It is impossible to dismiss it entirely from his mind, and there is an "overlay" of the researcher-respondent role still left in the ensuing interaction. This is the case if, for example, the same girl now becomes your student, or if she begins to date a friend of yours, or if you have to deal with her in some social capacity.

Another example is that of a woman who becomes a respondent in abortion research, revealing intimate details of her sexual life and aspects of her "situational deviance." This woman fleetingly becomes an unwilling participant in illegal abortion, an interaction that she herself sometimes defines as immoral, after which she then moves back into her regular respectable routines. Some time after the interview, in some unexpected capacity, the researcher meets this individual and is called upon to interact as though he possessed no intimate knowledge. Such interactions become problematic to both the respondent and the researcher, and each researcher must develop his own techniques for handling these difficulties.

Obtaining and Interviewing Respondents

Another major problem in deviance research is that of obtaining respondents. Although this problem is not unique with deviance research, but is common throughout sociology, the methodological problems in sampling techniques are multiplied when the sociologist researches deviance. In a small number of cases standardized sampling techniques can be used, but the population must be clearly defined in advance. Such techniques apply, for example, if one wants to generalize one's sample to a particular inmate population or to some category of arrested and/or convicted felons. However, where the population is not known, standardized sampling techniques cannot be used. And when standardized samples are not used, questions concerning the generalizability of one's findings are always left hanging.

Where there is a developed subculture of deviants and one is able to gain entry into that subculture and establish rapport with potential respondents, the recruitment of respondents is greatly facilitated. This is the case with my drug research. Drug users on a college campus ordinarily know several other users, and there is a communication or exchange network that exists among members of this subculture.

When, however, there is no developed subculture of deviance, the problem of gaining access to respondents is greatly increased. The researcher is then faced with a greater than usual problem of finding out who potential respondents are, as well as facing the usual problems of gaining entry or making contact with these potential respondents and establishing rapport with them. This is the case with abortion. Our whole legal approach to abortion has made it a secretive act that ordinarily isolates the abortionee from persons who could be of help to her in solving her problem (Henslin 1971; Manning 1971; Schur 1965). This isolation almost entirely prevents the development of a subculture of abortion. Abortionees, for the most part, remain individuated, without bonds growing between persons who have experienced the same deviance. This is not to deny that bonds between abortionees exist, but there is no widespread sharing of experiences, no common defining of the situation such as one finds with homosexuality, no public meetings held by and for abortionees, and, for the most part, there are no clubs or organizations centering around this deviance.

The problem that this individuating aspect of abortion presents for the researcher is that it is not possible to make just one major contact with an individual who has experienced abortion and then to be introduced, by that one individual, into a whole network of others who have been involved in the same deviance. This possibility might exist if the researcher were fortunate enough to gain the rapport of an abortionist who would then allow him to study his "patients." However, such contacts are ordinarily serendipitous since abortionists, understandably enough, appear rather hesitant to share information regarding their clients, their *modus operandi,* or other aspects of their work situation.

How then is the problem solved of gaining abortionee respondents? Since one is not able to locate a major contact and work through her to expand one's contacts, one must "send out as many feelers" as possible. I handled this problem by making abortion a possible topic for students doing original research in my courses in deviance and in social psychology, provided that they were able to gain interviews with friends or acquaintances who had undergone abortions and that they would tape these interviews and include them in their research papers. Additionally, I told practically every student with whom I was even slightly acquainted, and many that I didn't even know that well, that if they knew someone who had undergone an abortion, I would like to talk to her. Some of the students actively sought out such respondents for me. In some cases, potential respondents would not talk to me about the experience, but consented to be interviewed by their friends, who taped the interviews for me. Most, however, came into my office to be interviewed. In other cases, I had a sociologist-friend in a distant city administer a depth interview based on an outline that I supplied him to respondents that he was able to contact. He then taped these interviews and sent them to me.

The point that I am making here is that it takes ingenuity to gain interviews with respondents who have engaged in certain forms of deviance and who have something to fear regarding their own egos, their professional lives, or their social lives as a result of this information being leaked to others.[6] In situations in which an interview poses some threat to respondents or in which the absence of a subculture prevents respondents from being easily localized, the researcher must "push" potential contacts if he is to gain interviewees.

Having made contact with a girl who is willing to share such an intimate and frequently embarrassing experience as an abortion with a stranger, and a male at that, the problem is then one of establishing rapport, of maintaining rapport during the interview, and of applying interview skills. Basic to such an interview situation is the need for trust, and this trust comes primarily through the contact (if there is one) who arranged the meeting between the researcher and the subject. However, this trust must also be maintained, and it is in the maintenance of trust that the various validators of the interviewer's *front*—including the *setting* (such as an office), with its various props (such as books), the interviewer's general *appearance,* and the *manner* in which the subject is approached (hopefully a nonjudgmental approach that communicates "acceptance" of the person)—become the mainstays in maintaining rapport and trust (Goffman 1959:22–30; Henslin 1968).

Interviewing skills are something that have to be learned through the hard reality of interviewing itself. In open-ended interviewing, techniques such as *reflection* are extremely helpful—that is, when the interviewee stops speaking, the interviewer picks up a recent or last idea that was expressed, and he rephrases or paraphrases it, often in an indirect question form (for example, "Felt bad?"; "Petrified?"; "Again, huh?"), such that the interviewee then continues to talk about the same idea. Use of this and other probing techniques are especially important in maintaining a continuity in the respondent's answers that will enable one to reconstruct past events and understand the meanings of those events for her life.

Deviance research, as I mentioned above in regard to the moral problem of changing motivations to participate in the deviant activity, can lead a researcher into situations that differ sharply from his normal life, into a sort of "transient deviance" similar to that of the abortionee. For example, the deviant can test the researcher by asking him to participate in some deviant act, feeling that if he will participate, he must be trustworthy. In other cases, the research itself means participation in deviance, as in my cab research, when I automatically became a middleman for deviance by simply driving the cab, since, for example, call girls would take cabs to and from their johns. Also, deviance is sometimes expected of the researcher; because I was engaged in drug research, some students thought that ipso facto I must be a source of drugs or that I could at least put them in contact with a source. Similarly, a student who needed an abortion for a girlfriend asked me to supply him with the name of an abortionist. The researcher must, of course, handle such things according to his own feelings of morality and propriety.

This leads to the question of the extent to which one is willing to go in the pursuit of respondents. For me this has led to some rather humorous situations, such as an opportunity to interview an abortionee who was willing to travel a couple of hundred miles for the interview— but only if I would make a home for her two cats. Not being a cat lover, I passed this up, but I did consider the possibility of accepting the offer and merely finding a new home for the cats after the interview. Perhaps I should have.

This can also lead to some not-so-humorous incidents.[7] I wanted very much to be able to contact an abortionist, interview him, and be permitted to watch him at work. One of my students came up to me rather excited one day and reported that she had spoken with an abortionist friend who would let us both interview him and be present at an abortion. I also became rather excited at the possibility of joining in this firsthand observation. As I pursued the matter, my excitement was quickly replaced by anticipatory fear. It turned out that this was no run-of-the-mill (pardon the pun) abortionist. First of all, he had a serious criminal record regarding violence not related to that of abortion offenses. This was bad enough, but it turned out, moreover, according to his own admissions to this student, that on one occasion when one of his abortionees had developed complications and had demanded her $500 back, he agreed to return the money and arranged to meet with the abortionee and her boyfriend in another city. At the meeting site, he climbed into the back seat of their automobile and, instead of giving them the money, shot and killed them both. He had, moreover, never been apprehended for this. To what extent will one go in his pursuit of respondents? That question was decided for me rather quickly by the thoughts that kept going through my mind: "What if he is raided shortly after I have visited him?" and unconnected though it may have been, "What might he do when he is out on bail?" In spite of the commitments I feel to research, I passed up this "opportunity."

Motivations of Respondents

The problem of motivation of respondents in sociological research has not been adequately analyzed. In my own research I have steadfastly refused to pay my respondents. I am not only tight, but I am also suspicious of such motivation. There is not much question regarding the motivation of respondents who do not know that they are respondents (for example, "respondents" in covert participant-observation studies), since they are not acting as respondents but are playing their ordinary roles. Their motivations, then, are the motivations of people who are in the everyday process of revealing and concealing information about their selves—that is, presenting fronts and validating self-images.

In order to understand and properly evaluate information given by members of a group being studied by covert participant-observation, one must have an adequate understanding of their motivations to conceal and reveal information. The motivations themselves then become part of the data. For example, if it is a part of the common culture of a particular group to show bravado or to present the self in a particular form through jokes, joking, bragging, occupational anecdotes, and so on, the researcher must understand these behaviors as being part of the normative expectations of the group. He should not accept such behaviors at face value, but should interpret them within the framework of the motivations for information disclosure that that group has.

Knowledge of the motivation of respondents is also important for understanding and evaluating information disclosures that are made in depth interviews, since if the respondent is motivated to present a particular front, this will shape the data in a particular way. Unfortunately, we frequently know very little about such motivations for participation in this type of interviewing, and we know even less about the biases that we are incorporating into our results.

As Douglas says in "Observing Deviance," one must know what is being exchanged in the interview or other form of research if one is going to properly evaluate the motivations of respondents and the information that is gained through the research. Too often sociologists think of themselves as being the only ones receiving anything during interviewing. This idea of the interviewee as the giver and the interviewer as the receiver is quite inadequate, since interviewees are receiving as well as giving. Consequently, the researcher should always ask himself the question: "What is the interviewee receiving?"

One particular motivation that I have been able to tap in my research has been that of *altruism*. In the suicide research, for example respondents were specifically told: "Not much is known about suicide and what happens to families following a suicide. We need to know much more about this, and we would appreciate very much being able to talk to you." Furthermore, although it was not directly stated, the impression was implicitly left that their cooperation would somehow help other families in a similar situation. Tapping this altruistic motivation led to a high response rate and the establishment of solid rapport with the respondents in the suicide research. Supposedly what was being exchanged, at least on one level, was my satisfying their need for altruism in return for their giving me their cooperation.

I also frequently tapped altruism in the research on abortion. This was again altruism for the sake of science. Potential respondents and potential contacts with potential respondents were told that, although there are many abortionees around, it is very difficult to find women who are willing to discuss their abortion experiences with a researcher. I emphasized how little we know about the abortion experience, and how much I would appreciate it if they would talk to me or could arrange for someone else to do so.

There are, I am certain, many other motives for cooperating in research on abortion, such as a desire to share an experience with someone whom they feel they can trust, a desire to get things off one's chest through speaking to an anonymous listener, and so on. But, whatever the exchange that I have been able to offer, this approach has been rather effective, even to the point of getting a woman who had put in a full day at work to drive forty miles through rush-hour traffic to a university she had never been to before, to an office of someone she had never met, to speak to someone about intimate details of her life. This particular respondent, moreover, had not shared this experience with anyone other than her boyfriend and one girlfriend.

The motivation of respondents in drug research seems to be of a somewhat different nature. Although altruism for the sake of sharing knowledge for scientific gains is present in some cases, the motivation of drug respondents seems to be more on the level of curiosity itself— that is, respondents wonder what the researcher has in mind in his research and what it will be like to be interviewed or to participate in the research. Curiosity about the research appears to be the major motivation, and it is a good motivation to tap among drug users, at least among college students who are drug users, because college drug users appear to be very curious about experiences in life. Their curiosity, in fact, is perhaps one of the major motivations for initial drug usage.

Another major motivation of respondents in both abortion and drug research is that of responding to personal requests or meeting the expectations that friends and acquaintances have of the individual. In abortion and drug research, it is very seldom that I directly approach an individual to request his cooperation as a respondent. Rather, prospective respondents are approached for me by others who know of the individual's involvement in the particular form of deviance. This motivates the potential respondent to cooperate because of the expectations of the one who is requesting his cooperation—that is, to act on the basis of their friendship. It is, in general, difficult to refuse the request of a friend if the time required to satisfy the request is not unreasonable.

Deviants cooperate and give me research data, and I, on my part, give them such things as friendship, attention, understanding, acceptance, a sympathetic ear, anonymity, insight, satisfaction of curiosity, fulfillment of altruistic needs, self-aggrandizement, the chance to cooperate with that magical thing called "science," fulfillment of obligations incurred within a friendship network, and/or an opportunity to establish obligations that their friend must repay at some future date.

Ordinarily, that which is received by the respondent in exchange for the information that he gives must be inferred from certain aspects of the interaction. Very seldom is such an exchange made explicit by the respondent. However, this sometimes happens, as in the example above of providing a home for cats. Another exchange was most explicitly spelled out to me in a recent telephone call in which a male voice flatly stated: "She will come in and talk to you if you will give her the name of an abortionist." Again, the unanticipated moral decisions that must be made when one does research into deviance!

Notes

1. My apologies to the reader for referring so frequently in this essay to my own research. I ordinarily try not to do this, but because this article is meant to share with others some of the problems and experiences that I encountered, and to do so through a first-person approach, this is inevitable. Nevertheless, I feel somewhat uncomfortable about it.
2. From my field notes and files.
3. From a personal communication with Laud Humphreys.
4. One of my graduate students, Carol McCart, felt essentially this same role conflict in participant-observer research that she did for my course in deviance. She did research in a half-way house for exconvicts, and she wrote in her paper:

   How can you talk to a man who has been confined within two maximum security prisons (Alcatraz and Leavenworth) for 13½ years, with no interested human relationships, with no family or friends who give a damn whether he lives or dies, with no job and one disappointing interview after another, who is frantically searching for some shred of hope to which he can cling, and simply "walk away from him"? How can you not be involved? How can you feel his need and ignore it? How can you interview man after man who has been permanently damaged by the penal system and remain objective about that system? How can you objectively study a person as though he were an object only, when he is a human being?

5. Cf. "putative deviation" in Lemert (1951:56).
6. One form of contact that has probably been underused is that of direct advertising. Recently one of my students advertised in the student newspaper for divorcees, stating that she wanted to contact them for research purposes. She received an excellent response, including several faculty members who were willing to reveal intimate details of their lives to a freshman student!
7. A minor problem that is both frustrating and humorous that has arisen from my research into deviance is that of "bad words." If one aspires to ethnographic accuracy, it is sometimes the case that one will reproduce words that make the typical middle-class person blush. As a result, one typist refused to continue work on my cab-driving manuscript and even gained the concurrence of the divisional dean, who also wondered if it was necessary to use "words like that"! In another instance, the editors at the *American Journal of Sociology* changed such words in my text to read "fu**," etc., which I thought was perhaps motivated by puritanism but had the effect of giving the article a pornographic appearance. I then changed the copy on the galleys back to the original form without noting that I had made such changes, and the article went through as originally written (Henslin 1967).

References

Ball, Donald W. 1967
"An Abortion Clinic Ethnography," *Social Problems,* 14, 293–301.
Barnes, J. A. 1963
"Some Ethical Problems in Modern Field Work," *British Journal of Sociology,* 14, 118–134.
Becker, Howard S. 1963
Outsiders: Studies in the Sociology of Deviance. New York: Free Press.
Berger, Peter L. 1963
Invitation to Sociology: A Humanistic Perspective. Garden City, N.Y.: Anchor Books.
Caudill, William C. 1952
"Social Structure and Interaction Processes in a Psychiatric Ward," *American Journal of Orthopsychiatry,* 22, 314–334.
Davis, Fred 1964
"Deviance Disavowal: The Management of Strained Interaction by the Visibly Handicapped," in Howard S. Becker (ed.), *The Other Side: Perspectives on Deviance.* New York: Free Press.
Erikson, Kai T. 1967
"A Comment on Disguised Observation in Sociology," *Social Problems,* 14, 366–373.
Festinger, Leon, Henry W. Riecken, and Stanley Schacter 1956
When Prophecy Fails. Minneapolis: University of Minnesota Press.
Garfinkel, Harold 1967
Studies in Ethnomethodology. Englewood Cliffs, N.J.: Prentice-Hall.
Goffman, Erving 1959
The Presentation of Self in Everyday Life. Garden City, N.Y.: Anchor Books.
Henslin, James M. 1967
"Craps and Magic," *American Journal of Sociology,* 73, 316–330. (See also the attack on and the defense of this article in *American Journal of Sociology,* 74 [November 1968], 304–305.)
———— 1968
"Trust and the Cab Driver," in Marcello Truzzi (ed.), *Sociology and Everyday Life.* Englewood Cliffs, N.J.: Prentice-Hall, pp. 138–158.
———— 1970a
"Why Craps and Cabbies?" (unpublished paper).
———— 1970b
"Guilt and Guilt Neutralization: Response and Adjustment to Suicide," in Jack D. Douglas (ed.), *Deviance and Respectability: The Social Construction of Moral Meanings.* New York: Basic Books, pp. 192–228.
———— 1970c
"Changes in Perceptions of Sexual Experiences of College Students While Under the Influence of Drugs," paper delivered at The National Academy of Sciences, Washington, D.C., February 1970.
———— 1970d
"Sex, Drugs, and the American College Scene," in Edward Sagarin (ed.), *Sex and the American Scene.* Chicago: Quadrangle Books.

——————— 1971

"Criminal Abortion: Making the Decision and Neutralizing the Act," in James M. Henslin (ed.), *Studies in the Sociology of Sex.* New York: Appleton-Century-Crofts, 113–135.

——————— and Mae A. Biggs 1971

"The Sociology of the Vaginal Examination: A Study in Dramaturgical Desexualization," in James M. Henslin (ed.), *Studies in the Sociology of Sex.* New York: Appleton-Century-Crofts, 243–272.

Humphreys, Laud 1970

Tearoom Trade: Impersonal Sex in Public Places. Chicago: Aldine.

Lemert, Edwin M. 1951

Social Pathology: A Systematic Approach to the Theory of Sociopathic Behavior. New York: McGraw-Hill.

Lofland, John 1969

Deviance and Identity. Englewood Cliffs, N.J.: Prentice-Hall.

——————— and Robert A. Lejeune 1960

"Initial Interaction of Newcomers in Alcoholics Anonymous: A Field Experiment in Class Symbols and Socialization," *Social Problems,* 8, 102–111.

Malinowski, Bronislaw 1922

Argonauts of the Western Pacific: An Account of Native Enterprise and Adventure in the Archipelagoes of Melanesian New Guinea. New York: Dutton.

Manning, Peter K. 1971

"Fixing What you Feared: Notes on the Campus Abortion Search," in James M. Henslin (ed.), *Studies in the Sociology of Sex.* New York: Appleton-Century-Crofts, 137–166.

Matza, David 1969

Becoming Deviant. Englewood Cliffs, N.J.: Prentice-Hall.

Polsky, Ned 1967

Hustlers, Beats, and Others. Garden City, N.Y.: Anchor Books.

Psathas, George, and James M. Henslin 1967

"Dispatched Orders and the Cab Driver: A Study of Locating Activities," *Social Problems,* 14, 424–443.

Roth, Julius A. 1962

"Comments on 'Secret Observation,'" *Social Problems,* 9, 283–284.

Sarbin, Theodore R. 1954

"Role Theory," in Gardner Lindzey (ed.), *Handbook of Social Psychology,* Vol. I: *Theory and Method,* Chap. 6. Reading, Mass.: Addison-Wesley.

Schur, Edwin M. 1965

Crimes Without Victims: Deviant Behavior and Public Policy. Englewood Cliffs, N.J.: Prentice-Hall.

Seeley, John R. 1967

"The Making and Taking of Problems: Toward an Ethical Stance," *Social Problems,* 14, 382–389.

Sullivan, Mortimer A., Stuart A. Queen, and Ralph C. Patrick, Jr. 1958

"Participant Observation as Employed in the Study of a Military Training Program," *American Sociological Review,* 23, 660–667.

Yablonsky, Lewis 1968

The Hippie Trip. New York: Pegasus.

Problems of Access and Risk in Observing Drug Scenes

James T. Carey

There is a growing literature on the feasibility of participant-observation for sociological research.[1] In a sense, it is an attempt to recover or rediscover an approach long ago regarded as inappropriate to scientific objectivity. Sociological attention seems to have shifted from the ethnography of various facets of urban life that was popular in the 1930s. The tools for exploring gangs, occupations, and unusual life styles fell into disuse with the growth of quantification in the social sciences. The same factors that Becker suggests led to the decline of life history usage can also be said to have led to the decline of the other research procedures linked with participant-observation: concern with the development of abstract theory, separation of social psychology from sociology, and the fact that use of participant-observation techniques does not produce the kind of findings that sociologists expect research to produce.[2]

The reawakened interest in participant-observation seems partly related to an awareness of the limitations of survey methods[3] and partly to the realization that the difficulties inherent in field methods can be overcome and that full and detailed accounts of specific organizations, communities, local milieux, can be theoretically relevant.[4] Another basis for renewed interest in field methods is the recent discussion of the utility of a narrow and exclusive cultivation of purely technical research standards and education in sociology.[5] What was formerly conceived to be an indispensable condition of objectivity in the social sciences is now being seriously questioned. The implication of this discussion is that the sociologist must be aware of his own values and the fact that these are not necessarily shared by participants in situations under study. It also implies an obligation to get as full and complete a description of what is "out there" as possible, in terms that are understandable to the participants.

McCall and Simmons[6] summarize the major issues in participant-observation and perform an invaluable service for sociologists by indicating its advantages, the situations in which it can most appropriately be utilized, and a wealth of suggested solutions to the problems it poses for the field researcher. However, their discussion of establishing relationships with subjects, while treated as a problem of the first order, does not offer many suggestions. Polsky[7] is more instructive on this point in his discussion of field study with career criminals. He suggests the researcher go where criminals actually hang out and try to know them in their own settings. He also discusses how the researcher might deal with the hostility that is an inevitable concomitant of the researcher's intrusion. Both Polsky and McCall and Simmons opt for researcher honesty in briefing respondents on what they're trying to do and reject the observer-in-disguise role as too risky. Both discuss the character of the two-way contract that is established between researcher and subject, though Polsky is less inclined to dismiss money as an incentive for cooperation. McCall and Simmons enjoin the researcher to pay close attention to the problem of reward, especially of the social-psychological variety. They also deal more systematically with the problem of selecting informants and handling rumors or misinformation about what the researcher is doing than does Polsky.

Yet, as helpful as these codifications are, there are certain gaps in the existing literature that will be obvious to the sociologist who is looking for assistance in exploring deviant worlds, especially those with high risk potential for the researcher. This article is an attempt to remedy this deficiency by a discussion of four problem areas that are aggravated in observing an extreme deviant group: the problems of gaining access, the ethical dilemmas posed, the research bargain, and the handling of damaging rumors that emerge in the course of one's work[8]—more euphemistically described as "malfunctioning of the communication network." The extreme deviant group used as an example in this article is made up of persons who inject massive quantities of amphetamines intravenously and who, as a result of the chemical effect of the drug and the social relations that develop around its continued use, have a distinctive life style. Some discussion of the theoretical concerns that justify an exploration of the use of "speed," however, is in order before a consideration of the unusual problems of access and risk this particular enterprise poses for the researcher.

Theoretical Concerns

One of the most influential explanations of drug use in the past several years comes from anomie theory.[9] According to this theory, persons who evidence some inconsistency in life experiences and whose lives are out of kilter or who evidence the absence of integration or regulation would be considered likely candidates for heavy drug use. Hence, we could expect that those who had moved into a heavy drug-using group would have a number of qualities that would predispose them to drug use: they would have less consistency of life experiences than non-users; they would perceive their backgrounds as inconsistent; they would have greater than average feelings of insecurity and alienation; and they would be looking for something which would bring their lives back into a state of equilibrium.

Preliminary interviewing of a number of heavy drug users in the San Francisco Bay area suggested that these predisposing qualities were absent from most of those interviewed[10] and that anomie theory did not seem particularly appropriate to this group. An interview guide was therefore developed to get at the extent to which heavy drug use or particular patterns of drug use were related to the lack of integration and regulation in a person's life. The interview guide together with graduate interviewers were put at the disposal of the Haight-Ashbury Medical Clinic in San Francisco.[11] The plan was to query a sample of those using clinic facilities. The model of movement into drug-using was a two-step one: the first concerned with deficits, the second with the role of significant others immediately prior to experimentation with drugs. Preliminary analysis of the data suggested that whether individuals were "pushed" into the community by the lack of desired attributes or "pulled" there by a sense of adventure seemed less important to their drug-using patterns than what happened after they arrived. The presence or absence of what could be characterized, in short, as a "speed culture" was an important determinant of the careers of speed users. In my analysis, I found myself looking for the development of "organization and form, a body of customs and traditions, established leadership, an enduring division of labor, social rules and social values, in short a culture, a social organization, and a new scheme of life."[12] My major concern was to learn what the speed culture could tell us about the development of youthful social movements. I was struck by the parallels between the behavior of people involved in the world of speed and reports of nativistic movements such as the Ghost Dance of the American Indians and the Melanesian Cargo Cult.[13] Some of the graduate students, focusing primarily on the crucial role of the marketplace as a facilitating variable in shaping the drug scene,[14] were impressed with the parallels between the speed world in the Haight-Ashbury and the heroin world described by Fiddle.[15]

To proceed with any systematic observation, we needed assurance that we were actually dealing with a relatively enduring phenomenon rather than an ephemeral fad within the larger context of youthful rebellion. Our early interviews at the clinic indicated that speed was a highly social activity. It was not ingested in isolation. The social setting within which it was used lent itself to the development of fairly intense personal relationships, interaction, and values on the basis of speed. This was one indication that we were dealing with a culture or subculture. The second indication was that the people constituting any given scene knew each other or knew about each other—that is, they were not strangers. There was a high degree of concentration of one's most intimate and frequent interactions with acquaintances within the speed scene. We were fairly confident, also, that there was a subculture, anthropologically and ethnographically speaking[16]—that is, those deeply involved with the speed scene were, in fact, sharing a distinct way of life which set them off from conventional society. We observed that those heavily involved in the speed scene could not function in the "straight" world, at least not in many capacities. Individuals might be able to walk along the street, but a normal task was difficult unless it was something engrossing, intrinsically interesting and motion-effort-consuming. Because a scene typically involved persons going on long trips—36 to 72 hours, usually—it was frequented by very few who had steady jobs. It was not only the duration of the high that militated against a steady job in the square world but also the intensity and duration of the crash. The scene was so unique and time-demanding that it tended to become all-engrossing. The result was that individuals within it were sharply separated from conventional routines and people. This situation led to the third general indication that we were studying a subculture; this was the social-psychological factor—the degree to which identities revolved about the subculture and the degree to which members and nonmembers defined membership as significant, binding, and strongly indicative of the "kind of person" who belonged to it.

Access to the Speed Scene

The great upsurge in the use of illegal drugs in the Bay area in the late 1960s led to the development of the Haight-Ashbury Medical Clinic established to deal with the drug-related health problems of younger people in San Francisco. During the summer and fall of 1967 an increasing number of young people came to the clinic with health problems related to their ingestion of amphetamines. This situation lasted through the summer of 1968. David Smith and Charles Fisher, summarizing the activities of the clinic for the summer of 1968, reported that of the 310 patients seen 40 percent sought medical attention because of primary somatic symptoms or medical illnesses related to their use of speed:

Other than general debility with malnutrition . . . the major associated medical illness was hepatitis. Hepatitis is endemic to the Haight-Ashbury and, . . . it is a major problem in the medical population treated at the Haight-Ashbury Medical Clinic. . . . In addition to liver problems, we saw a variety of other gastrointestinal symptoms including nausea, vomiting and abdominal cramps, the latter occasionally being so severe that a diagnosis of appendicitis was initially entertained. Methamphetamine induced cardiorespiratory symptoms were often quite distressing to the patient and the drug induced tachycardia was occasionally interpreted as a "heart attack" or the mid-respiratory distress seen after shooting up was interpreted by the patient as a life threatening "choking."[17]

My role, with the assistance of several graduate students, was to gather information on the persons using or likely to use clinic facilities. To that end, three different samplings were taken six months apart to explore various patterns of drug use among people living in that community. Interviewing was conducted within the clinic and, later, at various gathering spots in the community. We were identified as clinic staff. Generally, our introduction, when we interviewed people on the street, included this identification: "We are from the H-A Clinic, and we want to find out what kind of people have used the clinic and the problems they are having so as to make our services more helpful." The work we were doing was defined as "medically related" (as indeed it was). The medical service relationship seems to be one that is generally understood in our society.[18] In an ideal doctor-client relationship the patient voluntarily places himself in the doctor's hands and brings to the relationship respect for the doctor's expertise, gratitude, and, in more conventional settings, a fee. Since the fee was absent, except in the more general sense we will discuss below on the research bargain, the feeling of gratitude among those who had used the clinic or knew people who did was stronger. The clinic was viewed as a medical quasi-underground by those illegal drug users who had reason to know of its operation. Anonymity was guaranteed, and the doctors who staffed it made clear their desire to treat what they considered to be almost exclusively medical—not legal—problems. The contact with heavy users was initially made under benign auspices, and the usual questions concerning the intrusion of sociologists were not forthcoming. The initial suspicions of the outsider which pervade illegal drug scenes—Are you a detective, undercover agent, homosexual, pusher, or what?—were allayed in this setting.

The generalizations that spring from this experience are fairly obvious: first, the auspices under which one operates must be favorably perceived by those whose trust is sought; second, identities or justifications that make sense to respondents and yet do not involve any deception are to be preferred to lengthy descriptions of who you are or to disguises of any kind. McCall and Simmons, in addressing themselves to the problem of what sorts of relationships are most advantageous for obtaining optimal information and most desirable in terms of ethical and humane considerations, suggest that the researcher teach respondents what the role of a researcher is:

...the subjects of a study are often totally unfamiliar with the research role, even if they have been led to accept the observer qua observer through his adoption of more ordinary ancillary roles, through presentation of legitimate auspices, and through strategic choice of sponsorship. Therefore, the observer must teach the subjects what the role of "researcher" is.[19]

This advice may be appropriate when discussing the researcher's role in a quasi-instructional setting, e.g., prison, hospital, or school, but it is unrealistic in a situation where the researcher is an intruder, attempting to relate to respondents on an equal status basis or where respondents are basically uninterested in what the researcher is trying to do and less than enthusiastic about helping, and there is no authority to back up the investigator.

Within six months it became clear that the proportion of speed-related problems coming to the attention of the clinic staff was declining. Some staff members interpreted this as evidence of the disappearance of the speed scene in the neighborhood. Interviews conducted with people who had been identified as knowledgeable in our survey suggested, however, that something else was happening. As one of the research staff reported it:

It was our guess that during this early period, the speed shooters were still fairly well integrated with the other residents, i.e., they had not yet begun to isolate themselves and develop identities separate from others within the community. Because they were widely dispersed throughout the community, a "speed culture," as such, was not present in which users could find support for their activities and where there could be an exchange of information about the drug and its effects. As a result many initiates perceived the speed effect as unpleasant, many suffered acute anxiety reactions and sought help. During this period the Haight-Ashbury Medical Clinic treated a large number of such reactions. As the use of speed increased, however, the number of acute anxiety reactions and other adverse subjective reactions to the drug (excluding such physical problems as hepatitis, abscesses, malnutrition, etc.) dropped off sharply. This may be interpreted as an indicator of an emergent speed culture.[20]

This is similar to the observations made by Becker[21] on the emergence of an LSD culture. A culture can be said to exist, he suggests, when consensus develops about the drug's subjective effects, duration, proper dosages, predictable dangers, and how these dangers might be avoided.

It was at this point—the realization that we had access to a very unusual kind of behavior but that our contacts would vanish unless we did something about it—that a decision was made to pursue the inquiry. The decision was made on the basis of several considerations: theoretical notions, and a belief that they could be extended by further study; a conviction that we were actually dealing with a culture; and an assessment of the legal risks involved.

Legal Risks

The laws against amphetamine use in the state of California are part of the California Health and Safety Code's Dangerous Drug section.[22] At the time my research was in progress, it was unlawful to possess restricted dangerous drugs for either personal use or sale; possession was defined as a misdemeanor for the first offense and as a felony with any prior conviction. At the same time, the fear of imprisonment for possession of amphetamines was slight in the speed scene. Such fear was largely mitigated by the fact that almost everyone was also carrying marijuana, which was then punishable by even more severe penalties. Marijuana was used to ease the period of crashing or in combination with speed to enhance the high. The fact that researchers were not likely to be in possession of dangerous drugs or marijuana did not alleviate the risks of studying the scene. Under California state law it was "unlawful to visit or be in any room or place where any narcotic [including marijuana] was being unlawfully smoked or used with the knowledge that such activity was occurring."

There is no privileged relationship between the sociological researcher and his subject similar to that enjoyed by the lawyer and client or psychiatrist and patient. The limited amount of research conducted so far on illegal activity has not provided sociologists with enough experience to recommend any definite course of action to follow when studying this type of activity. Some researchers have suggested informing the police of research inquiries and requesting immunity for the researcher. Yablonsky[23] has suggested pressing for legislation that would create a privileged relationship. However, Symonds[24] has pointed out that the creation of immunity would certainly hamper rapport and has very correctly observed that convictions have occurred not for being present when illegal behavior was taking place, but only for possession or use of marijuana, in short, suggesting that the risk to the researcher is minimal.

The fact that there were few convictions of researchers and no arrests at all in this kind of research situation was something we took into account. We still felt it necessary to allocate a certain amount of money for bail on the chance that we might be arrested. We also noted that in only a few states[25] is it required that felonies be reported, so that we were unlikely to be accused of having guilty knowledge. Although we came to no clear decision on what we would do if we were subpoenaed to testify, we probably would have tried to invoke the Fifth Amendment if such a situation had developed.

Distinctive Features of the Speed Scene

There are a number of distinctive features of the speed scene that pose problems for the researcher.[26] These characteristics are related to the chemical effect of shooting massive quantities of amphetamines intravenously; to other physical, psychological, and social effects of the drug; and to the impact of the law on social relations.

The first noticeable change after the exhilaration of the "rush" (a sudden overwhelming pleasurable feeling) has worn off is the tremendous physical hyperactivity of people who characterize themselves as "speed freaks." Pure quietness and stillness—often a goal of LSD users—is virtually unheard of in speed scenes. While high the person is usually bodily active, though seldom doing hard physical tasks. Rather, under heavy doses, the individual appears to have the "fidgets" and is unable to sit still. It is not uncommon for him to stay awake for two, three, or four days.

The duration of the drug-induced experience is characterized as a "run." During a run a person's appetite for food is severely suppressed, despite the activity and energy generated. A weight loss of from ten to twenty pounds, or even more, is not uncommon during a run.

The user experiences racing thoughts; he reports that things are happening very quickly inside his head. Thinking directed toward solving a long-run problem with no side adjuncts, that is, distractions, along the way is nearly impossible.

Concentration, so long as it is on a narrow path, is enhanced by the drug. Any number of immediate occurrences can lead the mind to wander along that path. There are reports of bizarre group behavior consisting of actions that are repetitive, immediate, and small, and which might be considered compulsive. This compulsive behavior, which is another characteristic of heavy users, is vastly different from past clinical descriptions of that phenomenon. The speed freak's compulsion is not focused on a single behavior like washing one's hands over and over again. Stringing beads, carving a wooden knife, memorizing the plots of all Italian operas and doodling for four consecutive hours are all acts that are intrinsically liked by speed users. Attention can easily wander and one can become wrapped up for hours in another "compulsive" behavior. There is no necessary utility in the acts performed. The action is its own reward since it is so enjoyable.

The enhanced concentration, coupled with high distractibility, leads to rapid mood changes. On methedrine a person seems to sail along without going very deeply into himself and deals with others in a swift but superficial manner. The mood swings reflect neither deep internal conflict nor deep mixed feelings about one's setting. Rather, the speed freak is engrossed in the here-and-now and exaggerates or invents flows in the social setting. These mood swings are quicker and stronger as the person's body wears out.

Hyperactivity often leads to a kind of "reaching out" that appears to be aggressiveness. Reports are frequent of sporadic violence which could be considered unprovoked under conventional circumstances. These acts are usually not premeditated but triggered by perceived insults or inconveniences. The aggression is likely to occur when coming down. It also seems that the extent and degree of violence increases with the duration of a person's run and the number of consecutive runs he has made. For heavy users, who keep their first five or ten runs not much over two days in duration, the incidence of violence may not be much higher than average.

Massive dosages of amphetamines seem to induce a kind of paranoia, which builds up over the duration of a run and during several weeks or months of running-crashing-running. Meth-heads report hearing police running down the hall to arrest them or little men with machine guns on the opposite roof tops moving in for the big kill. Others report fear of "moving trees" or suspicion of friends who are sitting with their backs turned to them. David Smith and Charles Fisher, whose experience was obtained in a clinic setting that included a high proportion of heavy speed users, report the same phenomena:

The amphetamine psychosis ... is associated with three diagnostic characteristics: 1) Visual hallucinations, 2) auditory hallucinations and 3) a well-defined system of paranoia including ideas of reference. Paranoia is a characteristic part of the reaction and makes treatment difficult because the individual is very concerned about entering a hospital or encountering the police. He feels comfortable only in a street facility and very often even there questions concerning the police arise. As an example, I saw an eighteen year old who had been having an amphetamine psychosis. He had a very well-defined system of paranoia in which he felt that the police were after him and that his roommate and he had come to the Medical Clinic for help. Except for this system of paranoia and distracting hallucinations, he was remarkably lucid. During our interview a staff volunteer of the clinic, wearing a black leather jacket, crossed in front of the door. The patient jumped up and said, "I knew it! You're part of the plot!" and tried to run out the door. While restraining the boy, I called the volunteer and indicated that this was a member of the clinic staff who just happened to wear a black leather jacket. He calmed down immediately. The movement in and out of a paranoia delusional system can be very dramatic, and the physician may suddenly become part of that system. If it happened to be a large or violent individual, the physician may be in some *immediate jeopardy.* [italics added][27]

Another characteristic is volubility. The most typical description of a heavy-use amphetamine scene is of a group of people in a room who are simply talking away at each other for hours or days at a time. Verbosity is so intense that four-person conversations are often impossible because everyone is speaking at once. The conversation is often just chatter, with little discrimination between what conventional people consider serious or enlightening and what they view as utterly banal. The frantic talking is punctuated by endless bickering and arguing. A common source of such friction is the accusation of theft, sometimes real, sometimes imaginary. This is usually related to the practice of "knick-knacking," which entails picking up or stealing small objects for the purpose of collecting them or playing with them. This activity provides an outlet for the tremendous energy and enhanced concentration that is a physical effect of the drug.

The "crash," or the experience of coming down from a speed high, is so extreme that even familiarity with a severe alcoholic hangover does not suggest what the phenomenon is like. The individual suffers from exhaustion and may sleep for a day or more, depending on the duration of the speed binge. Shortly after or even shortly before awakening, slight inconveniences greatly disturb the "crasher." Irritability is so intense that it appears to the outsider as intolerant selfishness. Arguments, to the extent of yelling and occasional hitting, occur for what appear to the outsider to be fairly insignificant reasons. The crasher feels that demands made on him are inconsiderate, insufferable, and impossible. Upon awakening, the person usually eats ravenously. A prolonged phase of profound depression characteristically follows the immediate after-effects of the crash.

If a person uses speed in great quantity, on many long runs, with few intervals between a crash and a new run, he will not only become emaciated but will report feeling muscle and joint pains and possibly twitches. Often the brain, as well as the body, feels the strain after awhile. There are occasional reports of overdoses resulting in numbness. Some users report being paralyzed and afraid to move; their thoughts either race too quickly or stop; their hearts throb. For others, the racing world gets out of control, leading to a temporary psychosis.

Rapid weight loss and irregular eating habits of speed freaks have led to some general health problems, for example, lowered resistance to colds and respiratory problems. More dangerous is the likelihood of catching infectious hepatitis because of the use of unclean needles and lack of attention to elementary sanitation problems. Occasionally someone goes on a bad trip due to shooting amphetamines which have been "cut" with an impure or harmful substance. Many cases of hepatitis or suspected hepatitis as well as of severe overdosing go unreported because of fear of any contact with the establishment and the inability to raise money for an examination and blood tests.

All this suggests a development that actually occurs: the gathering of speed freaks in freak houses, where like minded people get together to wile away the days. When a residence becomes "open," word gets around and crystal shooters flow into it until the limits of the particular house are reached. Houses develop reputations—as to how pleasant the atmosphere is, how fast and frequent the action is, and what types of persons on the periphery of a particular scene would be welcome. Common to all flash houses are frenetic action and crowded living conditions. There is always a shortage of money and meeting places, so speed freaks seem to move in and assume squatter's rights. If the person in charge of a given residence is not fully committed to the world of speed, the speed freaks flowing into and taking over his house will quickly force him to make a decision to be in or out.

Handling the Problems of Access

The speed scene poses unusual problems of access. The facts that people are very talkative, gather in particular locales to purchase drugs or take them, stay up for long periods of time, and do not have conventional jobs all imply, at first glance, that the access problems should be easily manageable. In actuality, they are not.

The volubility of a speed freak while high is so intense that it is almost impossible to conduct an interview, especially if more than one speed freak is present. The meaningless chatter, physical hyperactivity, and compulsive behavior all create major barriers for the fieldworker.

Persons who are high on the drug are unwilling to sit still for an inter-view or are constitutionally incapable of submitting to a focused kind of questioning because they are so highly suggestible to external stimuli.

In our research, a major part of the collection of life history data had to be conducted with knowledgeable individuals between runs. We found, however, that it was also possible to get information at the early stages of a run if we were alone with the respondent. The initial experi-ence of the drug is one of euphoria and expansiveness, and information about previous drug experiences, brushes with the police, and the tech-nical lore associated with drug-using could be obtained when the speed freak was in this stage.

The peculiar round of life wherein people stay up for three, four, or five days at a time and then sleep for several days posed enormous practical difficulties for the research. Our conventional commitments (family, friends, teaching responsibilities) had to be put aside for a time so that we could adapt ourselves more realistically to this youthful scene. As we became more familiar with this particular universe, we developed a crude sampling plan that called for observations at a num-ber of different gathering spots, and this relieved us somewhat from a very exacting round of life. If we were interested, however, in what hap-pened during the course of a run when a small group of people started shooting speed intravenously, it meant that one or two fieldworkers had to be present at the beginning and be relieved periodically by other members of the team until the run was over. Fatigue was a constant problem and suggests that more than one fieldworker is required in this type of research.

The health problems constituted more of an access than a risk prob-lem for us. We were continually reassured by our medical collaborators that the possibility of contracting hepatitis was extremely remote as long as we did not use the needles ourselves and paid a minimum amount of attention to sanitation. It caused constant concern while in the field, however, for every vague malaise was interpreted as the onset of hepatitis. The problem was a psychological one that we had to face. Our middle-class notions of hygiene led to feelings of revulsion at the physical conditions in one flash house where most of our observations were conducted. The health question was the one around which our general discussion of intervention revolved. This led to the explication of what we felt to be legitimate intervention, for example, taking people to the clinic if they were having strong drug reactions, pointing out early indications of hepatitis, informing participants of what was con-tained in street drugs that had been analyzed, and the like. Our discus-sions with concerned medical personnel reassured us that our initial antipathies to the unsanitary conditions we found were more related to our own culturally induced notions of cleanliness than it was to any actual health problem.

Ethical Problems

The literature on participant-observation is explicit about protecting informants so that they will not be harmed. When we publish our results, we are enjoined to give an accurate description of what we have found but to give it in such a way that we keep faith with our respondents.[28] However, the problem is more complicated than the novice researcher would be led to believe. Becker suggests that the solution to the problem of what to publish is the political adjudication of interest, and he recommends educating subjects, in a series of seminars or conversations, on the possible effects of the report. This remedy does not seem appropriate in a situation in which the researcher is not seen as a teacher. The model of the management conference that industrial sociologists have found helpful has little relevance to the speed scene described above: it is not that well organized or formalized, and there are no clear-cut lines of authority. A small group interview with informants helped to clarify our description, extend it, and possibly modify it and proved to be the most congenial setting to get feedback relating to the safety and security of the persons with whom we formed our research partnership.[29]

In addition to putting in jeopardy the immediate personal safety of respondents by being available to unenlightened enforcement strategies, that is, strategies that serve a punitive, nonrehabilitative, police point of view, there is a more general sense in which research can harm respondents. Research on underdogs is usually funded by the federal government or by national foundations who feel the need for information about underdogs. The uses to which the research is put, as Gouldner[30] has pointed out, can lead to a better understanding, to manipulation, or to management of underdogs by caretaking institutions. We have to be explicit about our own positions in this matter and honest with ourselves and our respondents. Honesty requires that we recognize that our work is not value-free, that it is conducted within a larger political context. This is not to deny objectivity, as Horton points out, but only to affirm that ". . . Knowledge is relational to man. They [proponents of the sociology of knowledge] do not deny objectivity, but contend that men are objective about quite different things. What things is a practical question of what perspective and what values for what purpose."[31]

The social facts we describe are behaviors seen from a particular perspective. That perspective must include some understanding and analysis of the link between the behavior under consideration and the master institutions of the society from which it derives. This is a difficult task, and we need further discussion of how it can be accomplished. Every study of deviant phenomena does not inevitably compel the sociologist to view the participants as victims, as Gouldner suggests. If it is true that our studies can only contribute to the suffering of our respondents (if not in the short run, certainly in the long run), then we would be well advised to withdraw from field studies of deviant behavior among relatively weak and powerless populations and focus on "overdog" deviance. This may be the position many of us will come to one day. It means that we will probably have to settle for something less than direct observation, since the powerful have the resources and wherewithal to resist our intrusions. High on our list of priorities in this eventuality should be the development of more ingenious methods that, in the absence of actual field observations or direct testimony, would enable us to ascertain the behavior of power elites. In short, we should focus on developing an appropriate battery of unobtrusive measures to aid us in our analyses of white-collar and corporate deviance.

But before we too quickly abandon our field studies, perhaps a closer look at their positive consequences is in order. Gouldner does suggest that one positive feature of underdog research is that it elevates into public view certain underprivileged aspects of reality. The effect of doing this may be to mobilize deviant communities for collective action to change the social arrangements that victimize them. This occurs in the context of two groups in contention: one that feels threatened and has the power and organization to do something about it, and one that doesn't. The sociologist conducting a study on underdog perspectives finds himself in the position of an advocate. A more careful analysis of what this has meant in different settings (homosexual community, differentiated groups of drug users, civil rights movement) might show this advocate role as indispensable to the later development of political consciousness.

The Research Bargain

It is clear what the researcher wants from the researcher-respondent relationship: introductions to certain people and access to data and particular sites. It is not always clear what the respondent wants or expects. Polsky[32] suggests that the respondent may see something in the work the researcher is doing that would be beneficial to him, may want to correct mistaken notions about what he does, or may be simply motivated by pride and status considerations. Hughes first touched on the research bargain in discussing pitfalls for the investigator in industry. His major concern was the danger of "passing"—that one's empathy might become one's identity:

If the relationship does not get so close that one is tempted to break the bargain, to step out of role, it is probably not a success. If William F. Whyte yielded to the temptation to help the Corner boys a bit with getting out the vote, it means that he was a success as a field worker. If he had yielded more fully and too often, he would have ceased to be a sociologist.[33]

Hughes did not discuss, however, the elements of the informal contract worked out with respondents.

The initial contacts with knowledgeable people in the speed scene suggested that we could be helpful in several ways: we could share our knowledge of drugs and drug reactions (expert role), we could facilitate getting medical services (expediter), and we could pay people for interviews (employer). This was the explicit contract (though not formalized in writing) worked out with three key informants during the first stages of our field research.

During the initial phase, participants also wanted to know what your "thing" is so they can place you. This involved giving not only a description of research aims but also information about personal ambitions, data about family life, and accounts of any experience we had had with drugs. These questions, though not asked all at once or exclusively in a group setting, constituted the first test that our respondents posed. Were we the kind of persons who could be trusted?

The next test was more crucial and made explicit one expectation that was not part of our initial understanding. We were asked if we would provide our informants with drugs from time to time, as a kind of payment, since we had access to drug supplies. This request, which we viewed as an attempt to structure our role in a particular way, was one that we had not anticipated. We asked for time to think about the request and clarify for ourselves just what it meant. Our conclusion was that if this constituted a fundamental condition of the research venture, then we must withdraw. Hence, we refused to cooperate in obtaining drugs. Our own views about the unpleasant features of the drugs being used and the emerging drug-related life style did not permit us to be maneuvered into accomplice roles. We fully expected that our research would be terminated at this point.

Our informants disappeared for a week or more and reappeared to ask for assistance when an underage friend was picked up by juvenile authorities. Our knowledge, skill, connections and influence were perceived as useful despite the fact that we would not supply drugs. The request for assistance was the third test we were asked to pass, and our success in this instance structured the relationship for the duration of the field research. We demonstrated that we could be helpful in "hassles" with authority, and we had to be prepared to render assistance in negotiating with the system in the areas of legal, monetary, and employment services. The closest analogue to the researcher's role in this setting is one of *detached gang worker*.[34]

Handling Damaging Rumors

The paranoia combined with aggressiveness, which is a pervasive feature of the speed scene, was always a threat to the disruption of the research partnership. Since access was achieved chiefly through reliance on several high-status people in the scene,[35] since the authority structure was primitive, and since the culture that was forming had not become differentiated enough to sustain enduring factions, the problems of the "malfunctioning of the communications network" and of alienating particular factions, usual in studying formal organizations or communities, did not exist. Rather, the rumors that developed and led to periodic breakdowns in our relationships were linked to the suspicion that pervaded the scene. We tried to deal with it by noting the circumstances under which it was likely to occur.

We observed that the paranoia usually occurred after there was police activity in the neighborhood, when there was likely to be some concern about who had brought them into the picture. In such a case, specific demonstration of our helpfulness seemed fruitful, for it underscored our role as medically related "detached workers." Essential to the maintenance of this role were the continued good relations with our initial high-status informants. They were expected to and did vouch for us again and again.

Another situation in which suspicion occurred was the response to theft of property, including drugs, or to "burns" (selling a substance incorrectly identified as speed or some other drug). These actions usually occasioned harsh and immediate retribution. Because of the limited possibility of observing such situations in which violence occurred—since we were known not to engage in drug trafficking, the likelihood of our being assaulted was minimal—we chose to rely on informant interviewing.

The third situation where paranoia was likely to occur was toward the end of an unusually long and intense run. In this situation, the suspicion seemed baseless, and there was some danger of physical assault. We attempted to deal with this by limiting the number of actual observations made of these behaviors and restricting our method of data collection about it to informant interviewing. Even then, if one of us were present in such a circumstance, the chance of physical assault was not as great as expected. The suspicious person in this context was usually highly distractible and subject to a flight of ideas. We found it useful to delineate the situations in which paranoia was likely to occur and to make a distinction between "social paranoia" and "individual paranoia"— about the former we could do something, about the latter, not very much.

Despite the potential for the disruption of our fieldwork, the communications network worked remarkably well. Some discussion of why it did is in order. The field study began after the examination of characteristics of sample clinic users was completed. It lasted for a brief three months. The flash house where most of the observations were conducted managed to survive for the duration of the fieldwork. This was very unusual, since flash houses are notably short-lived. The frantic action, the coming and going of strange-looking people, and the occasional violence did not lead to any major police raids on the house. This seemed related to the prevailing police policy, which at that time appeared to be one of containment. The house was located in the center of the community, surrounded by other residents who were sympathetic or neutral to what was happening there; hence complaints were minimal. As long as those using the house did not wander about the street, especially into adjoining middle-class neighborhoods, the police seemed to feel no need to make arrests.

It is very helpful for the researcher to know to what extent the police are informed about a given situation and how they are likely to react to it. This information can come from the police themselves or from those who are knowledgeable about police activity. Since we thought drawing our information from the police directly would compromise our investigation, we queried sympathetic agency personnel (social workers and lawyers related to juvenile court) instead.

If one is interested in the role of control agencies in the development of particular behavior, then we must acknowledge the tacit concessions granted by officials to the research enterprise. The problem is that we don't always know when and if concessions are being granted. But information about such concessions is indispensable to our analysis; for example, to what extent was the growing stability of the scene we were observing due to the emergence of new institutions and to what extent was it a result of the decline in police activity?

Summary and Conclusion

The researcher in deviance has always tended to be skeptical about "expert" portrayals of what the world of the deviant consists. This has generally led away from the viewing of official statistics as more than a mere index of agency activity. Interest in the personal perspectives of group members has inevitably resulted in fieldwork and has caused researchers to favor direct observation or testimony by participants. The reawakened interest in participant-observation in sociology in general has been a boon to the deviance researcher. It has provided an abundance of suggestions, guidelines, hints, and prescriptions. But the bulk of written material focuses on conventional kinds of settings and therefore does not attempt to deal seriously with the problems of access and risk in unusual situations like the one described above.

The experience in this setting suggests that access is gained by putting oneself into a situation in which a service that deviant members perceive as valuable can be provided. Access is maintained by an extension of these services and by continued good relationships with high-status members. One of the services that we provided was economic. Because of the impoverished character of the speed scene, a decision was made to pay those who worked closely with the researchers as research aides. The injunction mentioned by Jack D. Douglas, in his article "Observing Deviance," about not paying informants did not seem applicable to this situation. The primary task of the research aides was to interview other speed users who were inaccessible to the regular research staff, so the likelihood of undermining the validity of the inquiry by self-dramatizations was limited. No attempt was made to disguise the purpose of the research enterprise because we felt that a disguise of any sort would be: immoral, difficult to sustain in this situation, dangerous, and ineffective for exploring the kind of subculture under scrutiny.

A variable that is crucial during the fieldwork, but one that cannot be controlled by the researcher, is the "cooperation" or lack of it provided by control agencies authorized to do something about the deviance. The most the investigator can do is to be aware of official activity and how it affects the research role, member receptivity to being studied, and the evolution of the subculture itself.

The peculiar problems of access demanded an extraordinary amount of researcher flexibility in order to cope with the unconventional round of life and the differing norms governing face-to-face relations—norms so different that initially they did not seem to exist at all. Volubility, physical hyperactivity, and compulsivity called for certain adaptions of field methods to take these features into account and utilize them more systematically for a detailed description of members' perspectives. Health problems, another barrier to access, were discussed in two senses: first, the likelihood of respondents encountering particular medical difficulties and the sociologist's role in dealing with these difficulties; and second, observer concerns about becoming ill and the steps taken to address them.

The risk problems were related to legal-ethical dilemmas, the implicit understandings in the research bargain, and damaging rumors. The legal difficulties required the researchers to anticipate the possibility of arrest and prepare for this eventuality. Ethical problems inherent in this kind of research suggested a closer attention to what respondents' real interests were and the extent to which they would be jeopardized in publishing field studies. A more subtle and vexing difficulty is that research on underdogs might be used for "overdog" ends.

The partnership with respondents could be viewed as developing in several stages, each of which posed a test for the researcher, each of which had potential for disrupting the relationship. These tests inevitably resulted in a reworking of the initial research bargain. The trust that was generated in the course of the fieldwork was partly related to the conviction that the researchers were not on the side of the police. It was reinforced by the feeling that we agreed with some of the general justifications for using drugs, though this did not lead us to use speed, and by the fact that our concern for the participants was demonstrated by our giving them assistance with various problems created or aggravated by their drug usage. In Douglas's terms our participation could be viewed as a kind of "limbo membership." We commuted to and from the community and hung out with speed users. Our limited participation was a matter of researcher choice rather than the result of any barriers erected by participants to further involvement.

One danger noted in the literature is the likelihood of the sociologist's empathy for the respondents passing into identity. In our case, this did not occur because total immersion did not take place. The research team was sufficiently dissimilar from speed users in age, physical stamina, educational background, and commitments to conventional behavior to resist whatever attractions the speed scene may have held for us initially.

Apart from the fundamental human consideration—a desire to eliminate unnecessary suffering—the sociologist's final justification for exploring deviant worlds is his conviction that a particular theoretical area would be enlarged and extended by participant-observation. The theoretical rationale for this investigation was that the conditions for the emergence and development of a drug-related life style could be explored and comparative materials developed to add to the literature on youthful social movements. It is the sociologist's theoretical concerns which, in the last analysis, can be a corrective to simple prurient interest in the exotic.

Notes

1. George McCall and Jerry Simmons, *Issues in Participant Observation* (Reading, Mass.: Addison-Wesley, 1969).
2. See Howard S. Becker's Introduction to Clifford Shaw, *The Jack Roller* (Chicago: University of Chicago Press, Phoenix Books, 1966), pp. xvi ff. Becker (p. xvii) uses the metaphor of a "mosaic" to refer to the earlier work of the Chicago school and contrasts it with the brick "wall of science":

   > I use the term [the single study] to refer to research projects that are conceived as self-sufficient and self-contained, which provide all the evidence one needs to accept or reject the conclusions they proffer, whose findings are to be used as another brick in the growing wall of science—a metaphor quite different than that of a mosaic. The single study is integrated with the main body of knowledge in the following way: it derives its hypotheses from an inspection of what is already known; then, after the research is completed, if those hypotheses have been demonstrated, they are added to the wall of what is already scientifically known and used as the basis for further studies. The important point is that the researcher's hypothesis is either proved or disproved on the basis of what he has discovered in doing that one piece of research.

3. See C. Wright Mills, *The Sociological Imagination* (New York: Oxford University Press, 1959), chap. 3, "Abstracted Empiricism." For a comparison of methods that gets at the limitations and advantages of each see Arthur J. Vidich and Gilbert Shapiro, "A Comparison of Participant Observation and Survey Data," *American Sociological Review,* 20 (1955), 28–33, and Ivan N. Mensh and Jules Henry, "Direct Observation and Psychological Tests in Anthropological Field Work," *American Anthropologist,* 55 (October 1953), 461–480. Both selections are included in McCall and Simmons, *op. cit.*
4. Mills' attack on the atheoretical approach of the social pathologists, their interest in studying a discrete set of situations, and their inability to rise above a series of "cases" (C. Wright Mills, "The Professional Ideology of Social Pathologists," *American Journal of Sociology,* 49 [September 1943], 165–180, led to the dismissal of the contributions of the Chicago school generally, with its reformist emphasis and style of research. It is not necessary to point out that Mills was not opposed to these research procedures, for what better way is there to become familiar with particular vocabularies of motives and the situated actions to which they refer than field methods? What Mills did oppose was the lack of attention to theoretical concerns, as evidenced in his advice to sociologists:

   > Do not study merely one small milieu after another; study the social structures in which milieux are organized. In terms of these studies of larger structures, select the milieux you need to study in detail, and study them in such a way as to understand the interplay of milieux with structure. (*Sociological Imagination,* p. 224)

5. See Howard S. Becker, "Whose Side Are We On?" *Social Problems,* 14

(Winter 1967), 239–247, and Alvin W. Gouldner's rejoinder, "The Sociologist as Partisan: Sociology and the Welfare State," *The American Sociologist*, 3 (May 1968), 103–116. In a similar vein, John Horton, "The Dehumanization of Anomie and Alienation: A Problem in the Ideology of Sociology," *British Journal of Sociology*, 15 (1964), 283–300, explores the hidden value commitments of sociologists defining the concepts "anomie" and "alienation" today.

6. McCall and Simmons, *op. cit.*

7. Ned Polsky, *Hustlers, Beats, and Others* (Chicago: Aldine, 1967), pp. 122 ff.

8. Another key problematic area is the selection of informants. John P. Dean, Robert L. Eichorn, and Lois Dean, "Fruitful Informants for Intensive Interviewing," in John T. Doby (ed.), *An Introduction to Social Research,* 2nd ed. (New York: Meredith Press, 1967) (reprinted in McCall and Simmons, *op. cit.*), stress the search for insightful informants at the early stage of entry into an organization or community. They suggest a typology of informants who are especially sensitive to the area of concern and are more-willing-to-reveal. As applied to the illegal drug scene discussed here, their injunctions do no more than suggest that knowledgeable informants should come from all parts of the system, should include high and low status people, exusers, old-timers, and newcomers.

9. See Emile Durkheim, *Suicide* (New York: Free Press, 1951), translated from the French *Le Suicide* (Paris: Felix Alcon, 1897); R. K. Merton, "Social Structure and Anomie," reprinted in R. K. Merton (ed.), *Social Theory and Social Structure* (rev. ed., New York: Free Press, 1957), pp. 131–160; R. A. Cloward and L. Ohlin, *Delinquency and Opportunity* (New York: Free Press, 1960), pp. 179–184. See also M. B. Clinard (ed.), *Anomie and Deviant Behavior* (New York: Free Press, 1964).

10. During the early stages of my research, Helen Swick Perry provided valuable and sensitive insights into the character of youthful social systems in Haight-Ashbury and commented extensively on my early field notes. See her book, *The Human Be-In* (New York: Basic Books, 1970).

11. Joyce Clements, Charles Carey, and Anthony Poveda conducted a number of interviews and collected ecological information concerning hanging-out patterns in the community. Roger Smith and Harold Nawy assisted during the fieldwork phase of the research discussed in this paper.

12. Herbert Blumer, "Collective Behavior," in A. M. Lee (ed.), *New Outline of the Principles of Sociology* (New York: Barnes & Noble, 1946), p. 199.

13. Ralph Linton, "Nativistic Movements," *American Anthropologist,* 45 (April–June 1943), 230–240. See also James T. Carey, *The College Drug Scene* (Englewood Cliffs, N.J.: Prentice-Hall, 1968), chap. 8.

14. John Lofland, *Deviance and Identity* (Englewood Cliffs, N.J.: Prentice-Hall, 1969), chap. 4.

15. Seymour Fiddle, "The Addict Culture and Movement Into and Out of Hospitals," as reported in U.S. Senate, Committee on the Judiciary Subcommittee to Investigate Juvenile Delinquency, Hearings, Part 13, New York City, September 20–21, 1962 (Washington, D.C.: Government Printing Office, 1963), pp. 3–156.

16. These are the terms used by Goode in his discussion of criteria one could use to determine whether or not there is a marijuana subculture. See Erich Goode, "Multiple Drug Use Among Marijuana Smokers," *Social Problems*, 17 (Summer 1969), 48–64.

17. David Smith and Charles Fisher, "High Dose Methamphetamine Abuse in the Haight-Ashbury," in David Smith (ed.), *Drug Abuse Papers* (Berkeley: University of California Continuing Education, 1969), p. 1.

18. Erving Goffman, *Asylums: Essays on the Social Situation of Mental Patients and Other Inmates* (Garden City, N.Y.: Anchor Books, 1961), pp. 321 ff.

19. McCall and Simmons, *op. cit.*, p. 43.

20. Roger Smith, "Social Types in the Speed Scene" (unpublished paper; San Francisco, 1969), p. 5.

21. Howard S. Becker, "History, Culture and Subjective Experiences: An Exploration of the Social Bases of Drug Induced Experiences," *Journal of Health and Social Behavior*, 8 (September 1967), 163–170.

22. For a brief summary of California drug legislation in effect at the time of this study, see Donald E. Miller, "Narcotic Drug and Marijuana Controls," in *The Journal of Psychedelic Drugs*, 1 (Summer 1967), 28–40.

23. Lewis Yablonsky, "On Crime, Violence, LSD and Legal Immunity for Social Scientists," *The American Sociologist*, 3 (May 1968), 148–149.

24. Carolyn Symonds, in a letter commenting on Yablonsky's position, *The American Sociologist*, 3 (August 1968), 254.

25. See D. W. Broeder, "Silence, and Perjury Before Police Officers," *Nebraska Law Review*, 4 (1960), 63–103.

26. For a more detailed description of a similar speed scene, see James T. Carey and Jerry Mandel, "A San Francisco Bay Area 'Speed' Scene," *Journal of Health and Social Behavior*, 9 (June 1968), 164–174.

27. Smith and Fisher, *op. cit.*, p. 3.

28. See Polsky, *op. cit.*, and Howard S. Becker, "Problems in the Publication of Field Studies," in Arthur J. Vidich, Joseph Bensman, and Maurice R. Stein (eds.), *Reflections on Community Studies* (New York: Wiley, 1964), pp. 267–284 (reprinted in McCall and Simmons, *op. cit.*).

29. For a more detailed discussion of this procedure used in another setting, see Carey, *College Drug Scene, op. cit.*, pp. 200 ff.

30. Gouldner, *op. cit.*, p. 109.

31. Horton, *op. cit.*, p. 298.

32. Polsky, *op. cit.*, p. 125.

33. Everett C. Hughes, "The Relation of Industrial to General Sociology," *Sociology and Social Research*, 41 (March–April 1957), 25–26.

34. Irving Spergel, *Street Gang Work: Theory and Practice* (Chicago: University of Chicago Press, 1966). I am indebted to Roger Smith for pointing out the similarity between our research activities and street work behavior.

35. Since the social organization of this particular scene was relatively simple, we were like anthropologists gaining access to a primitive tribe. Our high-status informants were like chiefs.

Managing Fronts in Observing Deviance

Dorothy J. Douglas

A "front," in the context of sociological observation, is that facade erected, on the one hand, by the individuals in an organization the researcher proposes to study or, on the other hand, by the researcher himself in order to accomplish his ends.

Most sociologists make the assumption that, to some degree, every organization (or individual, for that matter) puts up a front which represents to outsiders an idealized version of what he or his organization is trying to accomplish, the way in which goals are met, and the motivations undergirding decisions and actions. Since the researcher must elaborate his approach to those whom he would observe in such a way as to facilitate his data collection, managing fronts becomes a major research problem. Both researcher and subjects, once in contact with one another (even if that contact is tenuous, as it is, for example, in a mail questionnaire), face problems in front management. They must detect, delimit, short-circuit, or undermine fronts devised by others while producing, elaborating, and protecting their own fronts.

If the researcher chooses to observe deviant groups (or supposedly nondeviant groups, such as ambulance drivers, cabbies, jazz musicians, and TV repairmen, that are engaged in deviant acts) successful front management becomes even more important. Such groups, by their very deviance, are forced to submerge much of their activity (and even ideology) when in contact with outsiders. Of course, an understanding of front management is also important in observing individuals or groups who more nearly conform to community norms. It is simply easier to investigate and lay out the mechanisms of front production and manipulation in terms of groups that deviate markedly from accepted

93

norms. It is precisely because those labeled as deviant are seen as somewhat defenseless that they become more vulnerable to being investigated. To defend themselves against unwarranted intrusions, the fronts these groups build up tend to be more elaborate, better constructed, and more ably defended.

The social scientist engaged in the study of an organization he defines as more or less deviant to ambient norms usually expects some degree of front production. If, on the other hand, he believes the organization to be relatively nondeviant, he will tend to be more accepting of whatever fronts are presented to him. Since, in general, *all* organizations engage in front production and front management it behooves the social scientist to carefully consider these phenomena.[1]

In my analysis, I am building on the work of a number of anthropologists and sociologists who are concerned with validity of data, the meaning of "real," and roles.[2] In addition to these more general sociological analyses, there have been several very interesting studies that specifically attempt to analyze fronts in research settings.[3]

Epistemologically, any investigator has to believe that the end result of his investigation will be the discovery of truth. To postulate that behind every front lies another front gets one nowhere. But to hold that immutable truth will reveal itself once a front is breached is an equally futile approach. One's interest has to lie in judging the validity of the data one collects regardless of the method used to generate that data. Probably there is no way for a researcher to be absolutely sure when or if he has penetrated a given front or, having penetrated it, whether his data is valid. It is my contention, however, that if enough researchers study a phenomenon from enough different angles and with enough attention to getting behind the fronts they encounter, validity of data will be increased. In presenting this study of the nature of front production, then, I am attempting to increase sensitivity to the question of data validity.

Fronts as Interactive Processes

Of course it can never be forgotten that front production and front breaching are interactive processes. Primary fronts, subfronts (to bolster the primary as needed), counterfronts (with their own panoply of primary and secondary fronts) are elaborated and retrenched by both defenders and intruders as need arises and imagination dictates. Goffman (especially in his *Presentation of Self in Everyday Life*)[4] implies that fronts are in some way necessary to preserve an organization qua organization. In other words, outsiders cannot be expected to completely understand the reality with which the organization is forced to work.

Therefore, in the process of interacting with outsiders, acceptable fronts must be presented to those not conversant with the organization in order that it may function without untoward interference. Using this line of reasoning one might say, for example, that no client would elect to ride in an ambulance if he knew that the driver and the aideman had no, or very little, first aid training. Therefore, one might argue, it is necessary for the company to project an image of competence in any way they can—by propaganda, outfitting the drivers in white coats or medical-style uniforms, and carefully devised advertising—in order for the company to exist at all. Similarly, a university presents the front that its professors are collectively and individually highly trained, competent scholars, able and willing to instruct students. A defender of this kind of front might argue that although some of the professors will be incompetent and/or unwilling to instruct students, the university *must* project this image in order to attract students and thus maintain its existence as a university.

This is one useful way of looking at this particular interactive process, but a slightly different analysis may provide additional insights. Multiple-front presentations can be looked upon as a form of social control. If an organization wishes to have a policy, a proposal, an idea, or even an ideology accepted by people outside the organization, they may slant their representations (propaganda, advertising) so as to elicit the desired response in the consumer or client. This brings up the whole issue of myth versus reality. Projecting the professional image of a doctor or a lawyer has traditionally been thought of as an essential part of practicing those professions. In traditional medical schools, for example, the physician-instructors are at some pains to convey to the students what is expected of them by way of adopting those mannerisms and other characteristics which set them apart as "doctors." Providing the neophyte with this type of front enables him to appear competent and skilled during his student days and tends to give nonmedical people confidence in his ability and competence regardless of the skill and knowledge he actually possesses (up to a limit of tolerance, presumably).

Social control can, however, work both ways. An organization may carefully construct a front for itself and propagandize its public until the representation is accepted as reality. The public can then turn around and insist that any characteristics contrary to this front be eliminated. In other words, they can force the organization to "realize" the fronts to some degree. Ambulance companies may attempt to project the image that their drivers and aidemen are medically competent to handle all varieties of accidents and other emergencies, whereas, in fact, their crewmen may have little or no training even in first aid. It is conceivable that if the propaganda is strong enough, clients of ambulance services could come to expect and eventually demand high-grade emergency care from ambulance crewmen. When that day arrives the companies will be forced to provide well-trained men for their ambulance crews. Alternatively, they could attempt to change the image of what constitutes a good crewman by projecting the notion that an ambulance crewman should only furnish transportation for the injured or the ill and that any type of medical intervention should be left until arrival at a hospital. In either case, a form of social control is brought about because of the discrepancies arising between the front and the reality it conceals.

The Negotiation of Front Production

In general, a front can be thought of as a formalized interpretation of observable reality offered in somewhat tentative fashion to an outsider. This interpretation may be more or less elaborate when first presented, but it is *always* negotiable, and especially so when first proffered. In a recent study of ambulance services I found many examples of this phenomenon.[5]

One ambulance owner, for example, wished to discourage me from actually riding in his rigs. He told me at first that it was against the law for any but the crew to ride on a real call. Without challenging the truth of the statement, I interpreted this as a front and offered to negotiate by suggesting that I had every confidence that he could wrangle permission for me in this *special* case. After a suitable time had elapsed, I broached the subject again and found that permission was now "pending," but I would have to write a formal letter requesting permission to ride. In due course, I got a reply to this letter stating I was permitted to observe from 10:00 A.M. to 6:00 P.M. for exactly five days. I accepted the offer in the naive belief that I would be able to gain a real insight into the problems faced by ambulance personnel and their ability to cope with the medical needs of the acutely ill persons they were asked to transport in that period of time. My initial approach was to ride with one ambulance crew (in this case the owner's son and his attendant) whenever they received a call between those hours which (I was led to believe) constituted a normal day shift.

During the first four days of riding, my observations merely confirmed conclusions I had already made from my experience with ambulance crews and their clients in an earlier emergency room project. On the fifth (and supposedly last) day of my observations, however, I took advantage of an opportunity to ride with another crew past the magic hour of 6:00 P.M. without the owner's knowledge. On that ride I finally caught on to the fact that the crew was able to communicate with their dispatcher by keying the microphone in a special way, so that, for example, calls could be transferred to another rig without my knowledge. By dint of a little guesswork and some insistent questioning I managed to find out that to an extent not then fully appreciated I was being "had." In other words, I was being formally shown a small segment of the real job that the crew performed in such a way that it might appear to me to represent the totality of their usual work load and mode of working. Up to that point I had been shown nothing that might contradict the usual lay image of an ambulance ride.

My problem then became one of finding some way of continuing to ride with the company in as unstructured a setting as possible. Therefore, I attempted to negotiate changes in the rules governing my activities by using a number of different techniques, in the hope that if one method didn't work, another would.

I started by simply "forgetting" to take leave of the crew I rode with that Friday night and staying with them until they went off duty at 10 A.M. the following Monday. By Monday morning I was dirty, disheveled, sleepy as any crewman and had been on enough "real" calls to lend an air of conviction to the following argument that I presented to the owner instead of my planned excuse. (I had planned to point out to the owner that since I needed his permission to continue to ride past my deadline, I thought it best to stay on the rig so that I would catch him as soon as he reported after the weekend.) I first thanked the owner for letting me stay the weekend (if he was surprised that I had stayed, he did not show it). Then I elaborated on the importance of the study and his contribution to it, stressing that if I were to get enough "cases" to make the study worthwhile, I would have to spend more time riding. When he asked how many cases I intended to collect, I offered the figure "fifty." However, I was careful to state that in order for a call to qualify as a case it had to meet very special and stringent requirements. When he seemed to be wavering, I added that I had a very insensitive, strict, and demanding boss (Julius Roth, the project's principal investigator) who would not look kindly on my reporting back to him with anything short of the stipulated number of cases. At this point, I suddenly found myself in an essentially open-ended situation, and from then on, whenever the issue arose of "finishing up," I was always able to say that I did not as yet have fifty cases that fulfilled the criteria for inclusion in the study.

This example nicely illustrates the essential elements in any negotiation. A position is stated by one of the negotiators (often, but not always, the one desiring to protect a given front). To challenge the position directly is undesirable, for, if the premises are false, the individual will not be happy to have this pointed out. On the other hand, if his position accurately reflects reality, you may be forced to concede this, rendering further negotiation futile. Instead, the position is relegated to the background, and a different and more acceptable approach is tried. This new approach, even if it achieves nothing else, permits sufficient time to pass so that the interaction can proceed and be tested in various ways. Finally, an attempt is made (perhaps through ambiguous wording, as in the example cited) to create as open-ended a situation as possible. This allows either participant to raise the issue of terminating the negotiated agreements but does not *require* that either do so.

The Function of the Lie in Front Management

One issue that needs to be considered is the function of the lie in front management. Since the concept of a lie has moral and ethical overtones, a real problem is sometimes created for the perpetrator and/or the defender of a given front. When an individual perceives that a given statement he is about to offer an intruder is, by his own standards, short of the truth, he must come to terms with himself.

The most common rationalizations that are employed to reduce tension resulting from such "necessity" for telling a lie seem to be predicated on the degree to which an intruder has a "right to know." Individuals volunteer information (correct or incorrect) on the basis of this "right to know," and most people will not hesitate to lie, or at least reply ambiguously, if they are questioned about something they consider private or secret. If someone is obviously not entitled to a certain type of information, he should be aware of the possibility that he will be "put on" or "fed a line" if he presses.

Another rationalization for lying is the notion that the unvarnished truth can wound. Most people are willing to tell another what they believe he wants to hear, especially if it is perceived to be in his best interest. Loyalty to an organization, therefore, requires that its important fronts be maintained, even at some cost, so that it can function smoothly, attain its goals, and reward its members, but also so that outsiders will not become disillusioned or discouraged about the benefit they believe to be accruing to them from the organization. (Even groups defined as criminal by some segments of society are seen as beneficent by *some* other outsiders.)

The third rationalization for lying is based on the notion that certain kinds of exaggerations are not lies. This appears to be the rationalization behind the type of story-telling ambulance crewmen engage in as they interact with their peers.

Although, from one point of view, this activity can be classed as a facet of front production (for example, seasoned veterans present fronts to neophytes in this way), it can also be seen as analogous to the conversations described by Thomas Kochman in his paper "Rapping in the Black Ghetto."

While often used to mean ordinary conversation, rapping is distinctively a fluent and a lively way of talking, always characterized by a high degree of personal style. To one's own group, rapping may be descriptive of an interesting narration, a colorful rundown of some past event.[6]

The content of rapping among ambulance men appears to be largely fabricated, and what is said is not taken very seriously. However, these stories serve a variety of important purposes. As Kochman notes:

...it is revealing that one raps *to* rather than *with* a person supporting the impression that rapping is to be regarded more as a performance than verbal exchange. As with other performances, rapping projects the personality, physical appearance and style of the performer.[7]

This type of story-telling helps the men in their efforts to establish their individuality and status among their peers. The style of the rap is important. Thus, the men who tell the most attention-getting stories are encouraged to elaborate and are listened to avidly.

The men often rap in a "Can you top this?" fashion on practically any subject at all (the kinds of loads they haul, the kinds of accidents they see, a hobby they are interested in, their girl friends). For example, the men once got into a discussion about the best way in which to learn Morse Code. (Most ambulance men are quite interested in radio, and some are ardent citizen's band radio enthusiasts. Learning to send and receive Morse Code is a formidable obstacle standing in the way of their becoming licensed radio amateurs.) The conversation was carried on over a period of a couple of days, with the men going 911 (ambulance code for "on personal business but still available for a run") in the rig to various electronics stores to pick up pamphlets on learning the code and spinning great plans about how they were going to accomplish this feat. One man thought that he could get a vaguely identified expert to teach him. This rap was "topped" by another man who stated that the Federal Communications Commission would not permit this. (No grounds were given and no authority was cited other than the man's statement.) Another man connected a nail that had a few turns of wire on it to a battery and was able to elicit a few clicks by bringing the nail in contact with a piece of metal. When someone objected that he could not distinguish between dots and dashes—all you heard was clicks—he topped this simply by stating that *he* could tell the difference and, as before, this was not disputed. Finally, as interest in this subject was beginning to wane, a driver produced what was recognized as the best rap of all by stating that he was going to send away for sleep-learning equipment. He went into a detailed description of how you put the Morse Code on a closed-loop tape. You can then play it on your tape recorder into a pillow-speaker while you sleep and in an unspecified period of time you will be ready to go and take your test. This was such an obviously inventive approach to the whole problem that it ended all discussion of the matter and the men took up another subject, never to return to the problem of learning Morse Code again during the few more months I spent with them.

Their raps having to do with the work situation are valuable as indicators of their general attitude toward their work, even if one takes it for granted that these stories are meant to impress and entertain the listener rather than to give an exact account of a factual happening.

One of the aides started telling stories about fat ladies he'd handled in his time. He said that he got this one gal, and when he loaded her into the ambulance she complained because he was handling her a little rough. So he told her he was busting his back for her and she'd better just shut up. He said, "God didn't make you fat, lady. He didn't just say one day, 'Zap, be fat.' You did it. You did it yourself. You just eat too much." Then he said, "Boy, that shut her up but quick. She didn't say anything more the rest of the trip, but when I unloaded her she thanked me, and I said, 'That's all right, lady. Just eat a little less.'"

They also told me about the time two of the men went out on a Code 3 (emergency call, red lights and siren authorized, with right of way at intersections assumed) to pick up a "jig" that had shot a cop. Two detectives got in the rig with the Negro who had done the shooting and who was pretty well shot up himself. The crew were told to do their Code 3 at 15 miles an hour or "I'll have your ticket." They said that the aideman sat there in the cab and dumped ashes from his cigarette in the guy's bullet holes—it was a nice detail.

On the other hand, certain subjects are considered out of bounds for rapping. For example, there are practically no stories told about accidents that involve the ambulances in their own company.

I caught a few hints that unit 418 had probably been creamed, but there's an unwritten code around here that if there's an ambulance accident, only the guy who's been in the accident tells you about it. Everybody else keeps quiet and makes excuses for the rig being in the shop. I saw this happen with the rig that Dan creamed. Anyway, it turned out, luckily, that Joe (the driver I was with) had been the one that racked the rig up. Apparently, he took the whole left rear fender and part of the bumper off in the accident. He didn't feel like giving me too many of the details and I didn't press him, but he said that one of the things that impressed him was that the owner never gives you any trouble about stuff like that. It's one of the things that happen. It goes against your driving record, and the owner figures that's enough punishment. Usually all he'll say is, "You god-damn stupid jackass," and you never hear another word about it. He mentioned that the fellows are good too. They never say another word about an ambulance crack-up, because they figure they might be next.

Men who exaggerate about their driving or first aid qualifications or credentials are quickly found out and are considered to be lying. Yet, as in most occupations without clearly defined requirements certified to by a recognized educational and/or licensing body, the men often fabricate those credentials that seem to them most useful for getting a position, elevating their status in the eyes of their clients or attaining an advantage over their peers.

Art (the driver) was interested in finding out what kind of fantastic story Arthur (the owner's son) had handed me about himself. When I told him that Arthur had told me that he had a degree in biology, he laughed as if he were going to split and said that he just couldn't understand why Arthur did things like that. It's true that Arthur had taken a biology course because he wanted to be a dentist (Arthur had told me he wanted to be a doctor), but he had flunked out of State College in his second year. Art said that Arthur was so shook up about this—he'd made plans to get married as soon as he graduated—that he was really near a breaking point. So his dad (as a pre-wedding present) immediately cut him in on half the business. That made Arthur feel a little better.

There are two remarkable aspects to this game of fabricating qualifications. One is that the men, providing they have not been formally blackballed, are usually hired on the strength of their stories and fired only if events prove that they have exaggerated about necessary abilities. The other is that the men's stories, although freely talked about and exposed among themselves, are carefully maintained for most outsiders. Thus, newspaper feature writers and sociologists, for example, have a difficult time getting a straight story from the men unless they spend quite a lot of time with them.

In some instances, the initial version of the front is accepted by the researcher without question either because he does not recognize that he is being presented with a front or because he prefers not to negotiate it.[8] When this happens, the front is often elaborated over time (sometimes in highly predictable directions). In fact, the researcher may consciously or unconsciously contribute to this elaboration. If he sincerely believes, for instance, that he is observing a highly trained ambulance crewman taking care of an accident victim, he may bring about all sorts of behavior that would not otherwise ensue. Moreover, he may, if he is medically unsophisticated himself, take the aideman's word for the validity of certain procedures, especially if they seem to "make sense" and/or if they are executed with an air of competence and confidence. On the other hand, the researcher may elect to help embellish a front just to see how far the subject will go with it. The following excerpts from my ambulance study field notes illustrate this process:

(The first day): The owner told me how he managed training. He said that, as far as he was concerned, you could put a guy in a classroom for three years and he'd never really learn how to handle emergencies. He believes in on-the-job training. He said he has two training platoons (each made up of a driver and an aideman) that he considers extremely well trained. He puts the new guy with one of these pairs. For the first week the guy just rides in the cab and observes; the second week he starts working with the aideman; and the third week he and the aideman handle everything—the driver just watches. During the fourth week he begins to learn a little bit about driving, although he's not allowed to drive, and continues to work with the aideman. At the beginning of the fifth week he's assigned to a partner and starts taking regular runs. "Every day," the owner said, "if I've got a new guy going, I get a report on him. If I don't wash him out, by the time he's finished with those four weeks he's pretty good." He said that they get doctors all the time to give them little lectures, especially orthopedic men, and that one of his men continually gives in-service training. They don't believe at all in this Red Cross training stuff. Sure they issue Red Cross certificates, but it's their own brand of emergency training. They've got their own Red Cross instructors, so they can do pretty much what they want with the course, and they do. They just don't buy the stuff that the Red Cross puts out.

   Much of what he said gave me the impression that he feels that ambulance personnel are not very much appreciated. He thinks he and his men are good. He talked several times about how people will question what he's doing in the hospital or will think he doesn't know how to operate a piece of equipment. He said specifically that he isn't trying to be a doctor, and he sure isn't trying to be a nurse, but he wants to be considered better than most nurses he's seen, and certainly above a garbage collector or an orderly.

   (One week later): Sandy (the "trainer") said to me, "You think these guys know something. You fell for that business the owner handed you about my training these guys and so on. That's a lot of hooey. They don't know anything. Sure I feel sorry for them. We get them off the street and we used to try to say, 'This is a pulmonator,' but they look at you and say, 'Duh, what's a pulmonator?' All I try to do is to tell them enough so they won't kill the patient before they get him to the hospital. These guys are really stupid, and they don't last long enough—the attendants don't—to learn anything anyway. The turnover is high. Lots of them are drunks. Sure they're running around with advanced first aid certificates, but the owner just hands those out. He shows them a film about ambulance driving, and their eyes bug out. If they bug out far enough they get a first aid certificate."

The Retrenchment of a Front

Because the front unfolds as a result of the interaction between the organizational defenders and the would-be intruder(s), the defenders do not foresee in detail the final form their front will take. To formalize and "perfect" a front requires gullibility and (to some extent) imagination on the part of the intruder. For example, during the first few days of my initial experience with an ambulance company, I was duped into believing that I was waiting for calls in a bona fide office, when actually I was sitting in the front room of a house belonging to one of the company's employees. Not only were certain pieces of furniture hidden in another room to help create this illusion, but in order to maintain it, the man's wife had to vacate the premises while I was there:

About 11:15 we pulled up at Station 2. It was a nice little house that had been freshly painted. We got inside and I was amazed at the way it was furnished. They had a front room fixed up as an office. In it was a rather nice rug, an old, broken-down settee and chair, and two old broken-down lamps. When I sat down on the settee I all but fell through the springs—they were that bad. Then there was a kind of bunk room with a box spring and mattress without any frame, just sitting on the floor along one side. On the other side was a little fold-up cot. They had all their clean whites (skivvy shorts, skivvy shirts, socks, smocks, pants, the works) all stacked up on this cot. There was an old desk in this room and a kid's planograph that, apparently, some of the guys were playing with. Some of the designs were rather nice. In fact, we spent some time exclaiming over them with two other guys who were there (whose names I can't remember) sitting around waiting for calls too. There was a small kitchen with a stove, table, and refrigerator. Then, of course, there was the bathroom. There were two other rooms they didn't show me. I guess they are private offices. The place is very sparsely furnished and is apparently used as a call station and a bunk room. The only reading material around was a whole stack of old *Life* magazines and one *Playboy* magazine that Pete, the driver assigned to Station 2, laughingly took and threw over on the bed when I started looking through the stack. Of course, there was a phone there—one of those fancy phones that has little buttons on it.

(About ten days later): George (the aide from Station 2) caught me in the dispatcher's office at the main office and talked my arm and a leg off about how Station 2 is the only one that does any business and what a show the owner was putting on for me. George said that the owner probably won't let me go out there again because he'd have to make George put all his stuff away again in that back room so I would believe it was a big office. He was laughing about what a big show-off the owner was and what a put-on he had arranged for me. "Boy, did he make us mad, all the stuff he did for you to try to make a big impression on you." I said something like, "I guess he knows now that I know what the score is." George said, "Oh, he doesn't pay any attention. He probably thinks you really believed all that stuff. What you really ought to do is just come out for a visit some night and stick around."

(The next day): I was talking to John (an aide) and was all set to ride with him and Terry (a driver). He was saying, "I hope it's not too quiet." The owner overheard this and he said, "I will tell you what I'd like you to do. Why don't you go to Station 2 with George and Pete?" (They were just about getting ready to take off for Station 2.) I played it a little bit cool and said, "Oh well, I've promised John I'd ride with him, and it's getting pretty late." The owner assumed a sort of seriocomic attitude and said, "Say, who's running this operation anyway? I said to go to Station 2, so you go to Station 2." So I said, "Okay, Station 2 it is," and got out fast lest he changed his mind.

I followed George and Pete in my VW. Pete drove and George was the aideman. When I got over to Station 2 George was very anxious to show me his house and his dog and his two parakeets and his color TV and his new stereo, and everything else. The house was just the same as when it was impersonating an office, except that now they had the TV and the stereo out in the front room. There was still just that one dim lamp in the corner by the *Life* magazines. The other one was now in the back bedroom. Also they had all the *Playboy* magazines out now. I had figured they were in hiding. The little dog was cute, and I played with him while I watched the damn TV. They watch it interminably.

As I found out much later, they had even arranged a code by means of which they could alert their dispatcher that I was leaving for the day so that he could tell the couple it was all right for them to reoccupy their dwelling:

Jeff (a driver) told me that he couldn't understand why the owner had insisted that he and Bill (an aide) go out to Station 2 to cover John and Hal (the other crew members) while I was aboard. He said that it was George and Pete's station and both of them were pretty upset about it. He said that he and Bill should have been downtown, where all the business is and where they enjoy being. I now realize that it was arranged in this way so that George's wife could be kept away from the house. Apparently that funny phone call at 6 P.M. every night was to alert George and his wife that it was okay to come home—I was leaving.

As a front crumbles, various modes of retrenchment and modification occur. The reality of the situation is not immediately (if ever) revealed, for there is an effort to see if the intruder will accept a modified version of the initial front. One mode of retrenchment is that of offering a humorous "explanation" of a crumbling front. If both parties to the interaction tacitly agree to allow for face-saving, then the whole front or portions of it can be passed off as a joke. To accept such an interpretation is often to the advantage of the observer, since he, by this means, puts the perpetrator of the front in his debt. It is also possible to use this joking approach as a vehicle for letting the intruder know that the defenders are very serious about keeping certain kinds of information from him.

During the ambulance study, for instance, one crew selected Halloween as an appropriate day to teach just this kind of lesson. That night I was treated to a number of events that were sufficiently ambiguous in nature to be construed as either threats or pranks. During a distinct "build up" over a period of several hours, I had the definite impression that my reactions were being closely monitored and "happenings" adjusted accordingly. Early in the evening, for example, my car was removed from its parking place (without the benefit of a key), and I was told it must be "lost or stolen"—that sort of thing happened to nosey people. Then shortly before midnight, during a stop for gas at the main station following a call, I was playfully "jumped" while I was leaning over the drinking fountain, blindfolded, and led along an unfamiliar route to a closetlike room. After tying my hands behind my back, they left me there for twenty minutes or so while they "went out for a beer." I hollered after them that they had better bring me back one, and they laughed at that. Shortly after 3 A.M., following another call, they asked if I wanted to see their haunted room.

I had seen the foyer of this room, with the sign saying, "Robert & David, Undertakers, Cheap Funerals $69.50 and up. If you can get a better deal, buy it." This beautiful, professionally done sign (lettered by the dispatcher, who is an artist) was placed in a lighted liquor sign holder. Right beside it was a sign saying, "We do not serve minors." They'd swiped a bank credit card emblem and a sign, "Credit Arranged," and—oh, everything in this room had probably been purloined. In fact, it must have taken considerable ingenuity to get some of these things.

Anyhow, I stood in this foyer, and they closed the outside door. It took me a little while to adjust to the semi-darkness, because filtering through the inside door—and, by the way, the carpentry work on this is amazing—was an eerie, psychedelic-type fluorescent light, purplish, reddish, greenish, and everything else, in which white glows orangish-blue. They had a hi-fi set going, emanating eerie sounds, and an inner door arranged so it creaked realistically. This was really something!

Before they took me inside, they put another blindfold on me. Then they fooled around locating the spot "on the trap door" where I had to stand. When they dramatically took off the blindfold, I saw that there, on the far side of the room, was a casket—a real casket. It looked like mahogany. Inside the casket was a "body," with a gruesome mask—one of those rubber masks— over its head, a stake "driven through its heart," and ketchup all over the place. It was Willy (one of the aides), moaning. They had a bar on the other side and mirrors set up so that they would reflect. The reason why Tony (another aide) wants a skeleton must be so that he can hang it up in there. (He keeps hinting to me that I ought to swipe him a skeleton from the medical school, and I keep telling him that I'm not a skeleton-swiper, but I kid him that maybe I can get him a cadaver.) Then they had two tombstones—real tomb- stones. They had obviously been swiped out of a graveyard. They'd swiped one of those little, stone colored boys with arms out for hitching posts, and they had a Ku Klux Klan hood on it. They had a Nazi flag. Then, too, they had swiped a number of metal ambulance slip plate designators from rival ambulance companies.

Tony told me he was going to frame the instructions for embalming people (from the Navy Corps book I gave him). He showed them to me under that eerie light. All those bodies, with their carotid arteries exposed, really looked gory. They had an undertaker's suit—the sort of half-suit that they put on bodies. Well, anyway, the upshot of the whole thing was that they'd spent a tremendous amount of time and energy rigging up this whole thing—even to the details of the hi-fi set. Certainly it wasn't done just for me—more by way of passing the long hours between calls. The pre-amp and one speaker of the hi-fi were located in the lower end of the casket, and they had the cord running up through the floor of the casket, so that if they didn't have a real live "body" in there, they could use a dummy and pretend it was talking.

After this incident, they "found" my car for me and let me know that they thought I was a pretty good sport and might be trustworthy after all.

There are, of course, other modes of modifying a crumbling front. On the other hand, an intruder can be gradually let all the way "in" until his motivations and goals become synonymous with those of other mem- bers of the institution.[9] Presumably, a researcher who would "go native" to this extent would immediately assist in rebuilding the front to safe- guard organizational secrets from outsiders—from the other side, as it were. Alternatively, a crumbling front can be salvaged by devising a substitute front even further from reality than the first one.

Problems in Front Penetration

As a defender's front crumbles, the intruder may suddenly find that he does not "like" the data that he now suspects lie under the surface, and subconsciously (or even consciously) he may begin to help the defender build (or rebuild) his facade. For example, if a researcher is committed to that view of medical ethics sanctioned by the American Medical

Association, it may be too traumatic to "see" gross infractions of those ethics, either "on location" or as revealed in a questionnaire or interview.

In most studies it is not unusual for some completed questionnaires and interviews to be thrown out simply because the responses are "too far out." That a researcher will not follow up leads or report fully his findings is a danger rarely considered in the literature. However, I believe it is important to recognize that, in spite of an attempt to be value-free, all researchers have some sort of stake in the phenomena they are researching—some more than others. My involvement with my own research (and the effect this involvement has on my findings) is an important consideration affecting the validity of my findings. For example, over an eighteen-month period, I came to know a number of ambulance crewmen and their families well. Some became close friends (and I still correspond with them); others I thought a great deal less of. Undoubtedly, my observations were affected by my positive or negative set toward the crew I was observing at any given time.

A slightly different problem arises (especially in participant-observation) when a researcher perceives that his continued or further penetration of a front will place him in a dangerous or even life-threatening position:

On one police call I was all but completely paralyzed by fear when I realized that there were real bullets flying around my head. My researcher's curiosity evaporated, and all I could think of was hiding behind the front fender of the cruiser and making myself as small a target as possible. Having gotten far enough behind their facade to become witness to a real cruiser call, I was at first too scared to follow the policemen into the house to see what was going on.

Even though it is readily understood that the researcher's eyes and ears can be partially desensitized by fear, the profession is less willing to admit that laziness and comfort-seeking behavior in general can also influence the researcher's dedication to getting behind fronts. The example that comes most readily to mind is that of the "curbstone" questionnaire or the "expanded" interview. But I believe this is a factor which must be taken into consideration in evaluating all research, even that conducted by a highly motivated investigator doing "his own thing." In my own fieldwork, I frequently became tired, bored, or disgusted and simply left the scene even though, on one level, I wanted and needed the data I could have gotten if I had stayed around a few more days (or even hours).

A more subtle variety of comfort-seeking behavior (but more serious in hindering front penetration) is the tendency to minimize contact with unpleasant people and uncomfortable situations. For example, I sometimes had to push myself very hard to ride with careless drivers, sadistic crewmen, men who threatened me, or those who simply made it clear that they would be much happier if I chose someone else to observe.

Stan (the patrolman driving the police ambulance I was riding in) really scared me by suddenly turning off the street into Fairgrounds Park, and there's nothing more deserted than a park early in the morning (around 3 A.M.). He took a turn and drove the cruiser (which doubles as an ambulance) across a lawn into a grove of trees surrounding an open grassy space. He pulled the rig up sharply and stopped it there. He looked over at me in the semi-darkness and said, "Do you know where you are now?" I guess I was shaking a little, but I said, "Yes, I'm in Fairgrounds Park." He said, "Well, that's what you think. I'll tell you where you really are. You're in our secret hideout." You wouldn't believe the thoughts that were going through my head at this point. I was even looking around for a flare to use as a weapon if necessary. It's hard to put across how this guy's whole attitude during the evening had affected me until I was ready to believe he was capable of almost anything. He said, "Well, Dot. I'm going to show you that although I know you're a spy, I'm going to trust you. I'm showing you this place because this is where we meet on the night shift when we want to sleep or just goof off a little." I began to calm down when I heard that, but I was still a little suspicious. He said, "What we do, all of us, is come here, and the caretaker either doesn't know about us or doesn't dare report us. One man stands radio guard so that he can wake up the appropriate guy, and the other fellows sleep. The reason I'm telling you this," and he said this in a sort of mocking, sarcastic tone—there was no sort of confidence in me expressed in it—"is because if you tell them"—I suppose by "them" he meant the powers that be, the "white shirts" or officers—"and they find out about this place, I'll know who told them and look out." (The implied threat was very, very clear to me.) With that he sort of gunned the engine, backed the rig up rapidly onto the road, and took off. He said no more about the incident, and all I can say is that I hope nobody finds out about their hideout before I get the hell out of town. From then on, I steered clear of Stan!

The researcher's commitment to obtaining valid data is also understandably lessened if, for example, he perceives that although he is getting at "real" data, he is gradually putting himself in line for, say, a beating or perhaps a jail sentence for participation in illegal activities.

Classification of Fronts

Fronts can be classified in various ways. First we should consider the question of who generates the front. One can learn a lot about a given front just by determining which person or group within the organization is responsible for setting it up. A front generated by a single individual can be different from the one set up by the entire organization. Consider, for example, the style and the complex elaboration of the front set up by the American Medical Association. Such a front is, at the very least, far less impromptu, requiring more cooperation from organizational members and more control of marginal members to preserve it, than a front set up by a less complex organization.

Another question to consider is who preserves the front once it is generated. As implied above, those who work hardest at preserving a given front tend to be those with the greatest stake in its preservation. Thus, one of the best ways to assault a front is through observing and talking with marginal members of the organization.[10]

Then there is the important analytical problem of determining what type of manipulation is required to set up and maintain the front. A distinction can be made between those fronts that require the physical alteration of the environment to create the desired impression and those that are erected solely from mental images that are conveyed by various means. There are other types of manipulation that lie on the continuum between these poles; for instance, an intruder can be physically isolated from a given set of events or allowed to see only a small segment of the total operation in hopes that he will accept the part as representative of the whole. Since physically changing the environment requires the greatest commitment to front production, one can assume, when the environment has been altered, that there has been sufficient time and cooperation to carry off the switch and that the organization has a lot to lose if an intruder were to discover the truth.

A front can be of a "technical" or "nontechnical" variety. All organizations have elements that are to some extent incomprehensible to an outsider. Sometimes this is simply because the in-group terminology is specialized, but occasionally the organization is recognized as being esoteric to a high degree. A researcher approaching such an organization does so with the conviction that he will not thoroughly understand or be able to interpret what is going on. As a result he tends to be a pushover for any insider who wishes to set up a technical smoke screen. One easy way to do this is to interpret the rules strictly for the intruder, even though the insider knows that the rules are not taken seriously by the organizational members and are easily gotten around. In fact, an "expert" can usually get away with making up rules that do not exist at all as long as they have an authentic ring to the intruder. It is easy to convince a nonmedical person, for example, that certain areas of the hospital are off-limits for *medical* reasons.

A far more difficult mode of analysis is trying to separate out the various fronts proffered by the parties to a given situation and to determine their interrelationships. For the sake of simplicity, I have been considering that there are only two primary fronts to deal with—that of the defender versus that of the intruder. In the real world, however, multiplicity of primary fronts (and *a fortiori* of secondary fronts) is the rule rather than the exception.

A researcher who studies one organization to the point where he feels he has penetrated most of its fronts may be in an advantageous position to study similar organizations, for he has a kind of standard against which he is able to judge data validity. That this can be a dangerously false assumption was made clear to me when I tried to "transfer" information gained about private ambulance companies to police-operated ambulances. I could not believe that I would find a whole new series of fronts to breach, and I therefore wasted a great deal of time getting "in":

I don't really think, in spite of my paranoia, that I'm being kept out of things, because most of the fellows don't even realize what I'm doing or even that I'm riding, and I haven't noticed any surreptitious codes going out over the radio. I'm sure Central Dispatching can't cooperate. I think this is just the normal way they handle things and that these few calls may really be typical.

(Later the same week): To my chagrin, Ralph (the patrolman) made me stay in the car. In fact, he rolled up the window and locked the door on me. I didn't quite know what to do. I had plenty of time to think it over, and I finally arrived at the conclusion that I was being had. This was hard for me to realize because I couldn't see how they could get to the dispatchers in the headquarters area in order to control the sorts of calls I got to go on. One way they may be handling me is by Ralph's prolonging any quiet thing he gets in order to keep me out of business (he likes to do this anyway). I'm really beginning to believe—in fact, I'm convinced—that Ralph had been thoroughly instructed to keep me out of police business and only let me go on "safe" calls.

Managing Fronts

In my studies of both ambulances and emergency rooms, I have hit upon a few general methods for getting around the various fronts I encounter. These methods illustrate a very practical facet of front management: How do you recognize a front, get behind it, and test what you find for validity?

Perhaps my most important technique is to rely on a low threshold of suspicion. If something just does not quite add up, I immediately suspect a front and try to see the situation from various perspectives. For example, I ask more questions, especially of marginal members of the organization, and check out one story against the other to see if I can verify my hunch utilizing a variation of the "divide and conquer" technique. The researcher may try to get at reality by approaching various members of the organization in different guises. To facilitate this cross-checking it is often useful to get people to trust you.[11] This sounds insidious and even unethical or somewhat immoral, but everyone employs this technique to some degree in everyday life. Thus, a researcher who suspects that there is more to the organization than meets the eye might approach a number of members of that organization of various ranks and responsibilities, in each case adopting a particular front calculated to elicit information on a particular point. He might, for example, sympathize with one group member who is feeling badly treated. With another he might adopt a critical stance. With still another he might present himself as not involved, as value-free. The point here is not the truth or falsity of his representation to the people from whom he hopes to obtain data but rather his ability to selectively present himself as possessing this or that set of attributes.

The researcher's aims would seem to be self-serving, and of course they are. But, at the risk of postulating a *reductio ad absurdum,* any presentation of self (to use Goffman's phrase) can be construed as self-serving. A more functional way of looking at this technique is to consider that a researcher, by presenting various fronts to different respondents, elicits slightly different data or slants on data from each respondent, and these varying viewpoints enable him to reconstruct reality, much as a jigsaw puzzle fan solves a puzzle. It thus permits him to obtain a composite view of the reality of the situation not available from any one respondent. In fact, this view of the organization may not be evident to any one of the respondents, for they may have a fragmented notion of the organization and, possibly, have accepted many of the fronts the organization presents to outsiders as part of reality.

Another technique is to use whatever insider's knowledge you possess. This can sometimes be parlayed to an amazing degree even with very sketchy knowledge, especially if you can convince the defenders that you know more than you do. For example, once I had spent some time in the first ambulance service to which I was reluctantly admitted, I had a fund of knowledge and "expertise" with which to approach a second company. Also, once one company had given me access, the owner of the second company found it harder to refuse me, lest it look as if he were not keeping up with the times or had something to hide.

Then, too, it is important to check a given scene at odd hours, on weekends and holidays, or at any time when you suspect that their guard may be down. Just hanging around for long periods can be useful. A researcher is often seen as a possible pipe line through which to channel information and grievances up (or down) the worker-management hierarchy. It is important to be around enough to be available for this type of service. Whether you actually *do* convey messages is another issue—much of the time people present you with their problems just to see whether you can be trusted *not* to convey them to anyone. Or they can be testing you to see which side you are on. The important point is that if you are not on the scene to some degree you will miss a lot of information that can help you understand and evaluate your data.

Finally, a researcher, to be effective, must use every means in his power to protect his own front so that he does not "blow his cover" and thereby endanger the project.

The Researcher's Front in Observing Deviance

Recently some social scientists have made a plea for granting legal immunity to those social scientists who, in the course of their research, find themselves observing (and thus being accessory to) deviant acts which are also illegal. It is argued that unless this is done many important areas of human endeavor cannot be subjected to analysis by behavioral scientists, lest the researcher be arrested and prosecuted as an accessory to (if not a participant in) the illegal act.

On the face of it, this appears to be a logical proposal, but upon closer examination, it can be seen that there is a gratuitous assumption basic to the argument—that all social science researchers are moral, upright, good, perhaps even saintly, but certainly incorruptible. Who is to guarantee that he who is made supra-criminal will not become a super criminal? A good example of the fallibility of human nature, regardless of initial motivation, is the small, but important, number of policemen who are co-opted by the "other side."

But even if a social scientist remains pure and single-mindedly dedicated to the pursuit of truth, putting him in an immune position vis-à-vis the group he is observing can have other consequences. He may find himself in the position of the cameraman who creates an incident simply because he was sent out to cover a riot and wants some "realistic" footage, or he may begin to function like the undercover narcotics agent (secure in his legal status) who promotes a drug party to "find out who the pushers are quicker." Both photographers and narcotics agents have, in some cases, been accused of manufacturing their "facts." How can we be sure that social scientists under similar pressures generated by their occupation and the exigencies of time would not also engage (no matter how subconsciously) in this kind of manipulation of reality?

There are obviously no simple solutions to the problem of how you get at data about groups (whether these be deviant or nondeviant groups, engaging in legal or illegal activities). One approach, not altogether satisfactory but highly developed by anthropologists, is to cultivate knowledgeable insiders as informants. Generally, marginal members of the organization are the most willing to act in this capacity, as they are not as dedicated to the preservation of the organization's fronts. The quality of their information is always suspect, however, if only because they are not fully "in" on important aspects of group behavior, motivation, and ideology.

Another approach is for social scientists to study groups of which they themselves are (or were) fully members. (Howard Becker's study of jazz musicians is a frequently used example, and the "sociology of sociology" is also becoming popular.) Loyalty to organizational fronts has to be considered as a possible contaminant in studies of this sort. Group membership requires group loyalty—even of sociologists. I am not implying that commitments to group fronts invalidate a study, but the possibility of some invalid data being generated as a result of such commitments cannot be overlooked. In other words, just because a social scientist is studying a group of which he is fully a member does not guarantee the validity of either his findings or his conclusions, for his commitment to some aspects of the group ideology may be so strong as to render him insensitive to data challenging a particular front.

Looking at it from the point of view of organizational defenders, a front may be protected (and even elaborated) by attempting to convert the intruder into a full member of the group. In order to bring about this conversion, it seems that the recruit must develop a *stake* in the reality such that he can be trusted to preserve those aspects of the situation the front was initially designed to protect.[12] But as the intruder is gradually admitted to defender status, his loyalty must be tested, preferably in noncritical matters first, lest he prove to be a spy. Of course, as has been implied above, it might be better for the study if the researcher only *appears* to develop such a stake, unless he can be co-opted to such an extent that he in a real sense ceases to be a researcher. Insofar as he is successful in convincing the defenders that he is worthy of becoming an insider, he develops a front himself which is designed to protect his own true purposes from those he would study. He usually begins his front production with a written or oral statement of the "purpose of the research," adds to it with "explanations" tailored to offset any adverse reactions in his subjects, and stabilizes it by oblique answers to questions they ask him about the purposes of the research and the uses to which he intends to put his data. Remember that even the generalized word "researcher" is a front designed to grant us as broad a mandate as practicable. As sociologists we try to safeguard that mandate by keeping our research aims as vague as possible when discussing them with the members of an organization we wish to study.

Notes

I am indebted to Julius A. Roth for discussing with me many of the notions advanced in this article and for his invaluable criticism of the various drafts.

1. Jack Douglas, *American Social Order* (New York: Free Press, 1971), argues that all organizations have public fronts and private realities because of the necessary moral conflicts in our pluralistic society.
2. See, for example, Erving Goffman's works, especially his *Presentation of Self in Everyday Life* (Garden City, N.Y.: Anchor Books, 1959); others of the "dramaturgical school" who discuss role-playing; George Homans' notions about exchange relationships, in *Social Behavior: Its Elementary Forms* (New York: Harcourt, Brace, 1961); and Peter Blau, especially in *Exchange and Power in Social Life* (New York: Wiley, 1964).
3. See, for example, the chapter on "Studentmanship" in Virginia Olesen and Elvi Whittaker, *The Silent Dialogue* (San Francisco: Jossey-Bass, 1968), pp. 148–199, and Arlene Daniels, "The Low-Caste Stranger in Social Research," in Gideon Sjoberg (ed.), *Ethics, Politics, and Social Research* (Boston: Schenkman, 1967), pp. 267–296. An earlier study that is also interesting in this respect is Gerald D. Berreman, "Behind Many Masks," *Human Organization* (Cornell University, 1962), pp. 17–21.
4. Goffman, *op. cit.,* pp. 22–30.
5. Dorothy J. Douglas, "Occupational and Therapeutic Contingencies of Ambulance Services in Metropolitan Areas" (unpublished Ph.D dissertation, University of California, Davis, 1969). This served as the final report for U.S.P.H.S. Grant #00044, on which Julius Roth and Dorothy Douglas were co-investigators and which had the same title. (All quotes in this article are from the field notes for this project.)
6. Thomas Kochman, "Rapping in the Black Ghetto," *Trans-Action,* 6 (February 1969), 27–34. (See also an unpublished paper by Shirley Cartwright, "Tripping as a Mode of Interaction in a Prison Setting," which contains an analogous discussion of the function of stories exchanged by prison inmates.)
7. *Ibid.,* p. 28.
8. Although, for convenience, the examples given here are developed in only one direction, this analysis applies equally to the subject, who must deal with the researcher's fronts.
9. The functional aspects of "adopting" a stranger into a group in order to gain some control over his activities first came to my attention in Margaret Wood, *The Stranger: A Study of Social Relationships* (New York: Columbia University Press, 1934).

10. However, some researchers have warned of the dangers inherent in becoming too closely affiliated with marginal or disaffected informants. See, for example, Peter Blau, "The Research Process in the Study of the Dynamics of Bureaucracy," in Phillip E. Hammond (ed.), *Sociologists at Work* (New York: Basic Books, 1964), p. 30.

11. See the discussion in Olesen and Whittaker, *op. cit.,* pp. 39–41, on "the friendship dilemma"—the dilemma the researcher is placed in when he develops close relationships with the subjects of his research.

12. Alfred Schutz suggests this in "The Stranger," in Maurice Stein, Arthur Vidich, and David Manning (eds.), *Identity and Anxiety* (New York: Free Press, 1960), pp. 98–109.

Participant-Observation of Criminals

John Irwin

It is widely believed by sociologists and criminologists that it is difficult and dangerous to study criminals in the open. Sutherland and Cressey comment that there

is no doubt of the desirability of securing information in this way [in the open], but it is clearly limited by considerations of practicability. Few individuals could acquire the technique to pass as criminals; it would be necessary to engage in crime with the others if they retained a position once secured.[1]

Moreover, it is believed that criminals are hard to locate, because they find it necessary to live clandestine lives. Once located, they are reluctant, for similar reasons, to give accurate and truthful information about themselves. On the other hand, it is believed that studying the incarcerated criminal is less than desirable because the sample is biased, the setting is not natural, the information is retrospective, and the criminal is often trying to make favorable impressions in order to secure favors or an earlier release.

In my own experience in studying criminals, both in the field and in prison, I have found that some of these notions are false, some exaggerated and others somewhat off the mark. My aim here is to clear up some mistaken beliefs and to offer some helpful suggestions for the methodology of observing criminals. To a great extent I will be commenting on, adding to, and occasionally disagreeing with Ned Polsky's generally excellent remarks on studying criminals.[2]

What Is Participant-Observation?

The most feared aspect of engaging in the study of criminals is the need for the researcher to be present when dangerous activities go on, for example, when robberies are being performed, safes being blown up, and so on. This fear is related to the false notion that in order to study a group you must observe all aspects of the lives of its members and stems from the fact that we take the label of participant-observation too literally. Participant-observation does not necessarily entail "participating" with the subjects in all their activities. In actuality, it incorporates a variety of techniques, some of which do not involve participating. For instance, McCall and Simmons state that it involves

some amount of genuinely social interaction in the field with the subjects of the study, some direct observation of relevant events, some formal and a great deal of informal interviewing, some systematic counting, some collection of documents and artifacts, and open-endedness in the directions the study takes.[3]

What we really mean by "participating" is being present to hear a lot of informal talk. Most data—histories, biographies, descriptions of events, meanings, concepts, patterns and categories—exist in and are conveyed to us through the informal talk of the subjects being studied. This is true because the structures and meanings that order a group's activities are constituted by their statements to each other—that is, by their on-going descriptions, discussions, and disputes.

Of course, there are nonverbal activities and events that are crucial to any group's activities. But even in the case of these, the collective or individual verbal renditions of the nonverbal activities, though they are distortions, are more important to the life of the group than the activities or events themselves. It is the social construction of reality that is important, and the social construction of reality takes place in the talk of the group.

Moreover, even when we directly observe some event or activity, we never see all. We always rely on descriptions of others to round out our observations. Usually the descriptions blend with the observations, so that our memory of an event is constructed from actual remembrances of the event and remembrances of the descriptions.

Doing participant-observation of criminals, like doing participant-observation of any group, is basically plugging in to the on-going world of natural communication. This means hanging around with criminals in natural settings for long periods of time, so that the researcher can immerse himself in their communicative behavior, and conducting long interviews with both informants and respondents.[4]

However, there are facets of the criminal's life that are important to the researcher and that cannot be learned in this way. To gain insight into these areas, the researcher must observe nonverbal activities. For example, there are many shared delusions in the criminal world, most of which are related to quantitative material. In general the actors themselves do not attend closely to exact amounts, number of occasions, hours per day, or numbers of persons, unless these things are particularly important to them. Most drug addicts claim to other addicts and to outsiders that they are using greater quantities of drugs than they are actually using. Likewise, thieves overestimate the amount of money they steal. One criminal that I knew for many years used to repeat in my presence how his "ex-ol' lady" used to make $800 a week hustling. Since I was spending a great many days with both him and his "ol' lady" at the time in question, I was able to observe that she did come close to that figure one week, but this was an unusual week.

This mutual support of each other's delusions among criminals is not simply dissembling. It is more a process of subtle distortion of reality by which they themselves are fooled. It is a process of selecting the most prestigious occurrences, amounts, and acts for retelling, and forgetting the less prestigious. In order to discover this distortion the researcher will have to add his own systematic observations over a period of time to bits of information he can acquire from a skeptical probing of his subjects.

Moreover, close observation of the criminals' routine will reveal processes that are operative in their lives but are ignored by them. These factors which affect or influence the criminals' lives, but of which they are not aware and which do not become part of their meaning world, have many social structural, psychological, and physical dimensions. For instance, the vast majority of criminals are probably not aware of the impact of the "labeling" process on their social-psychological development,[5] and most drug addicts ignore the fact that withdrawal symptoms are really many physical disorders of disparate causation lumped together into one single-caused malady.

Though these kinds of data cannot be explored simply by listening to and participating in the talk process of criminals, I am still convinced that the great bulk of material we seek does appear in their conversations. If we inspect Polsky's own statements on studying criminals, for instance, we find that all his examples of data secured in observing the natural round of life were items conveyed to him in verbal statements and not from observing nonverbal acts. For instance, the following three:

A long-time professional burglar has described to me his teenage apprenticeship to an older burglar.

A man in charge of a numbers operation grossing millions each year has described to me his entire career from the time he became completely self-supporting at the age of 12. . . .

A burglar tells me his line of work is best because "If you do it right, there are no witnesses." Another, indicating his superiority to pimps, told me that among his colleagues a common saying about a girl supporting a pimp is that "maybe she'll get lucky and marry a thief." And a robber, indicating his scorn of con men, proudly informed me of one of his scores that "I didn't talk him out of it—I took it off him."[6]

In the observation of criminals in their natural setting, what is important is not so much seeing every facet of their lives, as being present when "normal" discussions take place and holding many in-depth interviews. This, in part, removes one of the mythical obstacles to studying criminals—namely, we don't have to pose as criminals or be present during capers and other dangerous activities. We do, however, have to immerse ourselves in the conversational world of criminals, and this alone can be difficult.

Making Contacts

In order to engage in participant-observation of criminals you must first have contact with criminals. An initial major obstacle is meeting one criminal, or a few criminals, so that you may proceed from there and build a network of contacts. Polsky suggests hanging around places where criminals spend their off hours,[7] but this seems too slow and haphazard. It may take weeks to gain the confidence of one or two people, and these may turn out not to be good subjects. I recommend relying on *referrals*. Many people know a criminal or at least someone who can gain you an introduction to one. If a person with criminal contacts gives assurances that you are not a cop or social worker, it will save you considerable time, increase your chances of contacting someone who actually represents some significant element of the criminal population and get the relationship started on the basis of trust.

In many studies of criminals the initial contact was made in this way. John Barlow Martin, for example, was working on a crime story and needed a criminal for information. He therefore "arranged to meet Eugene . . . through a source . . . who knew him."[8] Subsequently, he wrote *My Life In Crime,* an excellent biography of a thief. William Foote Whyte, after making many futile attempts to meet people by hanging around Cornerville bars, finally penetrated the world through a social worker in a local community house who introduced him to Doc.[9] Though this wasn't a criminal world, and Doc wasn't a criminal, it did pose similar problems of entry, which were surmounted through a referral. The referral doesn't necessarily have to come from friends of the criminal, though this is the best source. In the example involving Whyte it came through a social worker, but it can even come from police. Sheldon Messinger and Egon Bittner, studying professional crime in a western city, made several good contacts through police.[10] After making the contacts, they were able to establish their identities as "neutral" sociologists and obtain good data, some of which could have been incriminating if turned over to the police. This indicates that the initial introduction by police didn't tarnish their relationships.

After the initial contact, you must keep up regular contacts in informal settings—that is, you must hang around with groups of criminals. This may prove difficult, however. The problem is not that criminals are unwilling to talk to you. In fact, after they decide that you are "good people," they usually enjoy talking to you, since this gives their lives a little more importance. The problem is that most criminals live rather chaotic lives, and they do not get together regularly for small talk. Occasionally, a cluster of a certain type of criminal will form and hang around for several hours a day in some bar, coffee shop, or pool hall, but this is usually short-lived. Either the "heat" descends upon them, they get "busted," or they pull a score and move on.

A method of solving this problem is to keep up contacts with one or two more stable criminals and then wait for groups of them to form from time to time. For instance, I kept up a regular relationship with one relatively successful pimp, set-up man, and occasional thief for ten years. During this time, three rather extensive criminal operations grew up around him and then disintegrated. But during the periods when they were operating, I was able to observe and talk to many of the criminals involved. Furthermore, through hours and days spent with my more stable friend, who was the center of these operations and who is articulate and intelligent, I gained a great deal of information.

Of course there is great variation in the stability and accessibility of criminal types. Thieves, or "professional heavies" as they have been called in criminology literature, are probably the hardest to contact and, when the contacts have been made, to find in group situations where information flows freely.[11] However, once trust has been established among a group of thieves, it has more expert value. Thieves respect and honor "rightness" more, so a reputation earned among them will be communicated to others.

Heroin users, on the other hand, are easier to keep track of because they have an anchor—their habit. They have to keep returning to some place or places on a regular basis in order to obtain drugs. Occasionally, they do move from one town or neighborhood to another or are arrested, but in between such breaks in their living habits most of them tend to follow regular patterns. However, when on dope, they are untalkative, are often irritable, and haven't much time for people who are not dope fiends or squares whom they can hustle. Because they tend not to care about impressions and have a limited need to be respected, they have little to gain from interaction with a researcher, unless he is seen as a source of money. However, when not on drugs heroin users become very affable and inclined toward group discussions. A great deal of information about them must, therefore, be gained in settings in which they are not using drugs, for example, "treatment" or rehabilitative settings such as mental hospitals, self-help centers, and jails.

Hustlers (thieves who do their stealing through "conversation," confidence games, pimping, gambling, and other "hustles") are very gregarious. They love to be seen, and they hang around for long periods in groups on street corners, in bars, and in big cars. But they are always on the hustle. In their world everyone is free game, a potential "trick," even their friends, and so is the researcher. Furthermore, they enjoy living and dressing expensively. It is not too difficult to penetrate a circle of hustlers; the problem is to maintain a viable, productive research relationship with them that does not cost the researcher too much money. Probably the best approach here is to latch onto one or two contacts with whom you can build a strong bond of trust and friendship.

One of the easiest categories of criminals to locate, establish relations with, and spend many hours with is made up of criminals whom I have elsewhere labeled "disorganized criminals."[12] This, the largest category of active criminals, includes the less skilled, less sophisticated thieves who spend most of their time while not in prison hanging around, waiting for something to come along, and engaging in unplanned, unprofitable petty crimes, often on impulse. Groups of these criminals hang around for hours and days in bars, poolrooms, coffee shops, and on the corners of most tenderloin and lower-class sections of every large city. It is not too difficult to immerse oneself in one or more of these groups, since they are not very careful about whom they accept as friends.

Defining the Universe

The foregoing are types of criminals with which I have had experience, although this does not exhaust the existing types nor are my descriptions of them complete. For example, I have ignored those involved in organized crime, since I know too little about them. This raises an important question: What is the nature of the universe of criminals? When we study a particular group of criminals, how do we know if we have a representative group of some type of criminal or that we haven't passed up a certain segment completely? One possibility haunts some researchers —that there are a significant number of really successful criminals who live a rather isolated life, who do not come into contact with law enforcement agencies, much less sociologists, and who are responsible for a lot of very serious theft. I do not believe this is possible, for there is some evidence that most criminals have wide contacts in the criminal world and that most go to jail at least occasionally. Most biographies and autobiographies of criminals and stories of large crimes present this picture.[13]

If it is true that most criminals have widespread contacts with other criminals and that most criminals go to jail occasionally, then we have a method both for defining the universe and for getting a fairly good representative sample of significant types. This is the method of snowball sampling, which entails gathering a sample by moving from contact to contact.[14] When using this method, one should concentrate on those persons who are known by many other criminals or who are at least highly recommended by a few. It is my experience that this technique tends to locate networks and, in fact, leads the researcher from group to group and from type to type because the social and cultural boundaries between criminal types are very vague.

Managing Fronts

Once we have established contact or contacts, we must do everything we can to blend with the group. This becomes a delicate matter of front management. The first problem is winning trust. Trust in the criminal world has special meanings based mainly on the concept of "rightness." Though rightness will vary slightly from one criminal type to another, there are common essential ingredients that must be understood by any sociologist who desires to circulate widely among criminals and obtain valid information about their lives. The primary dimension of "rightness" is related to passing information directly or indirectly to police or anyone else who has the power to enforce sanctions, such as administrators or employers. This, of course, means not "snitching." But it also means being generally close-mouthed in regard to potentially harmful information, since it may get to the police or others indirectly. The latter takes more practice but is very important.

Secondly, being all right, especially an all right square, means being tolerant of criminals. Though criminals make invidious distinctions among themselves—thieves don't particularly trust heroin addicts and hustlers; heroin addicts detest everybody; and hustlers think everyone else is a fool—vis-à-vis noncriminals they all feel some degree of commonality. When faced with derogatory evaluations by squares, they usually feel resentful and defensive. Conveying neutrality and a live-and-let-live, nonjudgmental attitude is therefore essential for the researcher.

To be all right, you mustn't be a phony. A phony is a person who puts up bogus fronts. Criminals are not against fronts. They are well aware of and skilled at front management. They admire persons who maintain good fronts, but they object to phony fronts. Putting up a phony front is making claims about yourself which aren't true for purposes other than humor or stealing, promising something at the moment for the sake of impression and not coming through later, or pretending to believe one thing and then by actions or words revealing that you actually believe something else.

We see from this that the researcher must strive to be honest among criminals. They will be searching for cracks in his front, and if they discover any, this will damage the relationship and the research. Of course, the researcher must present himself as a researcher. There is no other way because, first, you cannot take the chance of trying to pass and, second, trying to pass limits you (you are prevented from eventually being able to ask questions, poke around in areas, seek more contacts in a manner that would not be tolerated of anyone but a researcher). Furthermore, you have considerable trust already as an advantage for you as a sociologist. Criminals will probably trust a strange sociologist before they will a strange criminal.

Finally, being all right means that you can be counted on by friends when needed. In some groups this means complete sharing of resources and a willingness to take great risks of arrest and danger to help a friend. It at least means some willingness to go out of one's way when some help is needed. This aspect of rightness will probably cause the researcher many difficulties. He will find, as he gets to know criminals and gains their trust, that he will actually make friends among them; in fact, if he does not, he is not going to get very far in his study. As soon as this happens, he is going to find himself being asked to do things for which he might feel he doesn't have the time, resources, or moral inclination. This can be one of the most serious problems in his research, and it is one that I will explore more fully later in this article.

If the researcher earns the respect and trust of some group of criminals and is defined by them as all right, he will usually find that this reputation is exportable. A reputation for being "right," like a reputation for being a "jacket" (a bad person, usually an informer), will travel on its own or can be carried by the researcher's friends to other criminals.

DRESS

Managing fronts for the purpose of blending with groups of criminals usually necessitates adjustments in style of dress. Too little has been said in sociology about the role of dress in establishing identity. In the criminal world dress is an important aspect of identity, and in order for a person to be unobtrusive in the criminal world he must dress unobtrusively. First of all, you should try not to look too square; then, you should dress as much like a member of the criminal world as possible. At no time, however, do you want to stand out, even in the style of the particular group of criminals with which you are identifying. One way to accomplish all this as quickly as possible is to wear the particular kinds of cotton or synthetic cloth pants—levis, white levis, khakies, stay press, bell bottoms, and so on—worn by the group that you are observing. Preferred styles vary from group to group. The same is true of cotton or synthetic shirts, sweaters, and jackets. The key is to dress neatly, inexpensively, in the day-to-day style of the particular group, or at least some other style that is unobtrusive. Be sensitive to the fact that all day-to-day clothes are not alike. There definitely are preferred styles that can be learned and imitated.

My experience has been on the West Coast, where dress habits are generally more casual than in the East and Midwest. But even in California, some groups, for instance "high-rolling pimps and hustlers," value expensive clothes. In this case, the researcher should try to dress more expensively and fashionably. However, be careful not to try to emulate their style, which may be too flashy for you, but to dress in a manner that is nevertheless acceptable to them.

LANGUAGE

The use of language is another important facilitator in front management. As stressed earlier, a situation is built mainly out of talk. The *way* something is said as well as *what* is said will define the situation and shape the perspectives of the actors in it. The researcher must learn to blend into the normal conversational world of the group that he is observing. However, he must proceed slowly and quietly, at first acting as a good listener and only speaking enough to keep the conversation moving.

The researcher must aim, however, at some mastery over the criminal group's special language, since this is essential to fully understand their world. As he moves into an active use of their language, though, he must proceed with extreme caution and slowly feel out strange expressions and terms. If these are misused too many times or too often, the researcher will turn off his subjects because he is embarrassingly square or an "asshole." On the other hand, if he comes on too strong, too hip, too often, he will also turn them off. They are not there to listen to him, he is there to listen to them. The researcher must feel his way cautiously, not coming on too fast, but moving steadily toward a good understanding and active mastery of the language.

Immersion in Criminal Meaning Worlds

In making contact and then blending in with the criminal's world, what we are actually attempting to do is to become immersed in the meaning world, or shared perspective, of a particular group or category of criminals. This has to be done before any significant and valid data can be obtained, although the problem often has been passed over for another—that of being misled or put on by criminals. However, one will never be able to know whether he is being "shucked" until he has a good grasp of the language, the categories, and the meanings of the particular world he is examining. If the context in which people obtain information is not normal, they may feel that they are being lied to when, in fact, they are getting valid information, but from a shifted perspective. Until they are immersed in the meaning world and blend into the setting, they will obtrude upon situations and change them. As long as it is perceived that they are on a different "trip," that they represent a different perspective, their presence unavoidably alters the context. Instead of it being a group of people interacting within a particular shared meaning world—a criminal one—it will be a group of criminals interacting with some outsider. Even if the criminals try to be natural, they cannot. I saw this subtle but important shift occur repeatedly when I was joined by another sociologist in observing a group of criminals. His speech, dress, and perspective were obtrusive, and though he was liked by the group, they became visibly unnatural around him.

Sometimes it will appear to a researcher that his subjects are always assuming attitudes or putting on fronts. But this may not be true. In the presence of a sociologist, the context and, therefore, the perspectives of the subjects may be changed, and they may actually be talking and thinking differently than they usually do. An example of this is mentioned by Jack D. Douglas in his article "Observing Deviance"; he notes that Elliot Liebow, in his study of *Tally's Corner*, recorded too much talk about the black's relationship to the establishment and the white world.[15] It does not seem natural that the ghetto black could spend his whole day "telling it like it is to the middle-class white world." What possibly happened is that Liebow never stopped being an outsider, and as a result most situations were ones in which he was a representative of the conventional world to whom to "tell it like it is."

EXPERTS

Once contact and some degree of immersion have been achieved, taking advantage of experts may be one of the most useful research techniques. Most studies of criminals have been done through experts, in lieu of true immersion.[16]

The expert is a person who has an exceptional understanding of the implicit and the explicit, the esoteric, and the ordinary dimensions of his particular social world and an ability to articulate these. This usually earns him some special position. In primitive societies he is often the wise man or shaman. In criminal groups he is sometimes a group leader or a set-up man for various criminal operations, and at the very least he is a well-respected, skilled criminal whose services and cooperation are sought by other men. Because of his special position he is usually not hard to locate. His wisdom and sagacity are almost always recognized by other criminals, and once a network of contacts has been established, many persons should be able to refer the researcher to one or more experts. Furthermore, once located, experts are usually willing to reveal their expertise and will talk at length to the researcher. The researcher should exploit fully these valuable sources of information and interpretations in addition to immersing himself as fully as possible in the criminals' world.

GROUP DISCUSSIONS

As soon as the researcher has acquired some mastery over the meanings, categories, and language of a particular criminal world, he should move from his passive role to an active one by participating in the constant process whereby each member tries to bring his individual version of the shared perspective, the meaning world, the "generalized other," or whatever you wish to call it, into alignment with those of other members. This process, which is never completed and which is instrumental in maintaining the group's shared perspective, sometimes occurs in the form of arguing over interpretations or evaluations of some event, object, or person; at other times it takes the form of a direct discussion of a particular cultural component.

It is possible for the researcher to engage in this process because meaning worlds never exist as final, static entities among members of any social group. It is also necessary for him to do so in order to explore the subtle contours of a particular social world. Participation in this process allows him to probe the obscure areas, the areas of minimal or no consensus, as well as those of total agreement.

Of course, as the researcher starts taking this more active role in the group life, he must be particularly careful that he does not offend people. He must never appear belligerent or overbearing, for this will damage his relationships with most people and stop the flow of information. He must attempt to probe and pursue elusive material, and to provoke discussions and arguments over aspects of the criminal life, with extreme tact and agility.

Such probing can best occur when several knowledgeable persons have been brought together expressly for this purpose, but such a meeting is hard to arrange. As mentioned earlier, most criminals live fast-moving and chaotic lives, and a group of them are seldom available for regular talk sessions, especially at the convenience of the researcher. However, even in the case of criminals who live irregular lives, there will be occasions when the researcher will find himself riding in a car or sitting in a coffee shop or bar with some of them. These are good times to precipitate and actively keep alive discussions of the criminal world for the purposes of drawing out some of the more elusive dimensions. Moreover, it will occasionally be possible to bring a group of knowledgeable criminals together at the convenience of the researcher explicitly for the purpose of discussing their criminal lives. I have engaged in several such discussions, two in university settings. Herbert Blumer used this technique very frequently during the 1930s at the University of Chicago,[17] and at one time he and a group of graduate students met regularly with a select group of Chicago's heroin addicts. David Maurer reports that in gathering information for his book *The Big Con,* he pulled together several professional thieves for lengthy discussions of their lives.[18]

Bringing a group together expressly for the discussion of their world is perhaps one of the best techniques for both obtaining data related to very subtle material and testing the generalizations which the researcher has generated. The members of the group, in this situation where their expertise is being tested by each other in front of one or more observers, are often capable of probing deep into their lives, drawing the implicit into the realm of the explicit, exposing some of the shared delusions and revealing the areas of irreconcilable disagreement.

Dangers

PROSECUTION

There has been some concern expressed over the danger of arrest while studying criminals, mainly because the researcher will have firsthand knowledge of felonies and misdemeanors. Although this danger exists theoretically, it is my impression that in actuality it doesn't have much substance. I can think of no researcher of criminals who actually was in great danger of being arrested. To my knowledge the closest anybody ever came to having legal sanctions imposed on him because of his research was Lewis Yablonsky, who, while testifying in defense of Gridley White, one of Yablonsky's main informants in his hippy study, had the judge ask him nine times if he had witnessed Gridley smoking marijuana.[19] Yablonsky refused to answer because of the rights guaranteed him in the Fifth Amendment of the United States Constitution. Although he did not actually receive any legal sanctioning, he stated that the incident was humiliating and suggested that researchers should have guarantees of immunity. Despite this case, I feel that there is small risk of being prosecuted. If we keep our "heads straight" and avoid being sucked in or bowled over by the criminal world, and thereby do not slip or plunge into greater complicity than knowledge of crimes, we actually do have immunity.

ENTREATIES

As mentioned earlier, it is my belief that one of the grossly ignored problems of research on criminals is that of the entreaties for help which will surely come if the researcher is around criminals for any length of time. One reason that this problem has been ignored is because of a romanticized notion of criminals. The myth is that criminals, at least successful criminals, "make it" consistently—that is, they succeed in living a good life bothered only by arrest which comes seldom if ever. In my experience, this is simply not true; most of them stumble from one problem to another. In addition to the ordinary problems of living, like decaying teeth, bad health, and financial difficulties, they are involved in many legal "cases." I have never known any criminals of whom this was not true to some extent.

Consequently, the researcher will repeatedly be implored to give help. If he has made many friends in the criminal world, this will be especially hard to refuse, since mutual aid in the criminal world has a strong value. It will be impossible to do good research, to become closely involved in the lives of some criminal group or groups, and not to generate true feelings of friendship. Such friendship is not inconsistent with good research. As David Matza has recently pointed out, the spirit of naturalism in the study of human *subjects* is underpinned by *appreciation*.[20] One cannot study human beings without drawing close to them and embracing their viewpoint. And as one draws close, learns to appreciate his subjects, he will also develop sincere feelings of friendship and, thereby, in the case of criminal groups, an appreciation for their norms of mutual aid.

A wide variety of requests of assistance will follow. I have been asked to participate in capers, to help set up—"steer"—capers, to secure information from files to which I had access, to give advice on the feasibility of criminal operations, and to pose as a parole agent to secure the release of a jailed parolee. These were easy requests to refuse, because they all involved taking risks of arrest, and criminals understand not taking these kinds of chances. They themselves go through periods of refusing to risk arrest. But denying other kinds of help is not understandable, for example, small loans. One group of armed robbers borrowed and paid back twenty dollars four or five times in the course of two months. One thief with whom I have associated for many years has requested loans for bail money, transportation from Oklahoma where he was stranded, and general living expenses. The problem of loaning money will come up often, and I know of no solution to it. Besides requests for money, I have been asked to appear in court as a character witness, to loan my automobile for various reasons, mostly legitimate, and to put someone up in my house for short periods. Most of these requests seem petty, but they are important at the time to the persons making them. If the researcher does not intend to grant them, he should have good reasons that are understandable to the person.

There is another class of entreaties that are much harder either to refuse or to grant. These stem from the fact that many criminals want to change their lives. Although I completely agree with Ned Polsky when he argues that we must strip ourselves of our social worker orientation when doing research on criminals,[21] this does not solve one important problem. We will occasionally be beseeched with unsolicited requests to help criminals "straighten up their hands." Some will perceive the researcher as a person who has connections in the conventional world and can help them get a good job, into school, or assistance from some agencies in restructuring their lives in some way. These are hard requests to fulfill because the criminal is likely to overestimate the researcher's influence and is likely to have very vague ideas of the alternatives he is seeking. On the other hand, they are also hard to deny because the criminals have been helping you complete research that will earn you credentials, points in academia, or cash. Furthermore, while you were seeing how they live, they saw something of how you live and perhaps liked it. Now they might want an opportunity to change their lives. Though this can cut deeply into your time and resources, you will feel yourself strongly moved to help in this direction.

Grounded Theory and the Participant-Observation of Criminals

Once some degree of immersion has been achieved and some of the other difficulties have been solved or avoided, we are still faced with the most important research problem—that of deciding exactly what it is we are looking for.

Glaser and Strauss, in *The Discovery of Grounded Theory*,[22] suggest that to generate better theories we should pull close to the subject we are studying and let the concepts, categories, and theories emerge directly from the phenomena, from the data. Basically, they are arguing against approaching any area with the intention of verifying an existing theory, a procedure that they contend leads to distortion of the phenomena. With this basic idea of their book, I find myself in complete agreement. However, in developing their ideas further, they slip over a very important problem that must be addressed. They seem to be suggesting that the concepts, categories, and theories we seek are intrinsic to the phenomena we study and will be immediately evident to us if we look closely.[23] I could also agree with this if they had made one point explicit—that we bring to the phenomenon a perspective that enables us to experience it as "data." Besides carrying a commonsense perspective that allows us to make basic sense out of the meaning world of actors, we are also incurably burdened with some form of social scientific perspective, at least a set of pet concepts which aid us in making more abstract and general sense out of the world. Since it is useless to deny this, we should make these aspects of our overall perspective as explicit as possible and struggle to keep them flexible.

As symbolic interactionists or phenomenologists we are interested in the categories, dimensions, and characteristics of the meaning worlds of our subjects. Our data are primarily the dimensions of these meaning worlds, which we can enter because we too are human beings.[24] The concepts, the abstract theories, we generate from the observation of these phenomena will be directly derived from the actors' categories. From this standpoint, Glaser and Strauss's idea that the categories and concepts, and therefore the theories, will emerge from the data is true. But it is only true if we accept the view that the categories we seek are commonsense categories or higher order abstractions built upon these commonsense categories.[25]

In the participant-observation of criminals, therefore, the first level of material we seek is a clear, precise description of their meaning world. Often this is simply a description of the major folk concepts, such as "sucker," "hoosier," "snitch," "trick," "the heat," or "the man," which are clearly understood by practically all members of a particular criminal social world. However, there are many other commonsense concepts that are not as clearly or unanimously understood. These are more ephemeral, less consensual categories that are referred to in a variety of ways but definitely operate as shared meaning categories in the collective action of the particular group. For instance, in observing heroin users I have discovered at least four distinct meaning categories that orient the drug addict to drugs and the drug life. Only two of these are clearly and explicitly identified by most addicts themselves: (1) drugs as the cure of withdrawal symptoms, and (2) drugs as a means to "get high"—that is, to experience intense, peak, or euphoric feelings. The two less explicit meaning categories are: (3) drugs as a vehicle that removes them from "care," and (4) drugs as an engrossing life style. The meanings of these latter two categories are represented by a variety of statements about drugs that addicts make to others and presumably to themselves when they are planning courses of action. For instance, in regard to not caring while under the influence of drugs, they talk of "not giving a fuck" when a variety of normally embarrassing, stressful, or frightening events are occurring, and in regard to drugs as an engrossing life style, they talk of how dull life is or how they haven't anything to do to fill their time when they aren't "hooked" and don't have to "rip and tear."

But beyond exploring the meaning world of a particular criminal world and describing the existing folk categories in a more systematic, complete, and explicit fashion, we must strive to achieve more penetrating and more general descriptions, explanations, and understandings. Therefore, after embracing the particular target group closely and mastering its meaning world, we must step back and consider a broader perspective. I do not mean by this that we depart from the meaning world of our actors, but simply that, while paying attention to their meaning world, we also search for those factors that impinge on their situations and definitions but that are not known or clearly understood by them. I can think of two classes of such factors. The first is a set of categories, dimensions, characteristics which are knowable, but are usually not known or understood because of the complexity of the systems or processes in which the criminals are involved. For instance, a particular group of actors are almost invariably involved with or have their situations influenced by other groups who have different meaning worlds. Criminals are involved in regular patterns of interaction with squares, police, and people in courts, prisons, and parole agencies. Their understanding of the patterns of action of these other parties is partial, at best. In studying the careers of felons, I discovered that a fragile system of interaction exists between the parolee and the parole agent because neither party understands the perspective of the other.[26] They achieve a tentative accommodation, which is often upset by "normal" acts on the part of either party. To understand this kind of system of interaction, we must explore the meaning worlds of all parties involved and the patterns of interaction that emerge because the system is complex and there are disparate meaning worlds operating.

In this same class of factors are those influences that originate from the action of actors who are outside the immediate arena. For instance, the acts of public interest groups, legislators, and newspapermen affect the life situations of criminals, and to fully understand their lives, we must therefore take into consideration any group's action that is relative to the criminal. Furthermore, we will not be able to understand these influences by exploring the meaning world of only the particular criminal group we are studying; to get the *full* picture we must, of course, step further back and look at the influences on those groups of actors whose actions affect the criminal. This can go on and on until we have encompassed the whole world, so we must arbitrarily draw the line somewhere.

The second set of factors that impinge upon the life situations of the actors without the actors understanding them includes the physiological, psychological, genetic, social structural, and interactional constants that operate independently of time and/or place and that influence, shape, and set limits to the variability of the actors' thoughts, life situations, and actions. Many, perhaps most, social scientists believe that it is these factors which must be identified and described in order to produce a truly scientific theory of human behavior. It is my own feeling that, though these factors do definitely exist, most of the behavior that is interesting to us and that we are trying to understand occurs within the limits established by, or varies independently of, these factors.

Future Strategies

Before turning to an overall appraisal of the future of studies of criminals, I would like to emphasize three points made in the foregoing discussion or derived from the comments of others on the state of criminological research. The first point is that participant-observation of career criminals is not that distinct from participant-observation of most groups. The difficulties and ways of overcoming these difficulties are just about the same for all groups. To obtain good data we must always try to immerse ourselves in the meaning world of the group that we are studying. There are special problems of immersion in criminal groups, but there are special problems of immersion in any group. Trust must be won by proving yourself trustworthy according to the particular group's definitions of trustworthiness. Finally, researchers face no great dangers in studying criminals because of the dangerous activities in which criminals are engaged, since one need not become involved in these activities. The greatest threats to the researcher of criminals are not the threats of arrest or physical danger, but the threats to his self, time, and resources which come from the entreaties of persons who seek concrete help from him.

The second point is that many of us who study criminals and other deviants do so because we romantically identify with the underdog. This is the gist of the vilifying condemnation of "Becker" sociologists made by Alvin Gouldner:

...theirs is a school of thought that finds itself at home in the world of hip, drug addicts, jazz musicians, cab drivers, prostitutes, night people, drifters, grifters, and skidders: the "cool world." Their identifications are with deviant rather than respectable society.[27]

Furthermore, Gouldner argues that, in identifying with the underdog, Becker sociologists have been in complicity with the "overdogs" of the welfare state—the "Washington bureaucracies and New York foundations."[28] The result of this complicity is that the sociologists present the overdogs with a view of the deviant "making out," not a view of him suffering or striking back. This in turn does not help alleviate the suffering of the deviant.

The final point is that most criminals are not able to operate outside the law—that is, they cannot plan and execute capers and, at the same time, avoid being swept up by the controlling agencies. As argued earlier, the vast majority of professional and career criminals have considerable contact with police and correctional agencies. All criminals I have talked to confirm this. Some have stated to me that they have known one or two persons who have continued to engage in criminal activities for long periods of time without arrest, but this was mainly because of good fortune, not because of belonging to different criminal worlds. I have to conclude that most criminals, consequently, have their lives drastically influenced by these controlling agencies.

These points considered together seem to suggest a program for the future studies of criminals. First they suggest that the best direction is not the study of criminals exclusively in their clandestine haunts or their subterranean "underworlds," but the study of criminals in the round of their daily lives, which involves contact with various official correctional agencies. This is not a recommendation to study only incarcerated criminals, nor is it an invitation to continue to search for a class of really important criminals who live out a secret life of crime never being touched by controlling agencies. What we are after is the study of criminals in the field while they are engaged in criminal and noncriminal activities and have extensive involvements with official agencies, such as police departments, probation and parole agencies, and prisons.

Likewise, in studying career criminals in the round of their daily lives, we should not only explore the world of the underdog, but we simultaneously must fill in the view of the overdogs and the relationships between the two. More than likely this means taking the viewpoint of those middle-level superiors that Gouldner labels the "caretakers." However, as he has pointed out, this can open the door to the higher reaches of power, where real changes can be made:

It would seem that there is one way out of this impasse for Becker. He could say that it is not a matter of superiors and subordinates as such, but rather, of the *institutions* governing their relationship. He might maintain that the need is not to study social situations from the standpoint of subordinates as an end in itself, but of conducting studies with a view to understanding how some are crushed by certain institutions, and how all alike are subjected to institutions that do not permit them to live as they wish. As I say, this position would be one way for Becker. But he neither sees it nor takes it. For this undercuts his "infinite regress" gambit and leads research inevitably to the doorstep of power; it would force the research focus upward, fastening it on the national levels.[29]

Taking both underdog and overdog standpoints has broad implications beyond its import for humanistic social change, which is Gouldner's main concern. It is also important in a purely scientific sense. Gouldner argues that the conflict in Becker's sociological stance is that, on the one hand, he recommends that we take the view of the underdog, but, on the other, his main theoretical contribution stems from his focus on the overdog and the process of "labeling." If we want to explore the criminal viewpoint of the criminal, we must explore it in its full institutional context, and this includes correctional institutions and the viewpoint of the overdog. And, of course, Becker studies the underdog in this way.

In conclusion, I return to the first point: we should study the criminal groups in the same way that we would study any other groups. I would like to emphasize that researchers who study criminals need not be special types, have special connections, or have special access, any more than researchers who study many noncriminal groups; and such prerequisites are certainly less for criminal researchers than for students of the upper echelons of the business world or the class structure. Let us not be too cool or too hip about the task of studying criminals, which has been the posture of many researchers in criminal behavior.

Notes

1. Edwin Sutherland and Donald Cressey, *Principles of Criminology*, 6th ed. (Philadelphia: Lippincott, 1960), p. 69.
2. Ned Polsky, "Research Method, Morality, and Criminology," *Hustlers, Beats and Others* (Chicago: Aldine, 1967).
3. George McCall and Jerry Simmons, *Issues in Participant Observation* (Reading, Mass.: Addison-Wesley, 1969), p. 1.
4. Some persons have suggested that there is a basic methodological differ-

ence between the informant and the respondent. The informant is the one who is able to step out of his normal position and share the researcher's perspective. The respondent is a representative of his group, society, and so on. See, for instance, Donald T. Campbell, "The Informant in Quantitative Research," *American Journal of Sociology,* 60 (1955), 339–342.

5. Briefly stated, the labeling process refers to the impact on the individual of society or social agents categorizing and responding toward him as a deviant. See, for instance, Frank Tannenbaum, *Crime and Community* (New York: McGraw-Hill, 1951); E. M. Lemert, *Social Pathology* (New York: McGraw-Hill, 1951); Howard S. Becker, *Outsiders: Studies in the Sociology of Deviance* (New York: Free Press, 1963).

6. Polsky, *op. cit.*

7. *Ibid.,* pp. 130–131.

8. John Barlow Martin, *My Life in Crime* (New York: Signet Books, 1952), p. 5.

9. William Foote Whyte, *Street Corner Society* (Chicago: University of Chicago Press, 1943), p. 290.

10. Sheldon Messinger, "Some Reflections on 'Professional Crime' in West City" (unpublished manuscript on file at the Law and Society Center, University of California, Berkeley).

11. See Don Gibbons, *Society, Crime, and Criminal Careers* (Englewood Cliffs, N.J.: Prentice-Hall, 1969), pp. 255–257, for a description of the professional heavy. John Irwin, *The Felon* (Englewood Cliffs, N.J.: Prentice-Hall, 1970), Chap. I, describes this and other criminal types.

12. Irwin, *op. cit.,* pp. 23–25.

13. For example, see Jack Black, *You Can't Win* (New York: Macmillan, 1927); Edwin H. Sutherland, *The Professional Thief* (Chicago: University of Chicago Press, 1937); David Maurer, *The Big Con* (Indianapolis: Bobbs-Merrill, 1940) and *Whiz Mob* (New Haven, Conn.: College and University Press, 1964); Quentin Reynolds, *I, Willie Sutton* (New York: Farrar, Straus & Giroux, 1953); Martin, *op. cit.*; Donald MacKenzie, *Occupation: Thief* (Indianapolis: Bobbs-Merrill, 1955); Henry Williamson, *The Hustler* (New York: Avon Books, 1964); and Malcolm X, *The Autobiography of Malcolm X* (New York: Macmillan, 1965).

14. Ned Polsky, *op. cit.,* recommends this sampling method. Howard S. Becker, "Practitioners of Vice and Crime," in Robert Habenstein (ed.), *Pathways to Data* (Chicago: Aldine, 1970), describes this sampling technique and its usefulness in observing deviants.

15. Elliot Liebow, *Tally's Corner* (Boston: Little, Brown, 1967).

16. Three of the best studies of criminals have been done through the use of experts. These are Sutherland, *op. cit.,* and Maurer, *The Big Con* and *Whiz Mob.*

17. Herbert Blumer has recommended this technique to his students for years. Many of the early drug studies in Chicago that were undertaken under his guidance made use of groups of experts discussing their work.

18. David Maurer in his study of confidence men used this technique. See Maurer, *The Big Con.*

19. See Lewis Yablonsky, *The Hippie Trip* (New York: Pegasus, 1968), pp. 44–45.

20. David Matza, *Becoming Deviant* (Englewood Cliffs, N.J.: Prentice-Hall, 1969), pp. 15–17.

21. Polsky, *op. cit.,* pp. 134–135.

22. Bernard Glaser and Anselm Strauss, *The Discovery of Grounded Theory* (Chicago: Aldine, 1968).

23. *Ibid.*, p. 36.

24. For an excellent discussion of *verstehen* and its importance to the social sciences see Thelma Z. Lavine, "Note to Naturalists on the Human Spirit," *Journal of Philosophy*, 1 (February 1953), 145–154.

25. Alfred Schutz, in several articles, has brilliantly pointed out the relationship between "everyday" "commonsense" concepts and scientific concepts. See, for example, "Common-Sense and Scientific Interpretation of Human Action," *Philosophy and Phenomenological Research*, 24 (September 1953), reprinted in Maurice Natanson (ed.), *The Philosophy of the Social Sciences* (New York: Random House, 1963).

26. Irwin, *op. cit.*, Chap. 7.

27. Alvin W. Gouldner, "The Sociologist as Partisan: Sociology and the Welfare State," *The American Sociologist*, 3 (May 1968), 104.

28. *Ibid.*, 107.

29. *Ibid.*, 111.

Observing the Gay Community

Carol A. B. Warren

For many years, sociologists, psychiatrists, social workers, and religious leaders have attempted to grapple with the "problem of homosexuality." Since they perceived homosexuality as a problem, they were primarily concerned to find out the genesis of the problem and ways in which it might be eliminated. This correctional approach has, historically, taken many forms, from the hellfire rhetoric of the salvationist preacher to the sociologist's rhetoric of etiology. Where the preacher attributed the cause of homosexuality to mortal sin and the cure to God, the sociologist analyzed it in terms of a typology of family relationships and left the cure to practical men.

Until quite recently most sociology of homosexuality and of deviance in general has been of the correctional and absolutist sort, repudiating contact with the phenomena and substituting for this contact a set of scientific categories with which the data must conform:

Thus the early social scientists adopted a conscious policy of studying man in the same way one would study any physical object. Having presupposed these methods, they then adopted the stance which was most in accord with the method. They adopted the *absolutist perspective* on man and society. That is, they viewed *man as object* "causally" determined (totally) by "forces" outside of his self. In accord with this perspective they adopted an *absolutist (or objectivist) stance* toward everyday life, or what they normally called common sense or subjectivity; they assumed that the phenomena of everyday life could and should be studied only in terms of clear and distinct (scientific) formal categories defined by them in advance of their studies; they assumed that these categories should be both independent of and in opposition to the common sense categories of men in everyday life; they assumed that all decisions about how one would decide that his results were true or false could and should be made in advance of studies of the everyday phenomena; and they assumed that the goal would be one of controlling the everyday phenomena in the way scientists seek to control the natural world.[1]

With such theory and methods, absolutist sociologists did not, and still do not, get their hands dirty among deviants in their everyday lives. They maintain distance from their data, so that neither their categories nor their sensibilities will be violated by the unclassifiable or the unmentionable. Even when the researcher invades the subjects' world, he goes protected from unwelcome realities by various devices such as interview schedules and precoded questions. And even where realities successfully break through these protective barriers, they tend to be nihilated, denuded of their meaning, by the assignment to them of "latent" meanings known not to the subjects but only to the all-wise sociologist.

In recent years, however, a new kind of sociology of deviance has been developing—and a new kind of sociologist, also, who is not unwilling to get his hands dirty. This new approach is appreciative rather than correctional—concerned with analyzing phenomena such as homosexuality *as* phenomena, rather than simply as a species of the genus social problem. And to appreciate the phenomena, sociologists have begun to do field research in the natural settings of deviance and to observe the everyday lives of their subjects on their own terms, rather than in terms of some predefined categories of etiology or check-list of latent meanings.

However, the true sociological approach is not *purely* appreciative. It involves appreciation, but its *purpose* is the generation of theory grounded in empirical data. Thus, its language is conceptual as well as commonsensical, sociological as well as subject-meaningful. It is different both from absolutist sociology and from the naturalistic perspective of everyday experience—it is *theoretic sociology*: "To take the theoretic stance toward the everyday world is to stand back from, reflect upon, review the experience taken for granted in the natural stance. To take the theoretic stance is to treat the everyday world as a phenomenon."[2]

The method of theoretic sociology is participant-observation; its purpose is the generation of theory grounded in data obtained using participant-observation research. However, the sociologist who wishes to do fieldwork usually has been trained against a background of "recipes" for traditional methods that stress the verification of master theories rather than the development of new theory. Consequently, those few participant-observer studies that have been done have been limited in usefulness, primarily because little attention has been paid to the problem of doing research in different kinds of natural settings and even less attention has been given to the question of generating theory.

This article represents a formulation of some of the methodological problems and theoretical implications of doing sociological field research in the gay community. It also points out some alternative ways in which the most vital and fundamental problems can be handled. It is important to remember, however, that these comments are only guidelines—research in the gay community will still require considerable preliminary hard work to gain commonsense understanding of its language, its locales, and its customs. Methodological "recipes" are only of limited value in the real world.

Problems with Nonparticipant-Observer Research

Studies done so far in the general area of homosexuality may be subsumed within the following categories:

1. Incidence studies of homosexual behavior
2. Etiological studies of homosexuality
3. Studies of homosexuals' personal/sociological characteristics
4. Studies of the organization of homosexual roles in prison

The best-known incidence study of homosexual behavior is that performed by Kinsey, *et al.*, in the 1940s. Many detailed criticisms of this study have been made elsewhere, but from the sociological perspective, there are two major problems. The first is the problem of representability, since Kinsey's sample is a nonprobability sample of volunteers. Many critics have argued that this factor alone would suffice to indicate that his sample is representative not of the general population but of a much more specialized population of those individuals willing to talk about a socially tabooed topic. The second is the problem of accuracy—did the subjects accurately remember their past sexual behavior? If they did remember, did they reinterpret past events in the contemporary situation in order to reinforce their current presentation of self?

Etiological studies of homosexuality are similarly problematic. Such studies conceive of homosexuality as a disease or condition, with a cause, a course, and (possibly) a cure. One such etiological-psychiatric work is Bergler's study of one thousand homosexuals. He states: ". . . homosexuality *is* a disease, and *is* curable."[3] According to Bergler, the cause of this disease is located in childhood, in early relationships with the mother:

[The unconscious masochism of the homosexual] depends on events which occurred behind the scenes, within his unconscious mind, during his nursery past. These events, and the way he originally reacted to them, have shaped the approaches, attitudes and conclusions attached to every minor and major crisis in his life.[4]

As in the case of simple incidence studies, the past data upon which the etiological interpretation rests is contaminated by factors located in the present. Again, the individual under psychiatric care may have memory gaps; he is certainly reinterpreting his biography through the medium of his present situation. And one element in the subject's presentation of self may be self-explanatory systems derived through feedback from the mass media. For example, most people in our society are aware of the Freudian etiological explanations for sexual behavior (for instance, the Oedipus complex), and it is not unlikely that they will incorporate these explanations into their thinking and feed them back to the analyst.

In addition, etiological theories tend to be arbitrary. The analyst is, usually, already committed to a particular theoretical stance when he begins his study, so that the data are fitted into a preexisting framework, and little or no attention is paid to their unique features. Thus, data are given imputed meanings, based more on the analyst's beliefs than on empirical referents; often, different imputed meanings—sometimes opposed meanings—are given to the same phenomena, since analysts tend to have different and even opposed beliefs about reality.

Studies of the personal and sociological characteristics of homosexuals are problematic only if the researcher attempts to utilize methodologies based on the theory of probability sampling or to generalize his findings to a larger population. In a recent study done in England, Michael Schofield makes both types of errors. Schofield's methodology is that of the interview survey; he acknowledges that he does no field research. He uses a nonprobability sample of 300 males and lists some of their sociological characteristics—which is legitimate. However, he then proceeds to use p-levels (the probability that his quantitative findings were obtained by chance) to assess the "significance" of his results, erroneously implying both a random sampling base and statistical generalizability to a larger population. The major and most fundamental distortion in Schofield's work is, however, his generalizations from data obtained by the interview method to the real world of homosexual subcultural interaction.[5] This is not to say that no valid information is obtained in the interview situation—it is simply to say that *the interview setting becomes the natural setting when the purpose is to study homosexuals in the interview setting; when the purpose is to study the gay community, the interview setting is unnatural.*

Studies of the organization of homosexual roles in prison are essentially studies of the development of sexual institutions within a unisex total institution. As Gresham Sykes points out, the organization of homosexual experience in prison is a function of the prison environment; sexual behavior revolves around the fact of heterosexual deprivation and is tied in with the prevailing system of distributing scarce goods and services. As a result, the prison argot expresses specifically *prisonized* homosexual roles: the "fag" is a "natural" homosexual; the "punk" engages in sexual behavior for payment; and the "wolf" buys gratification.[6] Such studies tell us little about the gay community in the real world.

Participant-Observer Research in the Gay Community

Most of the participant-observer reports on the gay community done to date have been either insider reports or journalistic accounts. (The major exception to this is the work of Evelyn Hooker,[7] which is quoted several times in this essay.) The most famous insider reports are those written by "Donald Webster Cory," a gay psychiatrist, which are useful in themselves and as data on the self-concept and perspective of one particular homosexual. As Cory says, his work is highly ego-involved and polemical—in fact, a "spiritual autobiography."[8] However, many of his comments about the gay community actually parallel the findings of sociologists such as Hooker, Leznoff and Westley,[9] and myself, providing further evidence of the plausibility of the participant-observer method for finding out, in Hooker's words, "what is really going on."[10]

Many of the more interesting participant-observer research studies, whose insights also parallel many sociological findings, are journalistic accounts, such as that of Martin Hoffman.[11] But there are, from the sociological perspective, serious weaknesses in such studies. For example, Hoffman cites a case study:

I interviewed a physiologist who, *looking back, realizes* that he has always been gay, has never had any sexual interest in women, and has had sporadic overt homosexual contacts since childhood. Nevertheless, he did not *realize* he was homosexual until he was 27 and did not come out, in the sense of defining himself as such and entering the gay world, until after his 28th birthday. [italics added]

Hoffman adds that one possible reason for the failure of realization was: "the strong repressive forces that prevent people from *knowing* what their *real sexual feelings* are (italics added).[12]

As we have seen in the above discussion of etiological and incidence studies, descriptions of past events are not to be taken at face value as evidence about past events but, rather, should be carefully analyzed as indicators of the present. For example, the sociologist would ask—where the journalist does not—what is the meaning of the concept of "*real* but *unknown* sexual feelings"? Why does the subject present this particular front to Hoffman? What kind of relationship does this biographic reinterpretation have—if any—to the biographic norms of the gay community?

Thus, it is important not only to do participant-observer research on the gay community, but to do it with all the tools of the sociological trade; otherwise, the data may be distorted by too facile analysis. It is important to do field research in order to find out the real nature of the phenomenon under consideration, apart from the definitions given to the phenomenon by agents of social control such as the police or definers of others' realities such as psychiatrists, because what is significant, from the standpoint of theoretic sociology, is the realities of the gay world as defined by the participants, not as defined by those concerned merely with categorizing and curing social problems.

Only field research, participating and living with the members of a group, can give this kind of understanding. Secondhand sources— "reviews of the literature"—and studies done in unnatural settings, such as the interview or the psychiatrist's couch, cannot, in Hoffman's words, give any real sense of "what the homosexual world looked like . . . its texture and color."[13] Such sources give, at best, only secondhand understanding, or, at worst, total distortion of the data based on the presuppositions, wishes, fantasies, and vested interests of social control agents.

The Population

The first decision that must be made by a researcher who wishes to study the gay community—unless he has unlimited time and money to spend—is *which* gay community he wishes to study: the world of exclusive private gay clubs for businessmen and professionals? or the dope addict transvestites so vividly depicted in *Last Exit To Brooklyn*? or the sado-masochistic leather boys? Any extended preliminary observation will make it objectively obvious that "the" gay community is divided— fairly loosely at the boundaries—into a hierarchy linked to some extent with status and class criteria in the "real" world.

My research indicates that there are three major types of gay communities: elite, career, and deviant.[14] These labels, and the normative hierarchical placement implied by them, reflect *subjective* judgments of homosexuals as well as *objective* judgments of the researcher. The following statements illustrate such subjective judgments:

Interviewer: Do you think there's more than one kind of gay circle?

Sebastian: Oh most definitely yes.

Interviewer: What kinds are there?

Sebastian: Well, you go all the way from the low class, the real trash

Interviewer: Um.

Sebastian: to the very nice elegant people.

. . .

Interviewer: How many of these levels would you say there are?

Sebastian: How many levels? Well, let's see, there's the low class, middle class, and high class.

Interviewer: Is this true in the gay world, do you think?

Sebastian: Oh, I think so. Yes, certainly. And I know people from all levels.

Ronnie: I have so many different types of gay friends that sometimes I have to be what one would term very prissy, very elegant, and very pulled-together. And some of them like to go to very nice places for dinner. Others are more, much more fun-loving and very crazy types I call them, and, er, like to camp and scream and have a very good time, which I can enjoy myself, and these are usually the people that drink a lot, and so when you're with them you drink yourself. . . . I usually only associate, I mean, my friends—gay friends—are like myself; we, er, work very hard for a living and, um, conform pretty much to what society dictates—that you're, you know, O.K., well, you're gay, well, you'll have to still act a certain way, don't, um, embarrass us or bug us or anything like that, and, um, but then there are the other ones that are living in very— what would you call it?—tenderloin areas, especially in big cities, like where I am from, San Francisco, um. There's one area where there's a lot of drag queens, who live in drag all the time, uh, male prostitutes and, er, people who don't, who aren't very aware of where they're going or what they want or what they can get out of life if they only tried, through education and, and travel and, er, want of the finer things of life.

Jerome: I think it's too bad that, that so much of the world judges all gay people and all gay kids, both girls and guys, by a few of the social deviants that, you know, throw a bad light on all of us. . . . Certain people . . . get carried away with the idea of drag, and they become transvestites. But talking about these people is quite foreign to me because I neither socialize or know people like this—they're completely in another dimension, you might say, from us.

Ted: . . . we're living in a double standard of society, because I'm living in one and other people are living in another, and you also have classes within that society. You put yourself on your social level within that particular group, and the majority of people that you meet are on your same level. . . .

Jerome: Well, basically I think you can categorize gay kids the same as you can any other social environment, religion for instance. Because you have, er, low, trashy type people that I feel consist of the cruisers, you know, on the streets, um, possible deviants that do prey on younger children, and then you have business people that are really trying to make something out of their life.

In a general sense, the elite gay community corresponds to Leznoff and Westley's "secret" group, in which the gay side of life is masked in public deference to the work world. For an elite homosexual, his job is at least as important as his leisure activities in the gay community. He may socialize only in private homes and may rarely or never visit a gay bar.

The career homosexual corresponds to Leznoff and Westley's "overt" homosexual. He is likely to be younger than the elite homosexual and to be of a lower or of a "homosexual" occupational category. Most of his life energy is transmitted into the round of gay leisure activities, especially the bars; this, rather than his work, is his "career." This "career" classification does not correspond exactly to Leznoff and Westley's category, however, since career homosexuals do not reveal their homosexuality to nonhomosexual and work groups.[15]

The "deviant" gay category represents, for me, a residual category; I have been told about it by my subjects, but I have no research experience with it. It denotes, provisionally, a grab bag of persons and groups who are considered deviant, sick, or peculiar by most elite or career groups. Those within the deviant category include, at a minimum, men with a sexual orientation toward prepubescent children, those who engage in sado-masochistic practices, and transsexuals and transvestites. It is evident both from the label "deviant" and from the disparaging tone of the above remarks that homosexuals divide their world into categories of normal and deviant sex behavior, as do heterosexuals in the "real" world. The label that sociologists use for "normal" homosexuals is, in turn, applied by these "normal" homosexuals to those whom *they* consider deviant.

The researcher should keep in mind, however, that this division of the community is more situational than absolute, as should be apparent from Ronnie's comments (above) about his different types of friends. Of course, some individuals associate only with specifically elite or career cliques, but many move from clique to clique and engage in both elite and career-type socializing. And, similarly, there is some overlap of career and deviant cliques, especially in the large cities.

The researcher's choice among these alternative communities is limited, in the first instance, by the geographical area in which his research is to take place. If he lives in San Francisco or Los Angeles, he will probably find representatives of elite, career, and various deviant groups. If he lives in a small city, he may find few deviant or career groups; probably, for instance, he will not find a "leather" (gay) bar

in a city with a population of 250,000. The following discussion illustrates the problem:

Tom: But where I come from, in Illinois, you had to drive ninety miles if you
had wanted to go to a gay bar, and it really wasn't worth the trouble or the
hassle.

Interviewer: Um.

Tom: And it was a small town, about 10,000. . . . Well—

Interviewer: The place you lived in or the place the gay bar was?

Tom: No, the school town was 10,000, and it was close to my home town,
which was 25,000. And there was a small group in each town

Interviewer: Um.

Tom: who got together occasionally, in sort of a loose manner. . . . Neither one
had a bar. . . . The bar was ninety miles from the big one [in Springfield].

Interviewer: And this was the only one in the state capital?

Tom: Only one I knew of.

The Initial Contact

Once the researcher has decided, within fluid and realistic boundaries,
what general kind of community he wishes to observe, he must attack
the problem of making the initial contact. This can generally be made
in one of three ways: by accidental personal contact with a homosexual,
by "hanging out" in a gay bar, or by contacting a homophile organization.
   There are pragmatic problems associated with each type of contact.
During the lifetime of a sociologist, it is not unlikely that he will somehow discover, or be told, that a friend or acquaintance is a homosexual.
This type of first contact is described by Hooker:

My original access to the community was not deliberately sought for research
purposes, but developed quite accidentally in the course of normal processes
of social interaction with a group of friends to whom I had been introduced by
a former student—a highly successful businessman. After a period of testing
my capacity to accept their behavior in a non-judgmental way, while divesting
themselves of their protective masks, they made an urgent request that I conduct a scientific investigation of "people like them." By "people like them,"
they meant homosexuals who did not seek psychiatric help, and who led relatively stable, occupationally successful lives. They had read clinical literature
on homosexuality and felt that much of it was irrelevant to an understanding of
their condition. With their offer to supply unlimited numbers of research subjects and to provide entree into homosexual circles and public gathering places,

I accepted the research opportunity. Thus, the original relationship was not that of researcher to research subject, but of friend to friend. With the expansion of contacts through networks of mutual friends, the research role became more clearly defined and separated from its social origin. Independent contacts with official homosexual organizations led to other social strata in the community. Participation in the community and deliberate efforts to locate representative members of varying sectors of it, such as male prostitutes, bisexuals, bartenders and bar owners, adolescents and the aged, produced ultimately a wide cross-section.[16]

As Hooker's statement illustrates, the revelations of a personal acquaintance may serve as an impetus toward research into the gay community; however, such revelations are not certain to occur, serendipitously, as soon as the research has been planned.

As I have indicated above, the problem of finding a gay bar or homophile organization is partially dependent on city size. A city the size of San Francisco, Los Angeles, or New York may support several homophile organizations; a city the size of "Sun City" may support none —in fact, "Sun City" has no such organization. Again, a city the size of "Sun City" will probably have several gay bars—"Sun City" has approximately eleven at present count—but one the size of El Centro may have none.

The second problem connected with contacting people through homophile organizations and gay bars is that of publicity—how are such places to be found? Homophile organizations come within the definition of the political or pressure group organization and thus may be moderately well publicized, especially among groups defined by homosexuals as nonpunitive, such as psychiatrists and sociologists. However, no homophile group is nearly so well publicized as groups of equivalent size and power that are not regarded with public opprobrium, so that many of the general public will not know of the existence of such organizations, let alone their location.

The gay bar, on the other hand, is a less publicized but better known gay institution. Most towns that support several gay bars will have at least one that is well known to tourists from the straight world; for each one of these, there are several which are unknown to anyone except the gay community, the police, cab drivers, and social welfare workers. Thus, for the moderately resourceful sociologist, knowledge of the existence and location of gay institutions in his area is easily obtainable.

As opposed to the homophile organization—which has a relatively small and specialized membership—the general importance of the gay bar to the gay community cannot be overemphasized. It is rare to find a committed gay individual who never goes to gay bars, no matter how elite his socialization patterns or how high status his "real world" occupation. This is because the gay bar functions pivotally in the gay world, as a source of sexual partners, as a socialization agency, and as an exchange for friendship and acquaintance interactions.

Apart from private functions—which are often made up primarily of "married" couples—the gay bar is one of the few places where a male homosexual may legitimately seek homosexual partners. (Other places include beaches, public baths, theaters, parks, and public toilets, but police harassment may be greater at some of these.) Generally, he cannot look for partners at work, among friends of his family, or in straight bars and restaurants—but he can in a gay bar. He can also go to a bar to meet gay friends and to generally "let down his hair" without fear of hostility from others.

Gay bars open and shut extremely rapidly, but the number usually remains fairly stable for a given population, indicating a stable demand. For those who travel, there are many bar guides listing bars in all fifty states and in most of the countries of the world, including even the USSR.

The importance of gay bars in the lives of those in the community is illustrated by Tom, who is an average bargoer:

Interviewer: Do you go to gay bars?

Tom: Mm—all the time.

Interviewer: How frequently?

Tom: Well, really, just to go out on the weekend I'll go. Last night we went to one after I got home from work. We just had a couple of drinks and helped the, er, the bartender—a friend—clean up the bar, and we had him over for breakfast.

Interviewer: Till a quarter to five.

Tom: Till a quarter to five, a quarter after five.

Interviewer: So you go on the weekends but not usually on the week nights?

Tom: Not usually. I try not to go on the week nights just because it's too expensive to go every night. That and the fact that I work till midnight. . . .

Interviewer: In an average week, how much would you say you spend from, um, Monday through Sunday on drink?

Tom: In a seven-day period?

Interviewer: Yes.

Tom: I wouldn't be afraid to say twenty—twenty-five dollars.

Each of these locales for making an initial contact—personal contacts, the homophile club, and the gay bar—may lead, at least initially,
to very different groups of homosexuals. For instance, the personal
acquaintance who has just unburdened himself to the researcher may
associate only with anonymous faces in public toilets or he may be a
member of a small, closed "S and M" (sado-masochist) group. Our
commonsense expectations, however, would lead us to expect that such
an acquaintance would lead the researcher to a fairly large elite group,
from which he could then make contacts within the elite and career
groups.

Contacting homosexuals through a homophile organization might
initially lead to a highly unusual group of homosexuals—those who are
willing to (fairly) publicly define themselves as such. Few studies have
been done on the membership of such organizations; but, from what we
know of the "grapevine" quality of gay life, membership contacts would,
probably, eventually lead to contacts with more secret elite and career
homosexuals.

Perhaps the most useful way for the researcher to make the initial
contact is by "hanging out" in a gay bar. The names of the more publicly
known bars are easy to obtain, and the clients of these bars can then
provide the researcher with leads to others, and thence to the more
private aspects of the life of the gay community.

The Research Role

Once the researcher has found that he is able to make contacts for his
research and has decided upon its limits in terms of population, he must
be prepared to decide what role he will play during the process of
participant-observation. The choice of role is limited, initially, only by
the sex of the interviewer; beyond this, questions of research aim and
of personal bias will delimit the researcher's role choice.

The problem of bias in the early research stage of role choice is less
philosophically complex than the question of bias *during* participant-
observation, but it is one that must be faced. If the researcher is neutral
toward homosexual behavior or feels sympathy with the social situation of homosexuals, he will be able to choose his research role in
accordance with considerations of purpose and of dramaturgy. If, however, he has a negative bias, he must take into consideration the problem of coping with sexual and quasi-sexual situations.

A young man playing the role of the homosexual in participant-
observer research may, if he is young and attractive, be the recipient
of sexual propositions. At the very least, he will be expected to participate in "normal" quasi-sexual activities such as dancing. Even if he

decides to play the role of the sociologist and do overt rather than covert research, he may receive sexual propositions and will very probably be asked to dance at parties. If the researcher cannot work out, within himself, a way of coping with these problems without becoming judgmental or emotional, he had best not undertake the research. As Hooker says:

Gaining access to secret worlds of homosexuals, and maintaining rapport while conducting an ethnographic field study, requires the development of a non-evaluative attitude toward all forms of sexual behavior. Social scientists tend to share the emotional attitudes of their culture, and thus do not find this an easy task. . . . Only if I can achieve and maintain an attitude such that non-evaluation is constant, and that whatsoever I hear or see is simply a matter of sheer interest, will I be able to establish the necessary conditions of trust for complete frankness.[17]

Once this preliminary problem has been faced, the nature of the population and the researcher's own dramatic abilities remain as indicators of research role. From my own research experience, I should like to suggest several possible roles that are recognized within the gay world and some of the implications of each for the purpose of participant-observation.

Covert Research

One possible role in the covert, or secret, research category is the male heterosexual "tourist" in the gay world. However, this is a negatively rather than a positively valued role within the community and, thus, is probably the least suitable of all for the purpose of obtaining entrée into, and rapport with, the community. As one subject said: "If there's a show in the bar, it doesn't bother me. . . . If they're just coming to a gay bar just to look, then I don't like it."

However, if the researcher wishes to pursue covert research and at the same time present a heterosexual identity, he might consider using a female assistant with whom he would adopt the role of the married couple who have gay friends. Such a role is not exactly positive, but it is not particularly negative, either, so that there is room to maneuver, as individuals, into a position of acceptance or rejection. If the couple is accepted, they will be regarded as "wise" rather than as "tourists"; a "wise" heterosexual is one who knows about gay life, accepts it, and even enjoys it. This is a plausible research role for a man and woman, or for a single woman, but will very rarely be so for a single male. Bud describes one such "wise" couple:

I know that, er, there's one family in "El Sol"; I was at their home once, and I didn't return again. They had a ten-year-old boy. They entertained fifteen or twenty men, er. It was, a, on Saturday and Sunday afternoons—barbecues, swimming, whatever.

A woman engaged in secret research may assume a homosexual or a heterosexual identity. If she chooses a heterosexual identity, she will be assigned the role of "fag hag" (in other parts of the country this may be "faggotina" or "fruit fly"); she will not be called this to her face if she is liked and accepted, but she will almost inevitably be assigned this role whether she is liked or disliked. The argot term signifies a heterosexual woman who associates with male homosexuals for reasons that are a matter of speculation among male homosexuals. Usual interpretations are that she is asexual, she is frightened of sexual relations with men, or she is a latent homosexual.

If the researcher chooses to play the role of the female homosexual, she may be brought into contact with other female homosexuals and have to give some consideration to coping with sexual and quasi-sexual interactions. However, this would be a very minimal problem, since the overlap between the male and female gay communities is only tenuous, and, also, females do not engage in the persistent sexual searching that characterizes gay men.

In either case, the researcher will have to make her way within the community as an individual; there may be some prejudice against females in one clique, or against "fag hags" in another, or against "dykes" in another, but the decisive factors in acceptance or rejection will be interpersonal ones. For a female to become a significant other in a community in which maleness is the main status criterion is not easy, and the researcher should be aware that she may have to put considerable effort into becoming the type of person that the community will value. She need not necessarily be attractive—I once met a "fag hag" who weighed at least 300 pounds—but she must have some sort of noticeable personal style, make a suitable conversational contribution, and refrain from public sexual overtures to committed homosexuals.

Undoubtedly, the most problematic secret research role is that of male homosexual. Once the male heterosexual researcher has decided that he is able to play such a role without personal anguish, many problems remain. For example, it is easy to say "no" to sexual overtures—few homosexuals are determined rapists—but repeated "nos" would cast doubt on the authenticity of the researcher's role.

In addition, it is important to take into account the amount of preliminary time and effort that will be needed to learn the role: its presup-

positions, its cues, actions, habits, and language. Some of this can be
learned via the commonsense understandings of social life, although
some of these commonsense understandings provide miscues. For
example, it is quite well known that homosexuals refer to themselves
as "gay," and it is equally "well known" that most homosexuals are
effeminate in mannerism. However, the former knowledge is likely to
be useful as part of the role-learning of the researcher, and the latter
is likely to be the reverse—some homosexuals behave in a manner
that might be considered feminine, others in a "masculine" manner, but
most have a *self-image* with a strong masculine component. And such
role finesse is of extreme importance and is not part of commonsense
societal knowledge.

Perhaps the best role open to a single man who is quite determined
to do secret participant-observation is that of the homosexual who has
just "come out" into the gay world. Uncertainty about his sexual status,
which is subculturally recognized during the coming-out stage, can be
utilized to explain his "nos" to those sexual overtures; unfamiliarity
with the mores allows him to make faux pas as he learns about the role
requirements of committed homosexuals.

Male pairs engaged in secret research are able to present themselves
in the role of a sexually "married" couple, thus minimizing (although
not, probably, eliminating), the problem of sexual overtures. However,
the problem of role-learning and playing remains and, in this case, might
be tackled by playing the role—well established in the gay world—of
the "closet queen." The "closet queen" is one who refuses to associate
with other homosexuals because of the reputational dangers involved;
a pair of males might authentically present themselves as people who
have decided that the gay life is worth living despite the risks and who
are now learning their way around.

Overt Research

The researcher may, however, choose to take an overt research role
and to present himself to his contacts as a sociologist. The chief
advantage of overt research is that it enables the researcher to ask
for interviews and tape sessions; the chief disadvantage is, in sociological folklore, that the researcher-role alters the environment of
what is being observed to such an extent that the setting is no longer
natural.

In this context, the comments of Howard Becker in a recent paper
are extremely useful:

...the people the field worker observes are ordinarily constrained to act as they would have in his absence, by the very social constraints whose effects interest him; he therefore has little chance, compared to practitioners of other methods, to influence what they do, for more potent forces are operating.

[The people studied by a field worker] are enmeshed in all the social relationships important to them, whether at work, in community life, or wherever. The events they participate in matter to them. The people they interact with are people whose opinions and actions must be taken into account, because they affect those events. All the constraints which affect them in their ordinary life continue to operate while the observer observes.[18]

Becker does mention, however, that this analysis does not apply when the subjects regard the observer as someone important enough to constitute a *threat*. In this case, a protective show may be put on for the observer. I would add, in reference to the gay community, that this might also occur if the people observed regard the observer—say, a young and beautiful male—as important enough to be a *prize*. In a world where sexual contact is centrally important, other social constraints and social relationships become secondary upon the approach of an attractive partner. It is up to the *verstehen* of the sociologist to perceive, and use as data, his role as focal point within the environment.

Although I do not perceive as valid the entire concept of contamination, I agree with Ned Polsky's comments about the use of artificial aids during participant-observation, since this tends to make the researcher into an unusual, and therefore noticed, element in the environment:

Although you can't help but contaminate the criminal's environment in some degree by your presence, such contamination can be minimized if, for one thing, you use no gadgets (no tape recorder, questionnaire form) and, for another, do not take any notes in the criminal's presence. It is quite feasible to train yourself to remember details of action and speech long enough to write them up fully and accurately after you get home at the end of the day (or night, more typically).[19]

The group's conception of the researcher's role is important with reference to the amount and type of activity that he will be allowed to observe. In my research experience, I have found that individuals within the gay community have no special conception of the sociologist beyond the general societal one. I find that people I encounter in general social life perceive sociologists as politically liberal, unconventionally sympathetic, and vaguely connected with social work and do-gooding.

This generalized perception is also true of the gay community. But such a constellation of perceived characteristics is, for the homosexual, *also* seen as of potential benefit for the public relations image of the gay community. My subjects "knew," unproblematically, that my research was sympathetically oriented, simply because I was a sociologist. Frequently, the reaction of a contact who was a complete stranger to me was something like: "It's about time someone did a paper on us," or "It's about time someone told the truth about us."

Covert Versus Overt Research

The relative disadvantages and advantages of covert versus overt research are not simple, but the evidence indicates that overt research is both *less* complex—philosophically and pragmatically—and *just as* valuable, as covert research. Ned Polsky, with specific reference to criminals, comments:

The main obstacle to studying criminals in the field, according to Sutherland and Cressey, lies in the fact that the researcher "must associate with them as one of them." Few researchers "could acquire the techniques to pass as criminals," and moreover "it would be necessary to engage in crime with the others if they retained a position once secured." Where Sutherland and Cressey got this alleged fact they don't say and I can't imagine. It is just not true. On the contrary, in doing field research on criminals you damned well better *not* pretend to be "one of them," because they will test this claim out and one of two things will happen: either you will, as Sutherland and Cressey indicate, get sucked into "participant" observation of the sort you would rather not undertake, or you will be exposed, with still greater negative consequences. You must let the criminals know who you are; and if it is done properly . . . it does not sabotage the research.[20]

Although the situation is not as acute as it appears to be among criminals, Polsky's main points have some relevance to the question of secret participant-observation of the gay community.

In the gay community, the "testing out" process may have one or two phases, depending upon chosen role. The initial testing is of sexual identity and is based both on assumptions and on direct and indirect questioning. If a single male is hanging out in a gay bar, his sexual identity will tend to be assumed until some incident makes it problematic. At this stage, direct and indirect questioning may be used to provide an identity. In either case, he will probably eventually undergo the second testing phase—a sexual overture.

The sexual identity of a woman or a "married couple" hanging out in a gay bar will also, probably, come into question and may be tested out by observation and conversation. However, this is not always the case, since the sexual identity of a woman has little relevance for members of the gay community, so that the initial testing-out phase assumes little importance. And, for the "fag hag" or "wise" heterosexual couple there is no second testing-out phase.

For the researcher playing the "gay" role, the likelihood of exposure as a fake is both constant and serious—since, after all, being gay is a fairly serious game to those who *are* gay. But the likelihood of exposure for a secret researcher playing other roles is neither constant nor serious, both because the testing out process is less rigorous and significant, and because in an existential sense, he or she is not a fake. It is very probable that the role of "wise" heterosexual is backed by genuine feelings on the part of the sociologist, and the role of "fag hag" is situationally *true* while the researcher is engaged in the process of participant-observation. Thus covert nongay roles are fairly plausible research alternatives within the gay community, if not within the criminal community studied by Polsky.

The main advantage of the gay role is that the researcher is enabled to view many more situations and be involved in different types of interactions than the researcher who takes another role. For example, a "gay" researcher may be invited to social occasions where sexual acts are taking place; the frequency or existence of such occasions may remain unknown to "straight" researchers. Similarly, a "gay" researcher can experience firsthand the interactions and maneuvers that characterize a sexual overture between members. More generally, and much more importantly, he can more fully be a member of the community than a researcher playing any other role, in the sense that the behavior of the members toward him will be the behavior that they present *to another member.*

"Wise" heterosexuals or "fag hags," on the other hand, will be reacted to as members not of the gay community, but of these subsidiary, quasi-member categories. However, as is stressed so importantly by Becker, in all cases the researcher will be able to observe, equally well, all interactions in which he or she is a relatively nonsignificant other.

Most of the advantages and disadvantages of the secret nonhomosexual roles also apply to the overt researcher role, since, as I have already pointed out, these secret roles existentially approximate the sociological role. The overt researcher will be able to observe, in the same way as the covert "straight" researcher, all interactions that do not involve him as a significant other; in face to face interaction, he will be reacted to as a researcher.

Since individuals who play roles other than that of male homosexual are accepted into the gay community only under unusual circumstances, it is up to the researcher playing any *other* role to create these circumstances. The covert researcher has one possibility: he can create these circumstances through his "personality" and become valued in the community for his personal contribution and characteristics. The overt researcher, on the other hand, has two possibilities: he can become valued as a person, and he can also become valued instrumentally, for the research itself, which indicates that the research must be presented to the subject as something that may ultimately benefit him. This is neither a difficult nor an immoral task, because *understanding* of the gay community is seen by the members as the most important function of the academic observer. And this understanding is, after all, what the researcher is trying to achieve.

Establishing Relationships

Obviously, the researcher will not become valued in the community if he does not succeed in establishing relationships of mutual trust with his subjects. Such trust is necessary to gain access to any world, and particularly necessary in the case of gaining access to a world labeled by many as "deviant" and whose members tend to perceive any alien as a threat. For example, in doing research in the gay community, it is easy enough to gain access to a gay bar. But in order to extend that access from the public bar to more private settings, such as cocktail parties, it is necessary to gain the confidence of the subjects, especially if they have professional or business occupations and have everything to lose by associating with an untrustworthy stranger.

Another, more pragmatic, reason for establishing trust relationships with the members is that it then becomes easier to obtain interviews at a later stage of the research. In my own research, I have found two types of initial reactions to the suggestion of a taped interview: positive interest, and hostility. Many gay people, especially in the career subculture, find the idea of being interviewed very appealing; others, especially in the elite group, find it dangerous and frightening.

However, without the establishment of a relationship, many of those who like the idea of being interviewed are not likely to be able to find the time, or be bothered, to actually carry the project through. Similarly, with the establishment of a relationship, many of those whose initial reactions were hostile become amenable and interested. The importance of making relationships was illustrated in my interview with Bud:

Interviewer: . . . you're sitting in a bar, let's say, and you're just talking to somebody in the bar, and he says he's a sociologist and he'd like to interview you.

Bud: I'd say, well that's very nice, goodbye.

Interviewer: Why would you do this?

Bud: Because I think it would be a waste of time.

Interviewer: Could you explain?

Bud: Well, yes. I'm not about to bare myself to someone that I wouldn't know

Interviewer: Um.

Bud: and wouldn't know anything of their background and why they were doing this. . . . I'm doing this with you because it's a friendship.

Interviewing

The purpose of interviewing subjects is twofold: to check on observations, and to generate new ideas for further research. The best method of interviewing is to use tape recorders, since the data is preserved fully and not collapsed in any way or forgotten by the researcher, as is the case with interview schedules or notes. Interviewing must, in general, be left until the later stages of the research. This gives the researcher time to develop the necessary trust and, also, enables him to gain an intuitive sense of the community, so that the taped data can be put into the correct context. This intuitive sense creates the context both for the researcher's questions and for the subjects' answers.

Essentially, the questions asked by the researcher during the interview are shaped both by the participant-observation *and* by the immediate situation; thus, they cannot be preplanned in any formal sense. From his knowledge of the community, the researcher gains a general idea of what he wants to get his subjects to talk about. But he may find —as I did, very frequently—that the subject expects and wishes to talk about something quite different.

For example, the single most popular subject of self-analysis and interest among my interviewees was the etiology of their homosexuality —something that I was not particularly interested in. However, I at no time attempted to force the conversation into other directions, since I felt that this might cause some unnecessary tension within the interaction. I also found that some "filler" conversation at the beginning of the interview (always a somewhat tense social situation) enabled us to enter a more relaxed phase, when I would gradually introduce the topics about which I wished to know more. I found out that it was perfectly possible to do this without *either* forcing the subject *not to talk* about certain things or compelling him *to talk* about other things.

The subjects' answers, as well as the interviewer's questions, must be put into context by using prior intuitive knowledge about the gay community. This is, essentially, because of three problems: negative representation, allusion comprehension, and front management.

The problem of negative representation is maximized where the population under consideration cannot be sampled representatively. Unless the researcher has previously been a participant-observer in the community, he has no way of ascertaining whether or not his interview subjects are expressing typical or extremely unusual perceptions and opinions concerning the gay community.

The problem of allusion comprehension is, simply, that to understand his subjects at all, the researcher must be able to understand their language and have some knowledge of the nature and location of their world. For instance, if he is going to interview a career homosexual he should know what the gay bars in the area are like; what "trick," "trade," and "mother" mean; what the word "hairdresser" connotes. Otherwise, either the interview will become a definition-seeking enterprise or the subject will not be understood at all by the interviewer.

The question of the management of fronts is extremely complex. In the real world, fronts range all the way from the below-conscious everyday presentation of self to the careful performance of the impostor. But it may well be that the majority of individuals have no conception that fronts exist as conscious alternatives. However, fronts are, very definitely, a part of the gay universe of meaning. In the following commentary, Ted discusses three possible presentations of self to his family: heterosexual, homosexual, or sexually nonspecific:

I was always just scared to death my family was going to find out, and *I would go to any lengths not to have them.* I think I am starting to adjust myself where I've gotten the attitude now, *if it happens, it's going to happen; we're just going to have to sit down and discuss it,* and I'm not going to worry about it....

I used to always, er, *date the girls from the office, always trying to put up a pretense.* I always made sure that my family, you know, knew who I was going out with. *Now I don't particularly do it,* er, and generally, er, it can be. *So many people, you know, in, in this life will never refer to two men together to their parents*—ex, constantly—and *I do now.* I'm either, you know, talking about Roger and Sam, or Dean and Bob, or something like this, and if it's girls they're generally two girls' names involved, and I'm never speaking now, er, as, er, Mildred and Rex or something like this.... (my italics)

In summary then, taping must be used *supplementary to,* and *not instead of,* participant-observation, and it should be used *after* some fieldwork has been undertaken. If interviews are used instead of participant-observation, the researcher will have no clues as to the representability of his subjects. If they are used before participant-observation, the researcher will have little familiarity with the argot and locale allusions and the situational fronts of his subjects. And he may, also, have difficulty persuading subjects to be interviewed, since he will not have established trust relationships.

Some Theoretical Considerations

As we have already noted, the purpose of doing research into the gay community is the generation of grounded theory about the everyday lives of its members—the essential task of appreciative and noncorrectional sociology. Theory and method are, of course, inextricably linked, so that this methodological discussion raises three major theoretical questions: the perspective of the researcher, the existential basis of sociology, and the sympathetic or empathic dimensions of the sociologist's role.

Hooker states that the advantage of participant-observer research is that it enables the researcher to find out "what is really going on" among and within research subjects. However, it must be kept in mind that the sociologist can never see the subject's world *through the subject's eyes*. At the simplest level, no two subjects see the world— American society or the gay world—in exactly the same way. And, more generally, perceptions of what is going on in the subject's mind are filtered through both the subject's behavior and the observer's interpretive system.

In any situation, obviously, there are two types of meanings for a given action—subjective, or actor, meaning, and objective, or observer, meaning. But for the sociologist there is a third type of meaning that is specifically sociological, since it involves a specifically *sociological interpretive system*. This system, unlike many other types of thought, uses both subjective and objective meanings to process data, although it is not a simple summation of these meanings. It has a gestalt of its own—the *verstehen*, the empathic understanding, of the sociological imagination.

As we have seen, the theoretical sociological interpretive system attempts to do two things that other systems of thought are not concerned with: first, it attempts to *analyze* the empirical nature and methodological implications of observer meaning; second, it attempts to discover, through observation of behavior and interaction with subjects, some of the properties of subjective meaning, while recognizing that it cannot achieve a full knowledge of subjective meaning. Traditional sociology has aspired to such complete knowing, through the medium of latent meanings, and has, in addition, postulated a subjective *true self* which can be known, identically, to both researcher and subject, once research biases have been *cleared away*. Imputed to this true self are true, nonsituational attitudes, values, responses, and biographies, which can be arrived at sociologically by a continuing refinement of scientific methodology.

Theoretic sociology, on the other hand, involves a definition of the self as situational, rather than as absolute. Further, it involves a definition of data—*all* data—as true, useful, and valid, rather than applying the definition of true to *some* data and false to other data. Thus, one of the objectives in theory-building research is *to analyze the differences* between data obtained on the same subjects in different contexts, as well as to describe the phenomena. To illustrate what I mean by this, I should like to cite an example from the early stages of my own research. I became acquainted with a friendship clique of approximately five to fifteen members (membership varied within these boundaries in different social situations), which included two individuals whom I shall call Ted and Dave. I interviewed these two members and found them to be extremely different in biographical, current, and potential future involvement with the gay community.

Ted told me that he had always been a homosexual, and is sure that he always will be one. At the present time, he stated, he associates almost exclusively with gay individuals and is much more comfortable with gay than with straight people. Dave, on the other hand, claimed that he had had many serious and less serious involvements with women and tentatively plans to get married sometime in the future. He said that at present he dates both men and women, and that he is no more comfortable with gay than with straight people—he bases his friendship choice on factors other than sexual identity.

Before and after the interviews with Ted and Dave, I observed them in interaction with other clique members, with actual and potential sexual partners, and with other members of the gay community. At all times they *both* presented a front suitable for interaction within the community: women and marriage were not specifically rejected, but were treated—or, rather, left untreated—as unproblematically irrelevant to the life of any committed gay individual. In fact, Dave warned me very thoroughly not to tell his current sex partner about his dates with women, since the partner would not approve. For all intents and purposes, the fronts projected to the community at large and to the clique members were *very much the same* for both Ted and Dave. However, the fronts projected to me, the interviewer, were *extremely different.*

With this data I can do one of two things. Either I can look for existential truth and decide that the truth about Ted and Dave is located in the interview situation; or, conversely, that it is found in their community interaction; or that it can be found in some other situation. Or I can conclude that I cannot know which, if either, situation is *the* truth and that there is, in fact, no *the* truth, or at least none that I can grasp.

What I can do before I come to any conclusions is describe the data that I gather from the interview situation and from participant-observation and then detail the differences between the fronts in the two situations. For example, I could state the boundaries of the interview situation: the subject has a preconception of the interview situation and of the process of sociologizing, probably gleaned from general societal knowledge; and I have other preconceptions about the same things. The subject has an opinion of me, and I of him; since we are in one-to-one interaction, we are, momentarily, very significant for each other in terms of self-presentation. Then I could, similarly, state the boundaries of a situation in which the subject is engaged with members of the gay community and I am present as an observer. My importance in the situation varies with the importance of others in the situation; as soon as there are others or another on the scene who is more important than I am, my subject's front will shift in focus, if necessary, into line with the new situation. And, since much of the behavior expected of members of the gay community is fairly stable from situation to situation, my subjects' fronts are likely to be very similar to each other, no matter how different their interview fronts.

The problem of sympathy and empathy is closely related to that of the existential base of sociology, but with the emphasis shifted from subject's roles to interviewer's roles. Douglas's distinction between sympathy and empathy (in his essay "Observing Deviance" in this volume) is extremely useful, but it implies too much of an unknowable existential truth: it is not necessary, surely, that a sociologist be permanently sympathetic or empathic; he may shift role and front, as the situation requires, from sympathy to empathy and back again.

For example, one of the motivations to do a particular type of research may be sympathy—just as hostility may provide a barrier to research interest. Stated another way, the sociologist's preexisting *bias* may be —probably always is—a significant factor in the choice of research orientation. However, once the sociologist is actually engaged in participant-observer research, his bias must give way to an open-spirited and empathic *sociological front,* with corresponding changes in focus, attitude, and understanding.

If this kind of role and attitude switch is impossible for the sociologist, then the question of bias again becomes relevant—that is, if the researcher is unable to switch from sympathetic or hostile to empathic understandings, he will not be able to properly carry out the participant-observer process, since he will constantly fit what he observes into his preexisting value framework.

If the researcher is unable to prevent his sympathy or hostility from invading and contaminating his sociological understanding, then he has been improperly prepared in the art of sociology. Many such one-dimensional individuals do become sociologists, partly because for too long sociology has been perceived as a science and sociologists as passive manipulators rather than actors on the social scene. Perhaps the focus should be altered, and individuals taught art as well as science and how to be empathic actors as well as competent statisticians.

The image here is of social interaction as a masquerade and of the costumes as the subject matter of sociology. Presumably, or perhaps not presumably, there is some existential truth hidden behind the ephemeral truth that is the costumes, but such existential truth is the province of philosophers or deities. However that may be, let us be sure, at least, that the sociologists' costumes are tailored well.

Notes

1. Jack D. Douglas, *American Social Order* (New York: Free Press, 1971).
2. *Ibid.*
3. Edmund Bergler, *One Thousand Homosexuals* (Paterson, N.J.: Pageant, 1959), p. ix.
4. *Ibid.*, pp. 7–8.
5. Michael Schofield, *Sociological Aspects of Homosexuality* (Boston: Little, Brown, 1965).
6. Gresham Sykes, *The Society of Captives* (Princeton, N.J.: Princeton University Press, 1958), pp. 96–98.
7. Evelyn Hooker, "The Homosexual Community," in John H. Gagnon and William Simon (eds.), *Sexual Deviance* (New York: Harper & Row, 1967), pp. 167–196.
8. Donald Webster Cory, *The Homosexual in America* (New York: Greenberg, 1951), p. xiv.
9. Maurice Leznoff and William A. Westley, "The Homosexual Community," in Gagnon and Simon, *op. cit.*, pp. 184–196.
10. Hooker, *op. cit.*, p. 168.
11. Martin Hoffman, *The Gay World* (New York: Basic Books, 1968).
12. Hoffman, *op. cit.*, pp. 137 and 138.
13. *Ibid.*, p. 10.
14. The interview quotations used here and later in this article are from my research notes. All the names are pseudonyms.
15. Leznoff and Westley, *op. cit.*
16. Hooker, *op. cit.*, p. 170.
17. *Ibid.*, p. 169.
18. Howard S. Becker, "Field Work Research" (unpublished paper, 1969).
19. Ned Polsky, *Hustlers, Beats and Others* (Chicago: Aldine, 1967), p. 124.
20. *Ibid.*

Fieldwork Among Deviants: Social Relations with Subjects and Others

Martin S. Weinberg and Colin J. Williams

To greater or lesser degree all human research involves social relationships between the investigator and his subjects. The character of these relationships may range from becoming a member of a group studied (as in some forms of participant-observation) to having little or no contact with subjects at all (computer-simulation studies, for example). To the extent that it is a social activity, research behavior is governed by sets of rules and expectations that regulate these relationships. Like other forms of social behavior, these rules can be clear or confused, consistent or inconsistent. It is a contention of this article that the social relationships involved in doing social research have important effects upon the quality of the knowledge gained and the way in which it is portrayed (cf. Jack Douglas's article "Observing Deviance"). Hence, the social relationships that are created, maintained, or altered in such endeavors are an especially important area of study.

Social relations are salient with regard to participant-observation studies in the following ways:

1. The research technique involves long periods of interaction with the subjects of study. Thus, the quality of the relationships with these subjects can affect what is learned about them.
2. Interacting with subjects in their natural settings can have a socializing effect, so that the researcher (temporarily at least) becomes a "different person." Since the data-collecting instrument involved in fieldwork is the investigator himself (versus, for example, a mailed questionnaire), the type and nature of the information gained (and/

or published) at different stages of the social relationships with subjects can have a different quality.

3. The nature of the fieldwork, as well as the change in role and self resulting from field experience, can affect relationships with persons other than subjects. The fieldwork can affect the relationships the researcher has with family, friends, and colleagues, and this in turn can affect his stance toward his subjects. This aspect of the sociology of research has been quite neglected.

In fieldwork, operating rules are problematic, especially where the subjects are deviants. There are initially two bases upon which researcher and subjects can interact. First, rules apply which hold for any institutionalized relationship with an anonymous other. This set of rules is inadequate in that, if the subjects are deviants, they often do not accept such "normal" rules of interaction. The second set of rules are those procedures laid down by the criteria of social science. In return for free access to information, the researcher will record the behavior of the group in "objective," confidential, and truthful terms, being guided by "professional ethics."

For two reasons this second set of rules is also an inadequate basis for a working relationship between researcher and subjects. First, deviants often engage in unlawful or sanctionable acts, and thus exposure is a prime concern for them. Naturally, they are often hesitant to accept a stranger among them (no matter what his credentials are) whose stated aim is to record their behavior. Second, the researcher finds he is faced with problems that methodology books do not solve; although general principles might be proposed, these are often impossible to apply in specific situations.

We have, therefore, an unstructured situation: the subjects generally have no clear rules for interacting with their researcher, and the researcher has no specific rules for guiding interaction with his subjects, as methodology texts do not discuss the specific problems that he confronts. What follows is a gamelike attempt, usually by both parties, to work out the various stages of their relationship. In so doing, each casts the other into different roles as the research enters different phases: it is the demands of these roles that structure the nature of the relationships that are part and parcel of the fieldwork experience. These self-same features also affect the researcher's relationships with those outside of the research setting—relationships that can also become strained by the character of the research. These various social processes affect what knowledge is obtained and published by the researcher, and the problems associated with these processes should be a prime concern for him.

This article examines some of the problems and solutions generated in researching so-called deviants. The research discussed is primarily research that was carried out by one of the authors with nudists and research that was carried out by both authors with homosexuals. A life-cycle model of phases of relationships with the subjects will serve as an organizing device for the discussion. We label the stages in this model respectively: Application, Orientation, Initiation, Assimilation, and Cessation. As we cover each stage, we discuss some of the roles in which we cast ourselves and/or were cast in by others—some of the facets of social relations which thus appeared at each stage. In general, we speak first of the relationships with the subjects themselves and then turn to how the character of these relations affected our relationships with others. How these stages affected our perceptions of ourselves will also be made clear. Finally, we shall consider the implications of both sets of relationships for the quality of the descriptions produced. The table below provides a schematization of the ways in which the fieldworker is perceived by subjects, others, and himself.[1]

The Fieldworker as Perceived by Subjects, Others, and Self, as Related to the Stage of the Research.

Stage of the Fieldwork	Viewed by Subjects as:	Viewed by Others as:	Viewed by Self as:
Application	Interloper	Voyeur	Salesman
Orientation	Novice	Inside dopester	Stranger
Initiation	Probationer	Pseudo-professional	Initiate
Assimilation	Limbo member	Public defender	True believer
Cessation	Deserter	Expert	Worker who has finished his job

Application

Application refers to the stage of research in which contact is initiated with the subjects. This is often the most stilted stage in the social relations of fieldwork. The following questions plague the interaction: To what extent do you reveal your true research interests? To what extent do you tell the subjects what they want to hear? Do you even tell the subjects you will be researching them, or do you engage in covert participant-observation? To what extent can you reveal the specific research interests without jeopardizing the study by giving the subjects a set—orienting the subjects with your specific interest or theory, so that they provide you with dramatic presentations of what you want.[2] These are "ethical" problems that methodology texts treat even though they provide little guidance. In the actual fieldwork situation, however, the researcher's approach often becomes less academic when it appears that the fate of his project is in question. Generally, the strategy we employ is to be vague regarding our research interests. We believe this is necessary in order to protect the project, and we explain this to the subjects.

Such vagueness, however, is often taken by the subjects as indecision or a lack of precision or articulation, which may lead to a questioning of the researcher's competence. (Or, they simply are unwilling to see the fieldworker as being as special as he would like to think.) At the beginning of some cross-cultural research on homosexuality, the officers of a homophile organization asked such questions as: How is the organization to know the competence of the researchers? What will its members get out of cooperating in the study?[3] What are the researchers out to prove? All legitimate questions, but ones that can make initial interaction awkward. It is difficult to prove your competence. You can provide letters of recommendation or examples of your work. If you do not want to spare the time for such investigation (or if you question your own competence), you can ignore the legitimate queries of the subjects by emphatically stating that you would not be in your present position or have received your grant, and so on, if you were not competent—a *non sequitur* if there ever was one.

Vagueness often reinforces the subjects' notions that sociologists are obtuse. Perhaps researchers often fear submitting their past work to their subjects because it would further support this. Sociologists do believe it true that generally only other sociologists (and only those of your own persuasion) understand what you are doing, so you again cut yourself off from entering into really open interaction.

Sometimes we have been confronted with the question, "What is a sociologist anyway?" We have never formulated a sufficiently clear explanation for laymen. In the nudist research, for example, many subjects were convinced that sociologists are no different from psychiatrists, who want to study them because they think nudists are "nuts." It was not until the researcher gave a nude lecture at their Sunday morning "services" that they learned some of the types of conclusions sociologists had reached regarding social relationships, which were enumerated in terms of nudists' relations with "clothed society." (More about the "nude sermons" will be said in the section on Initiation.)

A problem in the Application stage is how to "psych out" the "games people play."[4] For example, one issue is the determination of whether questions are sincere or are instead an attempt to gain control of the situation. After one homophile organization had put us "over the coals," we found out that the organization was delighted to have us do the research (at no expense to them), since they had previously decided to hire a research organization to obtain information on their membership. By the time we found this out, however, the organization had gained much more control over the research (for example, requiring us to adapt a questionnaire that we were using for their own use with their female members) than it would have if they had taken a stance in which we would not have feared losing their cooperation.

A related problem is whether the questions directed at you are to be used to help evaluate you in comparison with other researchers who have approached the organization. In planning our research on homosexuals, we soon found that there were researchers other than ourselves competing for scarce resources—the time and cooperation of the subjects. This led to an awkward situation, because we felt a need to convince the leaders of the homophile organization that our research should be given high priority, but at the same time we did not want to depreciate the value of the research of others (which we sensed they would have liked us to do, to help them get a better sense of who should get priority, and so on). The problem becomes more acute when the other researchers are people you know and respect; competition then means more than "contaminating the population" by their being overresearched or "scooping" the other with regard to research results.

In sum, "open interaction" can face some severe tests during the Application stage. If it is difficult to gain entrance to the research setting, then the researcher may follow the temptation to promise more than he can deliver. (For example, "We hope to change the social situation for the homosexual in the United States.") In effect, then, at this stage the researcher often feels like a salesman, while the subjects, on the other hand, often treat him as an interloper.

During the Application stage, the initial problem posed by people other than the subjects is the opposite of that posed by the deviant group. With the subjects, the true research interest is often couched in terms that help facilitate entry and cooperation. With other persons, however, there is less need for such duplicity, and the research aims need not be obscured. The problem that first arises is that the *reason* for doing the research is often questioned: one's motivation may be called into question with the amused demand to "come clean" and give the "real" reason for your interest in the particular deviants. It is often difficult to convince the layman that studying nudists, for example, presents an opportunity to study sexual modesty rather than an opportunity to see nudes, or that observing homosexuals allows you to examine minority group behavior and is not providing you with a sexual opportunity. To other people, the deviance researcher often appears to be a voyeur (especially when he is, for example, spending time observing homosexual acts in men's rooms or observing group sex at Sexual Freedom League parties).[5]

This questioning of motivation is not confined to laymen; colleagues in sociology (no doubt searching for "latent functions" or latent homosexuality) have also warned us of the sorry spectacle we present in mixing with social outcasts. Such questioning is usually more indirect and has taken forms ranging from concern with *our* careers ("nobody will hire you") to concern with theirs ("we wouldn't want anything to reflect on the department").

These pressures do have some effect. Especially with noncolleagues, you become less likely to broadcast your research and, when you do, you tend to employ justifications far removed from your original scholarly motivation; in one instance, one of the authors found himself justifying his research on homosexuals in humanitarian terms ("it will help them"). Perhaps this problem is felt most of all in the face of questions from family members. For example, explaining to one's family of origin what one is doing can be awkward, and is often settled by obfuscation. Also, an account and justification for the research may be asked of members of one's family of procreation. In the course of an interview for a teaching position, one author's wife was asked what her husband was studying. The resulting answer caused quite a strain in the ensuing interaction with both parties attempting to conjure up justifications for the research in order to make the situation more comfortable. She obtained the job but also learned that, in the absence of an adequate "disclosure etiquette," she should remain silent about her husband's work. Thus, in the Application stage, the problems in social relations that arise from the subjects themselves regarding the question of the "why and what" of your research arise, albeit in different forms, with other people as well.

These problems can have important implications for the character of the data produced and consequent descriptions of the phenomena. For example, the manner in which entry is effected is a crucial determinant of the type of description that is produced. This is because the observer can get locked into a role or set of relationships that restrict where he goes, what he sees, and to whom he talks. A danger of the salesman role is that an organization may take it too seriously, so that the observer becomes committed to studying things he had never intended.

Outside of the research situation, as we mentioned, things are reversed—instead of selling research aims, one may mask the "true" research aims for fear (in deviance research) that the motivation will be called into question. Here lies another source of distortion in description: because of the felt approbation of others certain activities may not be observed, certain places may not be visited.

In conclusion, the way in which the researcher presents himself and his research in the Application stage is crucial for the character of the data he will obtain. Not only is his intended research constrained by a variety of social relations at the beginning, but the social reaction implicit in those constraints can significantly color his own attitude toward his endeavor.[6]

Orientation

The second stage—that of Orientation—covers the beginning of the actual fieldwork, when the researcher must attempt to get his bearings in what is in effect a new world. Two problems initially confront him: his *purpose,* and his *plan* for achieving this purpose. Certainly there are degrees to which a researcher is aware of his purpose or plan when he enters the field—in fact his reason for being in the field may be "exploratory," in the sense that it is to locate a research problem. Confrontation with any field situation, however, forces a researcher to focus his attention, to depress some aspects of the situation into the background so as to be attentive to other aspects. In Schutz's words, "the world seems to him at any given moment as stratified in different layers of relevance, each of them requiring a different degree of knowledge."[7] This is a difficult stage, and a sense of confusion is implicit in it. The researcher, no matter how complete he previously thought his plan was, usually feels directionless. It is not uncommon to experience yourself, and to have others view you, as "lost." With regard to this new situation, Schutz points out that "its remoteness changes into proximity; its vacant frames become occupied by vivid experiences; its anonymous contents turn into definite social situations; its ready-made typologies disintegrate."[8] Part of the mental exhaustion that is associated with this stage of fieldwork results from paying attention to details typically ignored in everyday life and from trying to organize them into a coherent picture.[9] What is of relevance to the researcher is, by necessity, different from what is relevant to an acclimated member of the group being studied, but perhaps not so different, except in its level of abstraction, from what is relevant to a new member. Thus, subjects generally see the researcher as a novice, and he feels himself to be a stranger: "Hence the stranger's . . . oscillating between remoteness and intimacy, his hesitation and uncertainty, and his distrust in every matter which seems to be so simple and uncomplicated to those who rely on the efficiency of unquestioned recipes which have just to be followed but not understood."[10]

In both the nudist and homosexual research, there was a question of what one could say or do without insulting the subjects. To what extent do you ignore the facts of life that lead you to study them? How do you determine the culture and social structure of the group without creating complications for the research? Among the dangers is that the researcher can get overly identified with the least accepted members of the group because they are most available for social engagement. One of the things that must always be avoided in the field is getting identified in terms of the clique structure; otherwise you will never be able to view the scene from any perspective but that of a particular clique, since others will be closed to you.[11]

The first day of the nudist study, for example, the researcher ended up spending too much time with an unmarried male who, it was later learned, was held in disrepute. The motive imputed to this nudist as well as to other single nudists, was of being there to look at other members' wives. In the early phases of fieldwork, when one feels most alone, it is easiest to associate with those held in disrepute who often feel similarly; so one learns to keep on the move and neither spend too much time with those whose company is most pleasureful nor avoid those whom one finds least amicable. Again, one struggles with the most natural tendencies in personal relations, in order to safeguard the objectivity of his view of the field situation.

With homosexuals, the same phenomena were salient. It is easier to get the perspective of the "middle-class" homosexual with whom the researcher finds it comfortable to interact than to share the world of the "bitchiest of queens." Again, one becomes most aware of the who and what of his interaction and his cataloguing of what is happening around him. It is experienced as a most unnatural form of interaction. While the Application stage is akin to "psyching out the bosses," the Orientation stage is more akin to "psyching out the scene," with the researcher experiencing himself more as subject than object (the opposite being true in the Application stage).

Although this stage is fraught with hesitancy and confusion in regard to relations with the subjects of the research, it is often the most enjoyable in regard to relations with others. This is because one can move into the role of "inside dopester"—the person in possession of knowledge of a group that tries to remain concealed from the public while systematically flouting its rules. In the eyes of other people, you have trod where few have trod before, and replacing the questioning of motives there generally ensues a rise in status. It is difficult not to overreact to such a situation. In truth, the early days of fieldwork are extremely confusing: Which of all the myriad observations are the important ones? Is there something important that perhaps is being missed? Whose story can be believed? How generalizable are your "findings"? All these doubts make for the depressing feeling that the "scene" is elusive, chaotic, and certainly beyond objective methodology. (This is the point when you most wish you had sent out a mailed questionnaire.) In the face of all this, it is comforting to be taken by outsiders as someone who really knows what is going on—the role of inside dopester offers temporary relief. So the role is often played with excursions into the field being followed by various "missionary tales" of the sights seen, blasé use being made of argot ("You don't know what a 'tea-room queen' is?"), and opportunities being taken to trade on one's limited knowledge.

Not only is one propelled into the role of inside dopester with regard to the particular form of deviance one is studying, but there are invitations to examine or participate in other forms of deviance. For example, on account of studying particular kinds of sexual deviants, we found ourselves being initiated into the sexual underground of one college town. In one case, we found ourselves being invited to see pornographic movies in the most "staid" of middle-class homes.

A researcher who studies deviants may also become the "odd ball" of his university department. For example, whenever a student wants to do a piece of research whose content is outside the conventional realm colleagues often say, in effect, "Oh! go and see X; he's interested in weirdos." One also can become instant copy for the local newspaper and radio station, finding oneself continually contacted to provide sensationalism for the mass media.[12]

To summarize, when entry is secured, the researcher must begin to orientate himself to this new world, and this process of orientation also can have implications for the data produced. The confusion that may exist for the researcher at this juncture can provide an important source of false description: in his confusion, the researcher may grasp any informant, as long as he can assist in providing some structure to the situation, or may visit and spend too much time in "safe" locales, for example, a homophile organization, comfortable gay bars, and so on, rather than sample other places where research subjects can be found. Orientation is a relatively short period compared to others, and the disorientation experienced by the researcher is usually warning enough to treat observations made at this time with caution; however, social psychology has taught us that first impressions can be lasting no matter how biased they may be. It is therefore crucial for the researcher to be aware of this problem.[13]

To allay the anxieties of first days in the field, the researcher may come to play what we call the "inside dopester" role. This may also propagate incorrect descriptions. The positive reaction toward a "missionary tale" by those foreign to the scene can function as subjective validation of that knowledge so that the observer comes to take as truth that which he himself created. Not that the observer sanctions outright lies, but the script he prepares for outsiders (often based on skimpy knowledge at this stage) can come to have a life of its own, albeit unwittingly. Again, the source of false description centers around the researcher's attempt to reduce the anxiety associated with his enterprise. Perhaps a general methodological rule at this point is to scrutinize that data most easily gathered while thinking afresh of those situations conducive of anxiety that might have been avoided.

Initiation

In the third stage—that of Initiation—the researcher again experiences himself as an object, being constantly tested by the subjects with regard to any number of things, but especially his acceptance of them. As in Application, the researcher becomes a strategist in how best to make himself accountable. The "bosses" may have accepted him; now he must prove himself to the "masses." He only has probationary status.

In the nudist camp an initial test was undressing. Since, on the first day, the researcher was introduced as such to the membership, he did not think to undress. This was the first test explicitly put to him. A further test was whether he would bring his wife to camp, if he was married, or a girl friend, if he was not married. Being continually under test, he usually replied more or less honestly depending on the judged efficiency of the tactic. When the researcher explained that he did not have a girl friend that he knew well enough to ask (a lie), but would if he had, this got him off the hook. Later, the researcher learned that this was a good strategy, since the members did not want just "anyone" brought to the camp but only someone with whom one was highly involved.

With the homosexuals the test was less severe. Some questioned our ability to understand homosexuality or homosexuals without having a homosexual experience. But we sensed that they knew we were not gullible enough to buy this as a test, and that it was a tactful script in case we happened to be in the market for a homosexual experience. At homosexual parties refusing to dance even "fast dances" proved to be a more difficult evasion, since it is less obviously "homosexual." One of us avoided it primarily due to concerns of what "others would make of it." He found it most expedient to simply reply that "he didn't dance," although verbal pressure often followed. When the other author agreed to "rock," he was then put in the position of having to refuse to remain on the dance floor for the "slow dance" that followed.

At this point, one can feel a great alienation toward his subjects, and research can often terminate if the researcher decides to "lose his cool." Satisfying as it might be, telling a subject to "fuck off" can jeopardize one's research. Negative consequences have not followed, however, in those cases where subjects have had to be dealt with firmly. The researchers were understood by most subjects to be accepting of their practices and sure enough of their true feelings as not to have to be patronizing. The fact that the subjects who give researchers the most trouble are often those who are often least accepted by the group, because of their difficulties with others, can reinforce empathy and support for the researcher. It is, however, important, especially in a bounded setting (a small group to which you are limited for your research), not to alienate *anyone* so as to lose their position as a point of perspective.

During the Initiation stage of the nudist study, the researcher was asked to present a lecture in the nude for Sunday morning services. This went along with other requests (or expectations) to "help out." In effect, the lecture was honest enough in conveying the researcher's true feelings toward the subjects to bring to an end what had been an arduous period of initiation. Obvious tests of the researcher's acceptance of nudists ceased.

As well as initiation tests by one's subjects, there are sometimes efforts by other people to test your expert knowledge or to further shake you in the role of deviance researcher.[14] The role style of the inside dopester is coolness—a detached urbanity mixed with slight contempt for the outsider who has not been "there." It is not surprising that, in the face of such a stance, attempts are made to shake the "expert." These attempts are often a continuation of the jibes met at Application—now, instead of "You're studying homosexuals because of your latent homosexuality," it is "I guess you have a lot of sexual opportunities hanging around those guys." The content is different, but the form the same—an attempt to deal with their own discomfort and/or to call your status into question.

The problem, as with the subjects themselves, is one of acceptance, though in this case in a different guise. With subjects it is generally one's authentic self you want accepted—the person accepting and tolerant of them—whereas with other people it is more often an inauthentic self that is presented—the person who is already an expert. (This is the reverse of the Application stage.) Successful acceptance, however, has different results depending on one's audience. With the subjects such role acceptance is a welcome stage, whereas with other people it can have unsought consequences.

For example, there are requests to be taken to "gay bars" or be shown the "scene." These present problems in showing that your information is not, on the one hand, terribly esoteric or, on the other hand, terribly complete. In addition, there is the possible threat to one's standing in the deviant group at a time when you are carefully building up important relationships among the subjects. From our experiences, we feel that our research involved problems of probation almost as much from other people as from the deviants themselves. (It can be argued that becoming deviant, for real, involves this double-barreled initiation in many instances.) As an example of this, we found that any "conventional" person can, by word or gesture, call one's status into question just on the basis of knowledge of the research. They feel "morally ahead" and sometimes take the opportunity to show it. We have never ceased to be amazed at the slights and innuendos that come from the most casual of acquaintances when they learn of our research. It is at this stage that the attempt to shed the inside dopester role begins; one is less blasé and boastful; one shares that annoying problem faced by many deviants—knownaboutness.

A second aspect of this stage in relating to others is the counterpart of the problem faced in relating to the subjects. It will be remembered that it is quite possible to become alienated toward subjects who are testing you. The expression of frustration often takes the form of talking down one's "tribe" to others, of criticizing them in public; often one comes to believe that negative stereotypes have a basis in reality ("homosexuals *are* flighty and irresponsible"). Voicing this criticism represents a reversal from the Orientation stage (but not such a change from the Application stage). Both these problems—the reactions of other people and a more negative appraisal of one's subjects—are fairly strong pressures to retreat from the inside dopester role.

Sources of false description also occur in the Initiation stage. A typical test, for example, involves being presented with "false facts" or misrepresentations in order not only to determine one's knowledge of the scene, but also one's acceptance of it. Such "put ons" are not always inspired by malice; rather, they parallel "sounding," in finding out about the other (in this case, the researcher), so as to structure or terminate further interaction. The obvious danger here, of course, is to take such presentations as representative of something other than what they are.

The tests that come from persons outside of the research situation, we have suggested, are instrumental in the researcher's desire to leave the inside dopester role. A process *opposite* to that which affects descriptions when taking on the role can sometimes occur when the role begins to be divested (with as biasing an effect): as certain presentations one might utilize are challenged by others, it is possible that the researcher, during this period, comes to doubt other of his descriptions that might be less biased. A contributing factor is the sense of alienation toward one's subjects that is characteristic of this stage—observations that reflect positive aspects of one's respondents may be bracketed, whereas negative ones may be highlighted.

Assimilation

The period between Initiation and Assimilation (sometimes a substantial period of time) is usually the easiest. The problems are mainly practical ones, and the research becomes a matter of course.

As the research continues, however, the researcher often becomes socialized to the way of life of his subjects. If the researcher realizes this, it can be a revealing stage, prompting him to go back to his early field notes to check his prior perspective. Objectivity drifts when one becomes "a true believer," and the researcher can be surprised by the realization of how far he has taken over the perspective of his subjects.[15]

This was brought home to the researcher in the nudist research when an unmarried male had an erection while observing a camp beauty contest. Although the researcher had entered camp thinking this to be a natural, rather than unnatural, type of response (and in fact had written about the power of resocialization to the most taken-for-granted of views), he now found himself responding as a true believer—this person was some kind of "pervert" who had the wrong motivations for being in camp (which he knew many people initially had). A hostile private interview followed to find out "why and how" this erection could have occurred. When the researcher realized what had happened to his own thinking, there was a more profound realization of the linkage between mind and society.

The homosexual research provides another example: the authors found themselves at one point in a "confessional" with another researcher of homosexuals (all of us having scored as "exclusive heterosexuals" on the Kinsey scale) expressing concern that it was easier than we had thought to be socialized to homosexuality. In spite of having all supported the position of polymorphous sexuality, the first realization that we ourselves could be, for example, "turned on" by reading "gay novels" or watching a movie of homosexuals having sex, or that we could "understand" the scene, was a surprise. As a result of Assimilation, the researcher can become, at this stage, a staunch defender of his "tribe," while during Initiation and Application his frustration may have led him to take a more hostile stance.[16]

Becoming a "true believer" can also make the researcher feel that he is accepted by his subjects—after all, he can see the world the way they do. Despite this, and perhaps also despite his staunch defense of their way of life, it has been our experience that *complete* acceptance does not follow. Secrets may be shared, friendships may be built, but generally the researcher is not really "one of them." Rather, in the eyes of his subjects he is a "limbo member"—a role that involves the expectation of desertion in a crisis, for example, police raids, newspaper exposés, and so on. If the researcher is honest with himself and if he does not go completely native, he should realize that limbo membership is the most he generally can obtain. (We carry our own "thirty pieces of silver" in the form of identification cards that state our association with the Institute for Sex Research. We would be less than honest not to admit the comfort—whether warranted or not!—that such identification gives in that it immediately shows that, after all, we are not what we might be taken to be. It is a convenient passport back to the respectable world, a passport not enjoyed by our subjects.) At this point, therefore, when the researcher has all the data he needs, a recognition of socialization may lead him to decide to either truly "become a native" or enter into the Cessation stage. To our knowledge most researchers opt for the latter.

In relating to other people, the opposite of what happens at the Orientation-Initiation stages often takes place at the Assimilation stage. As a result of routinization, instead of trading on one's knowledge, an attempt may be made to hide it. Instead of seeking an audience to relate the latest "missionary tale" to, there may be no motivation to tell anything; in fact, there is nothing to tell, as what was once bizarre is now commonplace and "understood." Now it is others who seek you out to talk on this, to explain that. What was once an expedition into uncharted lands is now just a job and, like most jobs, routine, so that one avoids discussing the scene with other people. It is possible to find oneself taking the attitude of one's subjects toward "straights" and the "straight life"; at least the slights of others become less of a personal concern. As mentioned previously, one may become a staunch defender of his particular deviant group when the topic is imposed, whether the justifications are really believed or not.

Another occurrence at this stage is that social relationships can take on new meanings as one's knowledge increases. In terms of our research, there was a realization that there are more people who are homosexual than we had thought. It was also surprising to find out that particular persons were homosexual. For example, one of the authors received unsolicited evidence of the homosexuality of a colleague, which led to some hesitancy in discussing the research with him, as well as voicing "complaints" about our subject. This exemplifies the type of knowledge that one can unwillingly acquire and that can affect relationships with others.

Other instances also concern disclosures. Many people whom we did not know were homosexual disclosed their homosexuality to us, for example, through offers of help in the research. These experiences made us very careful of what we said about homosexuals to other, ostensibly straight, people. During the Assimilation stage we became less likely to talk down our "tribe" not only because of changed feelings toward them, but also because of increased awareness that we did not know who was a secret deviant or an affiliate of one.

In conclusion, being assimilated into the world of one's subjects and seeing things through their eyes, while being an important research aim, paradoxically also provides the greatest source of false description of any of the stages we have outlined. The taking over of deviant ideologies can undermine dispassionate description, can make important factors become routine and be neglected, and so on. What occurs is that the researcher can become insulated from any challenge to his descriptions, which now have a taken-for-granted status. Withdrawing from the inside dopester role also removes an important source of challenge in that different perspectives far removed from the field situation are not brought to bear on the field data. There are many other sources of bias at this stage, but we feel enough has been said by other writers on this aspect of observational studies to make further comments unnecessary.[17]

Cessation

In many ways Cessation is like a reversal of the Initiation stage, with some of the same sense of frustration. To some subjects, the completion of the research symbolizes a renunciation of their way of life. Disengagement can be more or less difficult depending on the extensity and intensity of the relationships. In general, the greater the extensity (that is, the more subjects and territories) and the less the intensity (that is, the diffuseness and totality of the personal relationships), the easier it is to disengage. In the homosexual and nudist projects, the homosexual project had the greater extensity and lesser intensity. Thus, the nudist project provided more difficulties of disengagement.

Part of the personal involvement in fieldwork can also include the structuring of a role for the researcher as "trusted confidant." Almost independent of personality, the confidentiality of his communications with subjects leads many to seek him out with their personal problems. Although a researcher may try to avoid the role of clinician, he may still accept it to some extent because of the data that comes with it. When hearing the complaints one person has about others, he gets an even more profound sense of the norms of the group. While he must avoid taking sides, his understanding can lead to a funneling of many of the covert types of information that he would never obtain. It was this role and an attempt to leave it that provided one of the problems of disengagement from the nudists. Phone calls would come at all hours of the night from people who wanted to talk to someone who "would understand their problems with other nudists."

The other main problem was the concern of nudists as to whether the researcher would become a nudist now that the research was over? Or, had he just simulated an attachment to the subjects to use them for research? Again, tests came regarding an acceptance of them and their way of life. After trying to explain a lack of interest in becoming a member of a nudist camp because of other leisure time activities and involvements, the researcher finally had his phone number unlisted. To this day nudists with whom the researcher is still in contact report that the speculations of insecure people still go on as to whether the researcher really loved them!

A further problem that arises is the demand to see the "results" of the research—what you have to say about the subject. The problem is usually in direct proportion to how the Application stage was handled. If one has been profligate in his promises, then the research results will show it. A glance at the published report will tell the subjects that they have harbored an untrustworthy person among them. Of course, this need not present a problem to an unscrupulous researcher who does not intend to research among a particular group again once he has his data. For most researchers, though, we assume that the subjects' responses to the report(s) are a concern.[18]

In our case, we have never been too specific over research aims (working in sex research has made this almost mandatory, since the word *does* get around) and so have avoided such crises. We have also tried to pay our dues by lecturing and acting as consultants to our subjects and by providing them with summaries of our results.

It is still an uneasy situation, however. For one thing, one is sometimes publishing facets of the subjects' lives that are most familiar to them. This again reinforces sanguine views of sociology (in a very real way it is just the stating of commonsense to them) which again can lead to the questioning of competence. A second source of unease is the publication of results that are contrary to cherished belief(s) held by the subjects. There is often the assumption held by many deviants that any research is good because it will bring the true facts about them before the public eye. When the results do not support their ideology or present them in a light that is bad for purposes of public relations, they tend to feel betrayed. One runs the risk of becoming a *bête noire* in their legends. (We had evidence of this during the Application stage also. Attempting entry among one particular group of homosexuals, one of the authors was asked what he thought of Evelyn Hooker's work. After replying that he admired it, he was refused permission to research the group on the grounds that she had published an article on how to prevent boys from becoming homosexual, a goal with which the group was not in sympathy.)

It is difficult but always possible to cease one's relationships with deviant subjects; however it is difficult but often impossible to cease being or having been a deviance researcher in the eyes of other people. One is always someone who is in possession of esoteric, somewhat salacious knowledge, a knowledge that is impossible to renounce. Especially after publication of the research, people put you in the role of expert—it is similar to facets of past stages except that now you know (and often admit to yourself) the limitations of your knowledge. Not only do people assume that you know more about the particular deviance than you do (we have been criticized for not knowing various psychological studies of homosexuals), but that you are an expert on other forms of deviant behavior (we have been asked to discuss cures for juvenile delinquency, and so on).

With regard to specific knowledge, one's knowledge may perhaps have been true a few years ago, but may since be outdated, for, as time goes by, the scene changes. In a situation like this it is easy to be unmasked by someone who has just entered the field that you had finished cultivating eons past in social time. The dilemma at this stage is one of temptation to play the role of expert ("after all, perhaps we do know more about these things than a lot of people") versus admitting ignorance of certain things. It is sometimes a difficult decision; no one wants to appear ignorant. However, we have found honesty to be the best as well as the most practical stance—it makes life less complicated.

The decision to cease observing a particular deviant group can affect its description. Are observations complete or does premature closure exist? Has the group been observed in all its situations and at enough different times? This is essentially a sampling decision that should have been made before entering the field, although on many occasions things are discovered that the investigator had not been aware of. Nonetheless, the researcher must eventually decide to end his data-gathering and begin his write-up.

Descriptions also may be affected by the successfulness of the socialization that occurred in the previous phase, there being no more opportunity for perceptions made at that stage to be modified.[19] Furthermore, debts incurred at early stages may be called in, so that the researcher finds that relationships that were carefully built up inhibit the use of certain data. Some researchers find themselves negotiating with their subjects both over the results and their publication.[20]

The researcher's being pressured into the role of expert by other people also has effects on the descriptions produced. For example, field notes are returned to and one's observations reinterpreted to fit symposia or reflect on theories that they were not designed for.[21]

Therefore, it might be near the truth to state that, in relating to both subjects and others, the researcher never wholly completes the Cessation stage. One becomes prey to a reputation that can be constructed above and apart from one's own desires and have consequences that are often unsought.

Conclusion

It is impossible to provide the student with a detailed set of rules whereby he may profitably structure his relationships while researching deviants. To do so implies a knowledge of certain facets of relationships which the research itself ostensibly seeks. At the same time, however, we feel that some general rules can be presented with regard to the researcher's social relations with both subjects and others at the various stages of research covered in this essay.

APPLICATION

Relations with Subjects: Don't promise (or intimate) what you can't (or don't intend) to deliver.

Relations with Others: There is no "illegitimate" area of study. Researchers must be willing to disregard conventional attitudes toward sensitive topics and have the courage to remain unashamed.

ORIENTATION

Relations with Subjects: Don't be discouraged by the first days in the field; be skeptical of what you see and hear at first. As first impressions, though lasting, are sometimes incorrect, the validity of field notes and observations at this stage should be carefully considered.

Relations with Others: Don't be defensive. Don't try to impress others, thereby disseminating impressions that may be invalid. Validation by most outside the field is worthless.

INITIATION

Relations with Subjects: Don't be shaken by the tests you may encounter from your subjects. It is natural for any group to test a newcomer; don't take it personally. Remember that such tests are often given to gauge your reactions.

Relations with Others: Again, have the courage of your convictions.

ASSIMILATION

Relations with Subjects: You are unlikely to be as accepted as you feel you are (or feel you ought to be) by your subjects; nor should you expect to be. Remember what you are there for; your subjects will.

Relations with Others: Don't cease from talking about your research at this stage. Questions and criticisms from those outside the field can help to jar the set you have about your data. Go back to your earlier field notes and see how your perspective has changed.

CESSATION

Relations with Subjects: Prepare your departure from the field; pay your debts to your subjects in whatever way you can to ensure a smooth transition from the field. Plan to have some further contact with them (if only in the form of a summary of your report), and let them know that you have planned this.

Relations with Others: Be honest as to what you know and the limitations of your knowledge. Avoid the temptation to embellish and generalize upon what is often scanty knowledge. If you accept the role of expert, keep up to date, go back to the field, and don't let the scene elude you.

Finally, it is easy to forget that you are not simply dealing with "subjects" and "others," but with people. It is easy and natural to dehumanize people in reacting to the problems they provide for the research. This ignores the essential humanness from which these conflicts spring, an important factor in creating those stages we have outlined.[22]

Notes

1. Richard N. Adams and Jack Preiss (eds.), *Human Organization Research* (Homewood, Ill.: Dorsey Press, 1960), pp. 3–10, provide an overview of fieldwork problems. For a detailed treatment of some of the more basic problems, see Aaron Cicourel, *Method and Measurement in Sociology* (New York: Free Press, 1964), pp. 39–72. For other classification of the phases of fieldwork roles, see Robert W. Janes, "A Note on Phases of the Community Role of the Participant Observer," *American Sociological*

Review, 26 (1961), 446–450, and Rosalie Hankey Wax, "Twelve Years Later: An Analysis of Field Experience," *American Journal of Sociology,* 63 (1957), 133–142.

2. Sociologists differ on the point of how much to tell the subjects about the research. Morris Schwartz and Charlotte Schwartz, "Problems in Participant Observation," *American Journal of Sociology,* 60 (1955), 343–354, warn of the danger that the subject may "produce" data for the investigator in accordance with his perception of what the latter wants. However, Anselm Strauss *et al., Psychiatric Ideologies and Institutions* (New York: Free Press, 1964), p. 27, suggest that it is often useful to tell subjects about the propositions in the study in order to get information for counter evidence.

3. On making the research meaningful to the subjects, see Chris Argyris, "Creating Effective Relationships in Organizations," *Human Organization,* 17 (1958), 34–40, and Stephen A. Richardson, "A Framework for Interpreting Field-Relations Experiences," *Human Organization,* 12 (1953), 31–37.

4. By this we mean tracking another person onto a particular sequence of interactions that progressively constrict alternate behaviors for him. Eric Berne, *Games People Play* (New York: Grove Press, 1964), describes the psychological dynamics of a number of such games. Here, we are referring more to social dynamics and obtaining a view of what is behind linguistic utterances.

5. Laud Humphreys, "Tearoom Trade: Impersonal Sex in Public Places," *Trans-action,* 7 (1970), 15, speaks of the "Sociologist as Voyeur" and counsels that the "... social scientist should [n]ever ignore or avoid an area of research simply because it is difficult or socially sensitive."

6. An important early discussion on the personal problems associated with fieldwork that has implications for deviant and nondeviant subjects is Schwartz and Schwartz, *op. cit.* For a recent, extremely candid account of what it feels like to sell oneself, see Herbert J. Gans, "The Participant-Observer as a Human Being: Observations on the Personal Aspects of Fieldwork," in Howard S. Becker *et al.* (eds.), *Institutions and the Person* (Chicago: Aldine, 1968). Some good general rules to follow in the Application stage are provided by John P. Dean *et al.,* "Establishing Field Relations," in John T. Doby (ed.), *An Introduction to Social Research* (New York: Meredith, 1967), pp. 281–283.

7. Alfred Schutz, *Collected Papers, Vol. II: Studies in Social Theory,* ed. Arvid Brodersen (The Hague: Nijhoff, 1964), p. 93.

8. *Ibid.,* p. 98.

9. The anxieties at this stage, for example, not being sure that one will be in the right place at the right time, having difficulty understanding what's going on, and being overwhelmed by the mass of data, are discussed by Gans, *op. cit.,* pp. 312–313.

10. Schutz, *op. cit.,* p. 103.

11. Many researchers warn against partisan identification in the early stages of fieldwork. See Rosalie Hankey Wax, "Reciprocity as a Field Technique," *Human Organization,* 11 (1952), 34–41; John Gullahorn and George Strauss, "The Fieldworker in Union Research," *Human Organization,* 13 (1954), 28–32; and Dean *et al., op. cit.* Robert L. Kahn and Floyd Mann, "Developing Research Partnerships," *Journal of Social Issues,* 8 (1952), 4–10, suggest "multiple entry" to all groups at the same time in the study of organizations.

12. For a discussion of relationships with the mass media, especially on being asked for "juicy copy," see Lee Rainwater and David J. Pittman, "Ethical Problems in Studying a Politically Sensitive and Deviant Community," *Social Problems*, 14 (1967), 357–366.

13. Blanche Geer, "First Days in the Field," in Phillip E. Hammond (ed.), *Sociologists at Work* (New York: Basic Books, 1964), pp. 322–344, warns that early fieldwork, though presenting little data, has important effects for the rest of the study. Strategies and concepts, especially, change, and these changes can transform a study completely.

14. Very little was found in the literature on this phenomenon and its influence on observations.

15. Gans talks at length on the problems of "overidentification" and involvement. He suggests that "unconscious elements of [the researcher's] personality enter into his study and into the relationships he forms during fieldwork." As this can bias his results, "...it may be wise for every participant observer *to spend some time on the analytic couch*" (Gans, *op. cit.*, p. 308; our italics). While agreeing with the effects of personality on fieldwork, we suggest that the identification that occurs, rather than being unconscious and "bad," is rather part and parcel of what Harold Garfinkel, "Studies of the Routine Grounds of Everyday Activities," *Social Problems*, 11 (1964), 225–250, calls the "seen but unnoticed" background features of interaction, which hardly require a psychoanalyst to elucidate.

16. Gans attributes identification partially to the fact that the researcher *is* a spy, acting dishonestly and deceiving his respondents. This makes "...the fieldworker both guilty and sorry for the people he is studying, and, in partial recompense, he identifies with them, taking their troubles to heart, and sometimes even accepting the validity of their causes" (Gans, *op. cit.*, p. 315). This is especially the case, he warns, with underdogs.

17. Many writers recognize the phenomenon of "going native." Cf. Raymond L. Gold, "Roles in Sociological Field Observations," *Social Forces*, 36 (1958), 217–223; Arthur J. Vidich, "Participant Observation and the Collection and Interpretation of Data," *American Journal of Sociology*, 60 (1955), 354–360; S. M. Miller, "The Participant Observer and 'Over-Rapport,'" *American Sociological Review*, 17 (1952), 97–99. George McCall, "Data Quality Control in Participant Observation," in George McCall and Jerry Simmons (eds.), *Issues in Participant Observation* (Reading, Mass.: Addison-Wesley, 1969), p. 133, suggests as a check on this to compare observations at earlier and later stages of the research.

18. The general problems of this stage are discussed by Becker. He notes that bargains made in the initial stages of fieldwork are often, of necessity, breached as the problems studied change throughout the project. He also states that conflicts over the results are usually unavoidable, so that the problem becomes not whether to harm but which people to harm. Howard S. Becker, "Problems in the Publication of Field Studies," in Arthur J. Vidich, Joseph Bensman, and Maurice R. Stein (eds.), *Reflections on Community Studies* (New York: Wiley, 1964), pp. 267–284.

19. This may affect the style of the write-up, which determines the picture provided by the report. Erving Goffman, for example, because of the satiric style of his book *Asylums: Essays on the Social Situation of Mental Patients and Other Inmates* (Garden City, N.Y.: Anchor Books, 1961), has been called the Charles Dickens of social science. See Severyn Bruyn,

The Human Perspective in Sociology: The Methodology of Participant Observation (Englewood Cliffs, N.J.: Prentice-Hall, 1966), pp. 244 ff.

20. The rights and obligations of sponsorship are discussed by Rainwater and Pittman, *op. cit.* They also comment upon the effects of publishing findings, especially the timing of publication and what can be done with the results by other people.

21. Schwartz and Schwartz, *op. cit.,* note that observations are continually being evaluated. They refer, for example, to "retrospective observation," showing how what happens between the event and its recording affects the re-creation of what really happened.

22. Schwartz and Schwartz, *op. cit.,* p. 347, comment:

> ... it is essential that [the researcher] recognize the importance of participating with the observed on a "simply human" level—relating with them not only in his specific formal role, but also in terms of the sentiments Cooley described as constituting the core of human nature. He must share these sentiments and feelings with the observed on a sympathetic and empathetic level. Thus the observer and the observed are bound together through sharing the common role of human being.... Through this type of simply human interaction, the psychological distance between observer and subject may be diminished and restraint in communication reduced....

Observing a Crowd: The Structure and Description of Protest Demonstrations

Charles S. Fisher

Collective behavior is often treated by sociologists as a residual category. To it they assign events whose forms are difficult to describe and whose contents are threatening to a stable social order.[1] Because of its amorphous character, most sociologists are hesitant to teach it as a distinct subject matter and are ill at ease with the term.[2] A few notable exceptions provide frameworks in which to study collective behavior, but these proponents fail to carry through in any systematic way detailed descriptions and analyses of those groups that lie at the heart of collective behavior—that is, crowds.[3]

Without embarking on an elaborate intellectual history, it is clear that most persons who have written about crowds and collective behavior have done so either as elite critics of the "mob" or as pseudoscientific experts in the direct or indirect employ of agents of social control.[4] Rarely have the authors of either category been proponents of social change or participants in the events under study, and the perspectives with which both sociological conservatives and outsiders are endowed radically skew their reports and analyses.[5] Despite Merton's unctuous Introduction to Le Bon's famous book, the work is a jaundiced portrayal of crowds by a man whose political opposition to and lack of familiarity with the behavior of persons in crowds made his descriptions fanciful and his abstractions disembodied.[6]

Attempts to explain collective behavior with the aid of academically imposed categories[7] have resulted in the view of crowds as undifferentiated entities under the sway of any pervasive forces. The word "crowd" itself is pregnant with frightening connotations. Crowds are assigned collective mentalities that are deviant, irrational, primitive, animal. Members of crowds are helpless victims of demagoguery and contagion.[8] In the social order, crowds act as hiatuses, which then threaten to become destructive mobs. Imagery of this kind is typical of reporters who are nonmembers of the events they portray.[9] Events are painted in terms of grossly defined descriptive categories which neither distinguish subtle variations nor give hints of the manifold ways in which crowds are assembled.[10] Such reports and the theories which inform them are intellectually sustainable only if the tradition in which they are embedded is carried on by persons who are either isolated from or bear a similar relation to the events that are the subjects of their reports.[11]

The professional sociological blinders which made LeBon seem other than an historical oddity are now rapidly losing their authority. With the decay of former pieties of professionalism and the emergence of participants themselves within the academic community, ideas about collective behavior are undergoing radical changes.[12]

Beginning with the Free Speech Movement (FSM) at Berkeley and the several hundred university "crises" that followed, colleges have become veritable laboratories of collective behavior. Sociologists whose claim to science rested on their disdain for action have found themselves thrust into the midst of chaos. Rather than trying to describe the events on their doorsteps, many over-thirty sociologists have, in the name of science, engaged in discrediting the student dissidents.[13] The extent of the generational differences in views of campus unrest is symbolized by confrontations that have occurred between sociologists and some of their graduate students in places like Wisconsin, Columbia, Berkeley, Chicago, and Harvard. Stemming from deep political differences, these occasional strikes and shouting matches are also indicative of the varying perspectives that derive from different relationships to events. The policeman's club in Harvard Yard, while inducing temporary dizziness, also engenders a student's view of the events that is quite at variance with a faculty member's view of the same events from a chair at a faculty meeting.[14] With the entrance of former student protesters into the ranks of professional sociology, a radically new view of much of the discipline will emerge. This should be particularly true of studies of collective behavior, where an intimate personal experience is helping forge new intellectual categories.[15]

This article is an attempt to construct a framework for an emerging sociointellectual tradition. On the basis of my experiences as both a participant in and an observer of collective events in San Francisco, Berkeley, New York, Boston, and Chicago, I discuss the *microecological structure of protest demonstrations* and how this structure necessarily conditions the ways in which the content of occasions can be known. I also comment on the relationship between descriptions of complex events and attempts to control them. Some of the concepts developed here can be generalized to other kinds of crowds, while many are peculiar to the semiritual of a protest demonstration. The points made about the ways in which events come to be known seem to me to be basic to all social description whether done by the actors themselves or by a social scientist. I have divided the discussion into four sections: The Objective Features of a Demonstration; Perceptions of Crowding and Danger; The Subjective Nature of Descriptions of Demonstrations; and The Duality of Description and Control.

The Objective Features of a Demonstration

In their searches for a consistent and uniform language to describe observations of social life, men such as Hall, Harris, Lundberg, Goodenough, Sacks, and Garfinkel have created ambiences in which to analyze the microecological structures of behavior.[16] In this section I assume a stance similar to theirs and put forward an objective description of some structural features of protest demonstrations.

To begin, an understanding of the complexities of crowds rests upon an examination of those aspects which are "out of awareness" or "not worth the telling."[17] It is exactly their triviality which leads to their not being reported. Actors take it for granted that the listener has experienced and is familiar with the minutiae that go to make up such descriptions as, "The store certainly was mobbed." Of course, since most listeners have not participated in crowds or lynchings, a reporter of these events assumes that his listener will borrow analogies like "mobbed store" in order to make the report intelligible and meaningful. This method of telling and listening covers the variations of "out of awareness" features that make an occasion a crowd rather than a social gathering. Distance between members, the arrangement of persons, the use of space, all go to make up the character of the event.

Demonstrations, almost by definition, are nonroutine, statistically deviant, unstable, evolving occasions. Their extraordinary character necessitates the development of more complex descriptive apparatus than is required to illustrate the ecology of static events. In addition, demonstrations are loci of historical conflict and thereby events whose outcomes have serious consequences for the participants. Hence, their microecological structure is most often (rightfully) ignored in the battle for larger stakes. The vocabulary I use to describe demonstrations leans heavily on dramaturgical and biological metaphor in the spirit of

Goffman.[18] Like Goffman, it employs the minimum necessary social psychology. In the discussion that follows, demonstrations are taken as accomplished facts—that is, a demonstration exists by reason of the fact that it disrupts the normal flow of business in a place. An examination is made of a temporal cross section of such disruptions. There is no discussion of the formation and dissipation of crowds. Nor is there any attempt to explain *how* they come to be or *why* people behave as they do in such situations. I will engage in mere description. When not explicitly documented, the evidence on which the analysis rests is derived from firsthand observations recorded in field notes and a series of papers written either immediately after or within a few days of the occurrence of the demonstration.[19]

SPACE AND ITS USE

The most primitive ecological category is physical space. From a bird's eye view, demonstrations can be conceived of as taking place within a *container*.[20] This container is the physical setting in which the relevant events occur. At a civil rights demonstration in the Sheraton-Palace Hotel in San Francisco in 1964, the T-shaped walls of the lobby represented physically inelastic boundaries, whereas Michigan Avenue in Chicago, the scene of the 1968 Democratic Convention protests, was bounded on one side by buildings with streets between them and on the other three sides by wide boulevards and an open park. A container may be composed of elements of fixed-feature space,[21] and these elements may acquire a certain routinized use; for example, a hotel lobby or a commercial thoroughfare. By its mere existence, a demonstration redefines the use of, and in a nonroutine way creates a new set of movements within, the container. Contrariwise, variations in containers set limits on the ways in which demonstration events can occur.

Maintaining the bird's eye or helicopter's view, we can distinguish *arenas* in which the action takes place. An arena may be literal, as in the Berkeley case, when FSM leader Mario Savio was dragged off the stage of the Greek Theatre before a crowd of 10,000 people.[22] Here the container—that is, the theater itself—provided for an arrangement of persons commonly oriented toward and, when the outraged audience surged forward, engaged in action. More often arenas are compounded out of the arrangement of the persons themselves. Blocking the entrances to the Sheraton-Palace Hotel, demonstrators sat in tight-knit, semicircular clumps that became arenas into which police, coming through the doorways to drag the demonstrators out, introjected themselves.

In both cases, the focus of attention became a *stage* on which interesting and reportable events took place. Such arrangements of people can be termed *focused* arenas.[23] The stage may be literal, as in the Greek Theatre incident, or it may be the central space formed within a group of people who, for example, are watching a policeman subdue and remove a disorderly person. Focus is created in a number of ways. At night, a penumbra of light from buildings tends to demark the limits of the potential stage. In the dark, TV lights also create dramatic foci. As blue ribbon commissions and police manuals point out, our media-besotted, spectacle-hungry public becomes immediately alerted to the possibility of action by the presence or sudden operation of news paraphernalia.[24] Police feel that these foci generate many unwanted instances of collective behavior. Similarly, noise and rapid movement of crowd members can create foci.[25]

An interesting characteristic of demonstrations is that they tend to be *serially multi-focused*. Main events spontaneously give way to new foci, for while most members attend to the main show, secondary foci attract attention in other parts of the gathering. The removal of a counter-demonstrator is a typical secondary focus.

Because foci are multiple and unstable, leaders often lose their stages. In Boston, for example, a self-proclaimed Polish Freedom Fighter who is a chronic counterdemonstrator is often able to steal the stage. He carries a large sign on which is inscribed red warnings against the Jewish Communist Conspiracy. He frequently places himself between a speaker and the audience and carries on a loud uninterrupted stream of talk.[26]

Another technique for creating a new focus is to create a rival stage. When, from a table top, a leader was trying to discuss strategy with her fellow demonstrators occupying the Sheraton-Palace, a man in a business suit climbed upon a table at the other end of the lobby and argued for leaving the hotel. He was not heeded, but for a moment he seriously threatened the leader's stage.

Heckling is yet another way of creating a new focus. Usually, the heckler intends merely to destroy the stage. This happens if the heckling creates sufficient distraction. Hecklers take advantage of the anonymity derived from being buried in the crowd. They also create foci and therefore risk becoming rival stages.

Arenas need not be focused. A typical picket line defines where the demonstration action is without orienting the participants and onlookers toward a common stage. Picketers converse among themselves and continually change the object of their attention. Onlookers attend to that section of the picket line which is immediately in front of them. The picket line itself is a stage, and the arrangement of onlookers surrounding the picket line forms an audience attending the same show. This defines the arena, but since there is no common point of attention, many more diverse reports can be expected than if the stage were focused.

Returning to an overview of a demonstration, we can distinguish a certain texture, or feeling, that is familiar to all crowds. For instance, the presence of a crowd can be detected from quite a distance. In a special sense, crowds *pollute*[27] the surrounding environment. Among the indicators of the presence of a crowd is an abnormal flow of people in one general direction. This phenomenon can be quite subtle. It is especially marked when an observer is walking parallel to the crowd, for then he becomes aware that lots (even though they are few in number) of people are crossing his path. (This, by the way, is also a way of locating a crowd. As in finding a hidden gun emplacement, only two sitings are needed.)

Other signs of the presence of a crowd are an abnormal number of policemen either directing traffic or just waiting around outside the area of the crowd ready for action. Such a presence of policemen was dramatically noticeable in Chicago during the 1968 Democratic Convention. The extraordinary movements of police in quiet residential neighborhoods and the visible gathering of police were indicators that there was or would be action somewhere in the city. Using a military metaphor, if the police are going to do battle, they have to bring up their forces. And one of the rules of crowd control is to never show your hand until the right moment.[28] Hence, for a crowd observer, an examination of what the police are doing *behind the scenes* is an indicator of what they intend to do. For instance, a cursory inspection that I made of a fire station near the Harvard Yard gave me a great deal of information as to when and how arrests of student protesters occupying the Harvard administration building were to be made. While assemblage of police forces, insofar as it is outside the arena, is behind the scenes from the viewpoint of a demonstrator, it is pollution of environment from the point of view of nonparticipants who usually use the area.

Demonstrators on their way to a rally also pollute the surrounding environment. Whether the demonstrators be hippies, John Birchers, or Women's International Terrorist Conspirators from Hell (WITCH), the presence of distinguishable persons who are not routinely part of the environment indicates that something is happening. In Chicago, during the summer of 1968, one had only to follow the beards to find the action. Persons such as hippies, when they invade an area, constitute a threat to the environment, and people who routinely use thoroughfares in the area often react to an invasion of hippies as if the hippies were human garbage and a real cause of pollution.

From a point of view closer to the center of action, crowds exhibit graduated but distinct *edges*. Hall puts the distance between members of a crowd somewhere in the range of 0 to 2½ feet apart—that is, somewhere between what he calls "close personal distance" and "intimate distance." Jacobs found that crowd densities at Berkeley ranged from 9½ to 4 square feet per person.[29]

Using either yardstick, edges of a crowd possess room for more members. Fringe members of crowds tend to be onlookers who act much like an audience. They assume relaxed poses and engage in much by-play. Their attention is often interrupted by their neighbors, and they are easily distracted by emerging foci. If one wants to get into relatively nonthreatening conversations about the events, one has only to take a tour of the edge of a crowd, where the relaxed atmosphere is conducive to action-related sociability.

Edges of crowds are usually separated from the main events by a more or less informal *boundary*. This boundary may be a feature of the container. During the 1964 Auto-row civil rights demonstrations in San Francisco, the broad expanse of Van Ness Avenue, along with the island running down the middle, made natural boundaries for persons (almost entirely onlookers) on the edge of the crowd. The action was on the side of the street on which demonstrators sat-in in the auto showrooms, while the island and the opposite side of the street were natural bleachers—the police tried to keep the street itself clear for traffic.

A boundary may also consist of just the arrangement of persons. A crowd looking at a group of picketers is separated from the picketers by unoccupied space. This space acts as a boundary both for the protesters and the onlookers.[30] Such a boundary is usually more *permeable* from the side of the picket line than from the onlooker side. Permeability depends upon two factors: the physical proximity of the persons composing the boundary, and the expectations of the person who may want to cross it. A front line array of people standing in actual body contact presents an apparently solid boundary. In riot control formations, the prescribed spacing between police officers is 30 inches. This distance is supposed to be held throughout the entire action. Its purpose is to give each officer sufficient working room yet to make it difficult for any single officer to become surrounded.[31] While it appears to be formidable, a police line may actually be quite porous, for detectives and newsmen may be allowed to pass through it. Leon Trotsky relates that during the February revolution a wink from a Cossack conveyed to the demonstrators their right of safe passage. "The officers . . . lined the Cossacks out across the street as a barrier to prevent the demonstrators from getting to the center. But even this did not help: standing stock-still in perfect discipline, the Cossacks did not hinder the workers from 'diving' under their horses."[32]

Just as the fear of an apparently impermeable array intimidated the

Petrograd proletariat until February of 1917, so most boundaries are viable because participants read them as boundaries and do not attempt passage. Easement of boundaries is often simultaneous with assumption of its having been granted, because the persons making up the boundary have no intention of laying claim to the piece of land which they temporarily occupy. For example, while picketing outside of the Sheraton-Palace Hotel, demonstrators, observing a number of large men in suits standing in the entrance, hesitated to make forays into the hotel. Individual demonstrators, although easily identifiable, found on trying to make their way through the crowded entrance that they were not stopped. This caused surprise, for the impermeability of the barrier lay only in their expectations.

The texture of the core of a crowd depends in part upon its density and the arrangement of the bodies of the participants. For instance, seated persons jammed together have very little mobility, and both the limitations on their ability to scan and the angular perspective from which they view events combine to create a much more enclosed and vulnerable presence. College protesters have learned by hard experience that the worst way to greet arresting policemen is in a closely packed seated array, whereas the best way to keep control over one's own forces is to keep them seated on the floor. A standing crowd is more fluid, for people can move about more easily. If the members of a crowd are not solidly packed, they tend to shift their weight from foot to foot, thereby creating a subtle waving motion in the crowd. Passage between persons is then most easily achieved when two neighboring members of the crowd have respectively shifted their weight to the foot farthest away from the other, thus making an opening. Such shifting also makes passage across a boundary much easier.

Movement is also facilitated if the mover avoids eye contact with the person upon whose personal space he is impinging. Eye contact requires the mover to petition the standing person for right of passage—because mutual attention creates personal selves with rights and obligations.[33] The temporary infringement of personal rights is more easily taken and granted (under the assumption of both parties that the situation warrants it) if the parties do not enter into negotiation. Hence, movement from the back to the front of a crowd is both more rapid and less stressful. Similarly, crossing a boundary from in back of the persons who compose it is easier.

Besides density and arrangement of persons, a curious property that I call the "distribution of the presentation of affect" determines the texture or feeling of the interior of a crowd. In other words, the intensity of crowd members' expressions of their involvement in action-related activities is relative to the members' proximity to the center of interest.

The nearer they are to the center of action, the more participants express involvement; the farther away or the more toward the edges, the less participants express involvement. An excellent example of this property is illustrated in a picture of the hostile Cicero, Illinois, crowd that greeted Martin Luther King's open housing march of 1965. The picture shows persons at the front of the crowd, closest to the civil rights marchers, gesticulating angrily, faces twisted with hostility and hate. The amount of hostility in the expressions of members of the crowd diminishes as one moves away from the marchers, until at the back of the crowd people wear normal, unemotional expressions[34] on their faces. A somewhat more mundane example is presented by a crowd of students waiting for their college mailroom to open. Jammed into a V-shaped funnel, enforced by the position of persons and not the container, the students in the neck of the V, closest to the door, fidget, shove, and chant that the door should be opened. They are oriented toward the door and do not engage in conversation. Moving out into the V, the intensity of entry-related activity, including attention to the door, diminishes. On the edges of the V, waiting persons do not chant but engage in such forms of sociability as conversation and horseplay. This phenomenon of the distribution of the presentation of action-relevant affect causes a member of a crowd to feel that he is indeed closer to or farther from the place where the action is. The significance of the grading of affect will be discussed in the section dealing with crowding and danger.

Having outlined some analytic categories in which ecological features of demonstrations may be discussed, I want to again note that crowds are extremely fluid scenes. As we have seen, a number of arenas or subarenas, foci, stages, and boundaries may be present simultaneously, and any of these may quickly merge into another set of such features. In the course of persons in the crowd engaging in their business (protesting, meeting friends, arresting, etc.), the configuration of the gathering constantly flows from one shape into another. In some sense, the essence of a thing called a "crowd" is just this spontaneous, unstable flow.

PERSONS

Along with the arrangement of persons in a physical setting, the social ecology of a demonstration includes some census of the typical kinds of persons present. In addition to the various kinds of participants in the demonstration, one usually finds such figures as police, everyday occupants of the area, newsmen, exploiters, onlookers, and antagonists.[35] There, of course, may be many other groups and subgroups of people present. The principal actors distinguish themselves by their appearance and actions and also by their characteristic use of space.

Of abiding concern to demonstrators is the recognition of police. Law enforcement officials either wear uniforms that are designed to be noticed or dress in ordinary clothes and wear inconspicuous insignia, mainly for identification among themselves. (At political rallies where the speakers are government members who feel the need to be protected, T-men [Secret Service investigators] and G-men [FBI agents] can be spotted by the small, variously shaped and colored shields they wear in their lapels.) Plain-clothes detectives also give themselves away by their sheer bulk and the ways in which they use it. Police, whether uniformed or not, tend to assert their presence by commandeering or arrogating space to themselves. This can be seen in the gait and demeanor of a policeman on the beat (especially now that riot stick twirling has come back into practice).

Commandeering space is functional. When disorder breaks out in a crowd, the immediate reaction of the police is to isolate the disorder. For instance, a hostile antagonist or drunk is immediately surrounded by several policemen. They isolate the disorder in two stages: first they move in so as to make room and use their bodies as a wall; then they turn toward the surrounding crowd and begin to move it away from the action, obscuring as much as possible the crowd's view of what is going on. Similarly, in crowd control formations, officers use their bodies and riot sticks in a massive, coordinated fashion to divide, disperse, and smash assemblies of people.

The arrogation of space also has some nonfunctional consequences. Plain-clothes detectives usually shove their way through crowds without asking or apologizing for their rough invasion of personal space. At one demonstration, a slight young man was arrested for impersonating an officer when he refused to yield ground to two detectives who were pushing their way through a crowd. His anger was similar to most people's when they receive such unjustified, impolite treatment. Later, in court, the judge threw the case out, for the law astutely provided that the alleged impersonator had to have intimidated his victim. The situation was clearly the reverse in this case.

This leads to my speculation that the police do not see or ignore the subtle distinctions among members of a crowd. In both overdisplaying the means of social and physical control at hand and overreacting, they treat all members of a crowd in much the same way—that is, either as potentially vicious participants or obstructing bystanders. This has been accounted for by the difficulty of their job, the routine ways they have handled crowds in the past, the danger involved, and masculinity problems deriving from their social background.[36]

Participants have developed some tricks of their own to counter attempts to control them. Here again space and body arrangement are purposively used. In one crowd I watched a participant systematically kicking policemen through the open legs of persons standing in front of him. Deftly and swiftly, without looking at the officer, he would launch a blow. When the officer turned around the kicker had so placed himself that the policeman had no way of reading who had kicked him. Similarly, if police are not in solid formation and are attempting to move a crowd, a member can begin turning in the direction indicated and then continue turning, if necessary several times, until the policeman has passed. If there is no eye contact, the policeman cannot exact the obligations of mutual attention and therefore sanction the member for disobeying. The only resource a policeman has, if he is continually monitoring the member, is to shove, and this escalates the level of violence. By using the technique of turning, I have found myself entirely behind police lines. Also, a woman with a baby buggy who repeatedly shouts, "watch out for the baby!" can exempt herself both from the attempts of the police and the general movement of the crowd. There are, of course, limits to all of these techniques.[37]

Newsmen move quite differently from police. They have two different styles. One is to petition for passage; they make themselves small and try to slip between the members of the crowd, saying, in a pleading voice, "Newsman coming through please." The other style is to let the TV cameraman lead and use the bulk of his camera, resting upon the newsman's shoulder, to open a path. A changing attitude on the part of both protesters and police is making it harder for the newsmen to use any technique. Hostility from blacks and radicals is matched by the police treatment of newsmen at Columbia University and the Democratic Convention in Chicago.[38] Newsmen now have more difficulty getting their petitions for access approved.

One other type of crowd member should be noted. He is the person who routinely uses a place in which a demonstration is occurring. When, despite the presence of a demonstration, this type of person demands that the space be routinely used, a potential for conflict emerges. Regulars appear to regard demonstrations as an aggression against their persons.[39] In trying to move through the place as they normally do, they often engage in pushing demonstrators. Little old ladies on their afternoon strolls plunge right through picket lines, muttering and shoving people aside with their umbrellas. Lunch-hour bustlers aggressively make their way through crowds, berating the demonstrators to go home and insisting that the sidewalk does not belong to them (presumably it belongs to the regulars). Other regular users take the demonstration as an occasion for entertainment and stop their routine activities in order to watch, thereby becoming members of the crowd who are onlookers.

Perceptions of Crowding and Danger

Ethologists view crowding as a physiological phenomenon.[40] Each species requires a characteristic amount of space in which to function normally. A radical reduction in *Lebensraum* produces pathological behavior. A behavioral sink in a crowded rat cage is a classical example.

In the case of homo sapiens, the problem of *Lebensraum* is more complex. A stringent reduction of space, such as close confinement, will produce pathological symptoms. But it is by no means clear that riding in crowded subways or just living in densely populated ghettos is responsible for the abnormal functioning of persons. Furthermore, most events labeled "collective behavior" involve pathologies of judgment— that is, participants act irrationally and the irrationality is not easily tied to physiological restriction.[41] Reinterpreting Smelser and others, we can view situations in which the options for action and for the collection of information are reduced as being constituent elements of crowding and, like crowding, as having potential for collective outburst. Clearly, the less a member can see and the less movement that is possible, the denser the crowd. A diminished ability to collect information and to test out alternate modes of action, in a sense a reduction in a member's ability to make choices, promotes a feeling of crowding. The degree of crowding corresponds to the degree of reduction.[42]

It can be inferred from the discussion in the previous section that, contrary to what most people think, there is a great deal of room in crowds for a variety of actions. This again is tempered by the density of the crowd. Hence, while there are reductions of certain options, there are also other options that are created by the situation. The relationship between these depends upon the particular characteristics of a given crowd.

It is also noted by ethologists that while containers temper the action which takes place within them, they in turn gain their social character from that same action. In other words, physical space is not absolute: with respect to actors and events, space is dynamic. Examples of this are plentiful. For instance, during the sit-in at the Sheraton-Palace Hotel, the lobby seemed more or less crowded, depending on what the protesters were doing. When 200 demonstrators entered the lobby and marched around silently, there seemed to be plenty of room for the guests to move about. The container was still an ordinary hotel lobby. Minutes later, 20 uniformed policemen entered, and although they did not greatly increase the numbers in the lobby, it seemed much more crowded. Some guests complained that they could not move about freely. For the demonstrators, the lobby became quite confining. Suddenly the lobby had been transformed into an arena of more consequential action. The presence of the police reduced everyone's options. Still later, in an attempt to coerce the management, the demonstrators marched around the lobby singing and chanting. Now the lobby seemed filled. Although some guests made their way through the chanting line, others cowered in corners as if crowded out of the way. Finally, the demonstrators blocked the three entrances by sitting on the floor in the doorways. Then, from the demonstrators' point of view, the empty spaces between the entryways and the high ceiling turned the lobby into a vaulted cavern. For the guests and the hotel personnel, the lobby had returned somewhat to normal.

It could be argued that a time span occupation of greater volumes of space occurred during the periods of chanting, and hence the lobby was actually more crowded at those times. This certainly contributed to the feeling of crowding. On the other hand, the presence of police transformed the scene—not particularly by their occupation of more space, but by the way in which the meanings of the use of space were changed.

Similarly, during breaks between classes, hallways in high schools may or may not seem crowded to students depending upon the sex of the students. For girls trying to protect themselves from minor sexual invasions, the hallways are extremely crowded. To male students hoping for accidental or contrived contact, the hallways are not too crowded for an entertaining, if not exciting, game. During the occupation of buildings at Columbia University, students transformed classrooms and offices into temporary living quarters. The remains of their domesticity, when viewed by returning secretaries, seemed the refuse of wanton destruction.[43] One can only speculate on the extent to which the secretaries would have felt crowded had they been present during the occupation of the buildings.

Perceptions of danger, like those of crowding, are derived from the structure of the setting and the activities that take place. Feelings of danger are tied to the degree to which a person feels himself to be a member of a seriously consequential situation. I argue from the negative. For instance, to be on the *edge* of a crowd is to be only a partial member of it. Persons on the edge of a crowd participate in little of the intense action. Persons on the edge are off the stage and partially outside the arena. This contributes to their feelings of insulation from the consequences of participation in the events. While police in the Sheraton-Palace Hotel none too gently removed demonstrators from the entranceways, a couple of guests from Florida, standing in the lobby, but outside the arena—that is, behind the row of persons standing behind the seated demonstrators—discussed the events in a relaxed manner. The terms of description they used expressed that the event was distant and that they were not part of it. They gave no indication of a sense of danger. Yet less than fifteen feet away, police and demonstrators were wrestling. The edge of any crowd includes similar fringe members.

Another element that contributes to feelings of participation and danger is the distribution of affect mentioned above. Intensity of the feeling of danger falls off rapidly the farther away from the action a participant is. At the Democratic Convention, standing one or two rows behind the front line of demonstrators being battered and maced by the police reduced significantly the sense of danger. In this part of the crowd, there was some room to move, and members did manage to carry on more or less mundane conversations.[44] The attenuation of affect with distance from the center of action seemed to contribute to the curious rules of battle etiquette that existed in Chicago. Police in battle array facing demonstrators were fair game. Yet isolated policemen standing in crowds of people were not attacked. Lone policemen who did not make hostile gestures were even obeyed when they gave instructions for the orderly flow of traffic. This can be accounted for by the fact that the stage for action was elsewhere and that both affect and the sense of consequential embattlement diminished as one proceeded back into the crowd away from the stage.

The Subjective Nature of Descriptions of Demonstrations

A characteristic of incidents of collective behavior is that reports of them are confused and fragmented. Unlike a press conference, at which statements are read and questions fielded, crowds lack frames to sharply define them.[45] For instance, the simple issue of who participated is problematic. This imprecision of description can be traced to objective features that account for the confusion and *irremediable subjectivity* of the reports.[45] That collective behavior, as a type of behavior, has a special structure that makes the subjectivity of descriptions of it irremediable will be made clear through an examination of the strategies to which reporters are forced to resort in order to construct adequate reports. This discussion of limitations arising from objective features and strategies employed to overcome them is a model of the problems of description of any complex public event.

There are two principal places from which to view a crowd: above it, and within it. A helicopter's view of a crowd enables an observer to catch some of the highlights of its ecological structure. Easily observable features are its size, density, arenas, and edges. If the landscape is open, then an overlooker may be able to grasp the whole scene in a glance. Clever use of a camera can reveal cross sections of people present and rates of entry into and departure from these cross sections. Because of the geometry of perspective, helicopter and camera deliver a minimum of information on the social character of the persons present (say even their race) and only occasionally discriminate the body orientation of the crowd members.

Entirely missing from the helicopter's view of the events are the texture of the happening and its social or interpersonal content. While we need not discuss the latter, the former's absence is germane. Certain of the objective features of a crowd are experientially known, but presence within the crowd is required to be able to observe their existence—that is, if one wants to report on anything that is dependent upon the texture of the crowd, the reporter has to place himself within it.

The inside of a crowd presents a number of immediate problems for the observer. First and foremost is its social ecology. Arena, edges, foci, boundaries, and stages both direct and delimit the observer's scope. As was indicated above, a typical demonstration has numerous events going on simultaneously. While a picket line, say, occupies the main stage, a number of substages and peripheral foci can draw the attention of people both within the core and on the edges of a crowd. The structure of an arena causes the stage to be the focus of attention. The arrangement of persons in an arena is such as to make the viewing of events elsewhere difficult. In an arena that is at all crowded, traffic from and attention to things not on the stage are inhibited by the physical and interactional orientation of the members. Therefore, the observer caught within an arena is partially bound by its structure.

Distance from the action, diminution of the presentation of affect, and diffusion of focus together reduce the intensity of the experience of the ongoing events for persons on the edge of a crowd. Reports from the edge of a crowd reflect these factors. Edge reports are distant, less emotional, and framed either because the observer can survey the scene or diffuse because he cannot quite tell what is going on. Persons on the edge of a crowd stand at larger distances from each other; they mill around and usually do not present indicators of whether they are coming, going, or intending to stay a while. This makes it extremely difficult for an observer to monitor the supply of people coming into or departing from the assembly. Edges do not generally have gates at which persons check in or out. Hence, attendance records are not easily assembled.

Because they are in part formed by expectations, boundaries exert a slightly more complex limit on the observer than on members of the crowd. Insofar as they compose the outlines of pieces of an arena, they encase domains of relevant action. From within a domain, an observer can tell a story that naturally exhibits the classical unities of time, place, and action. Insofar as boundaries are not physically solid, they present images of being more or less permeable. The observer, as a natural member of the assemblage, possesses expectations that partially define the permeability of a boundary. Therefore, the access that he has to various parts of a crowd are tempered by how he acts on these expectations. Crowds in which a lot is going on present many boundaries. If they are impermeable to the observer, then he will not be able to report firsthand on many of the pieces of action.

A further limitation on observers can be seen in the redefinition of the concept of "segment" developed by Bucher and Strauss.[47] A "segment" of a crowd is defined as that piece of behavioral action that a member perceives. This only partially coincides with the objective features of the gathering. An example of a segment of a crowd is the experience of a person who is marching on a picket line that is surrounded by a mixed audience of friendly, passive, and hostile onlookers. The movement of the picket line gives an episodic character to what the picketer observes. He catches only glimpses of what members of the audience are doing. If the picketer engages in conversation with his coparticipants, then he can monitor even less of what is happening both in other parts of the picket line and within the audience. Similarly, the action observed by a member of the interior of a crowd is limited by what he can physically monitor, by what he attends to, and by the way in which he reads the events. These limitations constitute the boundaries of a segment. Such a segment may be individual or shared, depending on whether a member "coparticipates," that is, shares a natural history with a group of other members.[48]

Finally, the social character of the observer conditions what he observes. As noted above, some typical members of the crowd carry themselves in special ways. The police, by reason of their aggressive manner and their obligation to control, look for certain things and precipitate special reactions. Hence, they obtain a particular picture of crowd events. This is illustrated in the testimony policemen give in court. Although such testimony is clearly constructed so as to gain convictions, it has, from the participant's point of view, additional strange qualities. Systematically, the police seem to see things differently.[49]

Similarly, newsmen's views of events are tempered by the way in which they move and the manner in which their work predisposes them to look for things. The apparatus that a newsman carries in order to do his work not only causes reactions in members of a crowd, but also precipitates major crowd events. At the Democratic Convention in Chicago, the large TV trucks were used by both the police and demonstrators, sometimes as obstacles and sometimes as audiences.[50] Other members of a crowd—the participants, regulars, onlookers, and so forth —also obtain views of the events that are tempered by the ways in which they behave and their predispositions toward the events.

The basic strategy employed to come to terms with the limitations on observation inherent in the social ecology of crowds is that of *social exploration*. Because crowds contain many pieces of action taking place simultaneously in various subarenas, an observer who wants to gain as wide a coverage as possible must move through the crowd. Movement multiplies the number of objective perspectives and allows the observer to view different stages and parts of the assembly. But movement also runs afoul of the structure of the crowd. Edges, arenas, stages, foci, and boundaries have to be taken account of and experienced in order to move and to observe each distinct setting. In fact, these structures may be said to partially constitute the setting.[51]

Diving into each of these structures requires initiative and sometimes even bravado. An observer has to make his way through the crowd. To engage in conversation with the onlookers, he has to take advantage of the sociability of the edge of a crowd. He has to move close to, or get on to, the different stages. He has to test the permeability of boundaries. This last matter is a particularly acute problem for observers. As noted abovo, the boundary created by a picket line is more permeable going out of the line than into it. This, taken together with the comment that the views of the events from either side are quite different, implies that an observer who cannot cross the less permeable side of the boundary further truncates his report. In short, if an observer wants to make all but the most oblique report, he has to engage in social exploration. In so doing he will make use of, uncover, test, and be delimited by the structure of the crowd.

What remedies are available for this *objectively structured subjectivity of observations*? The technique most often prescribed is team reporting.[52] News media do team reporting at conventions and are beginning to do it at other complex events. A research unit at UCLA sent a team of observers to watch and film the demonstrations in Chicago in order to get a true picture. The advantage of team reporting is the multiplicity of both perspectives and experiences of the events. Team reporting does increase the amount of information that can be collected about a crowd; it is, in fact, more than the sum of the individual reports. What it does not do is to overcome the constraints put on each of the observers.

The experiences of an observer may be thought of as a *sample* of the complex event. As in statistical sampling, some subset of a larger event is examined. A difference is that the observer's bias is neither random nor uniformly weighted.[53] The observer is a social being, and hence, the sample has built into it indicators of the extent of its own extrapolation[54] that are derived from the movements, social explorations, and reactions of the observer. Since each observer produces only one sample of the events, the team (provided they have common descriptive language with which to communicate) assembles only a few samples of the happenings.[55] Since these samples are products of the interaction between the observers and the structure of the crowd, they are subjective. And since there is no available smoothing assumption, as in statistics, team reporting is, therefore, not a remedy.

Other remedies for the subjectivity of observations rely essentially on the helicopter's view but, like the helicopter, are unable to report on the texture and complexity of gatherings. Hence, the subjectivity of reports of complex events is intrinsic.

The Duality of Description and Control

In a "deviant" demonstration, insurrection, or revolution, the agents of social control and the agents of change are in direct competition over the management of the outcome of events. The problems they face in this competition are similar although by no means equal. As is almost always the case, the defenders of the established social order have a tremendous advantage. The similarity of problems is illustrated in riot control manuals and books on the strategy of warfare.[56] In terms of game theory these conflicts can be seen as zero-sum two-person games in which for each problem of information gathering and intervention presented to one player there is an equivalent problem presented to his opponent. Since one side wants to change things and the other wants to maintain them, the initial move prompts a response. By calling a demonstration, protesters attempt to create events over whose outcome they exert at least partial control. In planning a gathering they become involved in its structure: they are both part of it and bound by it. Similarly, the agents of social control become part of and bound by the structure of the events. As competitors of the protesters, they endeavor to maintain control or at least keep the events in check.

In order to exert continuous influence over events, both agents and disrupters face the abiding problem of knowing what is happening. The kind of information needed depends on the outcome each side desires and the forces it can bring to bear on the events. The logic that informs protesters' actions is essentially a strategy of weakness. Protest planners rarely get beyond the stage of creating a situation in which people can assemble to express their opinions. Once events are under way, planners try both to precipitate happenings and to keep them in check. The former is usually done by way of public announcements, demonstrations, or calls to battle. The latter is accomplished by soothing words and generally ineffective systems of monitors. Agents of control, on the other hand, possess trained and disciplined forces that are designed for intervention in ongoing disruptions. Hence, these agents prepare for and theorize about demonstrations and crowds in a much more detailed and elaborate way. Although needs for information are unequal, both parties require a constant flow of descriptions of the events if they wish to intervene.

Descriptions of the events are of two kinds. The first are the models of events that planners use in order to try to think about and scheme for a desired outcome. It is in these models that we can uncover one half of the relationship between description and control: each control procedure that planners contemplate has implicit in it a description of how events can occur. Books on riot control are veritable picture shows of crowd events.[57] They catalogue the kinds of participants, give indications of how their varying characters will lead them to act, and illustrate everything from the special strategies of crowd dispersion to the psychological effects of a bare-fanged police dog. From a participant's point of view such books are caricatures and reveal the deep social and political biases of the agents of social control. For instance, in diagrams of riot control formations, the police are portrayed either as individual circles or orderly boxes, while the rioters are a black, solid, flowing mass. This corresponds to written descriptions of crowds as being made up essentially of the dupes of vicious demagogues who manipulate them. Despite their naivete and socially obnoxious connotations, riot manuals are not, to the agents who use them, absurd either as descriptions of the events or as plans for control. Correspondingly, strategy sessions of demonstrators are filled with descriptions of the events that might seem unrealistic to their opponents.[58]

The second kind of description of events is the description of the ongoing events that opponents collect in order to exert influence. These descriptions are limited by the objective features of the events and the normal perceptions of the observers, who are part of the events that they are monitoring. Their observations are collected not to satisfy the curiosity of some aloof academic tradition, but for the purpose of intervention and control. This illustrates the other half of the relationship between observation and control: for each description of the events, there is a potential plan for control. For example, my observations of how the police use their bodies could be the basis of counter strategies for the neutralization of policemen. Clearly, such observations by others were the basis of the strategy for kicking a cop without his being able to discover the culprit. Similarly, a description of the ecology of a given crowd is usually the basis of any plan to disperse it; it is wise to know where the rioters are and how they are behaving before attempting to deal with them. In any case, the agents of social control would uncover the ecology during their actual attempts at dispersal.

To find out what is happening, police and demonstrators put different kinds of observers in the field. Police borrow a military term and call their investigations "intelligence." Their intelligence forces range from helicopters to undercover men. Because of the complex structure of a large demonstration, the use of only one intelligence technique to observe such an event would be inadequate. Instead, partial pictures of the gathering, collected by several observers, are communicated to a central locale for piecing together. At the Democratic Convention in Chicago this was done both by radio communication—each officer had a small radio attached to his helmet, and many carried walkie-talkies—and by direct personal communication. It was through such communicative acts that undercover men betrayed themselves. In order to act like hippies, policemen have to unlearn their normal ways of carrying their bodies, and this is hard to do completely. A marginal hippie conversing with an obvious plain-clothes officer on the edge of a gathering was almost sure to be a cop. The implication here is that structure also limits the amount which can be conspiratorially observed. The more the members of one side want to know what is going on within the bosoms of their opponents, the more they have to become like their opponents. It is in the conveying of information back to one's own side that spies violate the rules of behavior of opposition membership and hence create the opportunities for exposure.

Some kinds of demonstrators are attempting to forge strategies that overcome the problems of observation, coordination, and communicative privacy. A currently popular concept is that of "affinity group"—a cell, or small group, of persons who trust each other and are working for a common goal. These people may be planners of or just participants in a demonstration. They try to formulate strategies beforehand and act cooperatively during a demonstration. The advantage of an affinity group is that members recognize each other, can communicate, and trust each other. Moreover, they remain in constant contact. This means that the group's monitoring of the events is both continuous and immediate. An affinity group is constantly sizing up the situation and making new plans of action on the spot. Their descriptions and plans for control are intimately bound together. There is little hiatus between their theories and applications. Each acts so as to modify the other. Of course, these advantages do not make affinity groups invulnerable. In fact, it is difficult to say whether affinity groups have had any effect on the character and evolution of demonstrations.[59] The obvious disadvantage of affinity groups is that in order to maintain their advantages they must be small and unencumbered by much paraphernalia. Therefore, when facing larger and better equipped opponents, they do not have the forces with which to win. In spite of the fact that a tank within an army of men is almost completely incapable of observing its surroundings, it very easily rolls over barricades.

Members of affinity groups are realists, as opposed to riot manual authors, who are social theorists or idealists. For affinity groups, control and description are intimately tied together. The group structure is designed to gather observations, evaluate them, and put into action plans for control almost simultaneously. Affinity groups are mired in the structure of a demonstration and are continuously trying to manipulate it.

On the other hand, agents of social control, partly because they have much larger bureaucratized entities with which to deal, use derived descriptions of idealized past events to construct plans for future action. There is a gap between the notion of how crowds are controlled and the actual control of them. In ongoing incidents, this distance breaks down, and the agents of social control use the descriptions they find at hand to face the real situation. In a similar way, any complex social group that wished to act in a coordinated manner within a complex event would have to decrease the distance between ideal conceptions of control and the real situation that they face.

CONCLUSION

This article has attempted to develop some basic categories for the description and analysis of demonstrations. With an understanding of microecological features such as "arenas," "foci," "boundaries," "stages," and "edges," an observer ought to be able to describe and dissect demonstrations.

Any good description would involve the observer as a member of the gathering. Taking cognizance of the way in which his membership is a function of the structure of the crowd will allow the observer to characterize the status of his description—that is, to show how the objective structure of the gathering gives a particular subjectivity to the report. Such an indication of the status of the description will enable the reader to evaluate what kind of report he is receiving. Without this indication, a report of a complex event seems to be incommensurable. Open recognition of the fact that sampling and social exploration are intrinsic to reports of demonstrations undercuts the apparent objectivity of a report but puts it into a much more informative frame.

In pointing out the relationship between description and control, I indicated that both require immersion in the events, and that they are complementary, for each control procedure has implicitly or normatively within it a description of how things happen, and, conversely, each description contains a potential plan of control. In brief, both the intrinsic subjectivity of reports and the duality between description and control are functions of the structures of complex events.

Notes

1. Robert Park and E. W. Burgess, *Introduction to the Science of Sociology* (Chicago: University of Chicago Press, 1921), especially pp. 865–869; and Roger Brown, "Mass Phenomena," in Gardner Linzey (ed.), *Handbook of Social Psychology* (Reading, Mass.: Addison-Wesley, 1954), pp. 833–876.
2. Dennis Brissett, "Collective Behavior," *American Journal of Sociology*, 74 (1968), 70–78, and personal communications with several well-known sociologists.
3. The unempirical approach runs from Gustave Le Bon, *The Crowd* (New York: Viking, 1960), through Herbert Blumer, "Collective Behavior," in A. M. Lee (ed.), *New Outline of the Principles of Sociology* (New York: Barnes & Noble, 1951), pp. 161–222, to Neil Smelser, *Theory of Collective Behavior* (New York: Free Press, 1963).
4. Taine, Burke, Le Bon, and Robert K. Merton are clearly elite critics. Knowledge of who the pseudoscientific experts are requires the dirty work of looking into the grounds for awarding grants to many so-called value-free sociologists. An example of one might be R. Conant; see his "Rioting, Insurrection, and Civil Disorder," *American Scholar*, 37 (1968), 420–433; "The Future of Black Protest," *The Police Chief*, 36 (1969); and "A Perspective on Student Unrest," Lemberg Center for the Study of Violence, Brandeis University (mimeographed paper, March, 1969). Disaster research falls within the work of this second group. For an interesting perspective on value-free science, see J. Ben-David and A. Zlocsower, "Universities and Academic Systems," in N. Kaplan (ed.), *Science and Society* (Chicago: Rand McNally, 1965), pp. 62–85.
5. George Rudé, *The Crowd in History* (New York: Wiley, 1964), p. 10.
6. Le Bon, *op. cit.;* see also the entry "Le Bon," *International Encyclopedia of Social Sciences.*
7. The notion of imposed categories comes from Bernard Glaser and Anselm Strauss, *The Discovery of Grounded Theory* (Chicago: Aldine, 1967).
8. See Blumer, *op. cit.* This view of crowds is also implicit in Smelser's notion of generalized beliefs that short circuit rational schema; *op cit.*, p. 72.
9. Most descriptions of crowds are authored by nonmembers, as a perusal of the massive footnotes to Smelser, *op. cit.*, will quickly indicate.
10. A forced articulation of categories can always be imposed, but they are then not grounded; see Glaser and Strauss, *op. cit.*, and W. Goodenough, "Componential Analysis," *Language*, 32 (1956), 135–216. For anthropologists' disputes on the matter, see Paul Bohannan, *Social Anthropology* (New York: Holt, Rinehart and Winston, 1963), pp. 90–96.
11. "Isolated from" may be thought of as a sociological version of Karl Popper's "falsifiability," while "bear a similar relation to" is a pragmatic criterion. Karl Popper, *The Logic of Scientific Discovery* (New York: Basic

Books, 1959); and Charles Fisher, "Mathematics, Interaction, and Truth" (unpublished paper, Brandeis University, 1967).

12. A mini-paradigm for emphasis on the processual aspects of collective behavior was put forth by Blumer, *op. cit.* A step forward can be found in Ralph Turner and Lewis M. Killian, *Collective Behavior* (Englewood Cliffs, N.J.: Prentice-Hall, 1957), Chap. 6.

13. Lewis Feuer, *The Conflict of Generations* (New York: Basic Books, 1969).

14. It is unnecessary to document the unreality of faculty meetings during times of crisis.

15. Max Weber's experiences with traditional forms of capitalism supplied a mold for many of his generalizations in *The Protestant Ethic and the Spirit of Capitalism* (New York: Scribners, 1958), especially p. 66; see also Reinhard Bendix, *Max Weber* (Garden City, N.Y.: Doubleday, 1960), p. 72. Although shackled by old rationalistic chains, M. Heirich's study of Berkeley, "Demonstrations at Berkeley" (unpublished doctoral dissertation, University of California, Berkeley, 1967), is a refreshing new start by a participant in the events.

16. E. M. Hall, *The Hidden Dimension* (Garden City, N.Y.: Doubleday, 1966); Marvin Harris, *The Nature of Cultural Things* (New York: Random House, 1964), pp. 30–52 and 133–150; F. Lundberg, *Foundations of Sociology* (New York: Macmillan, 1939); Goodenough, *op. cit.;* H. Sacks, "Sociological Description," *Berkeley Journal of Sociology,* 3 (1963), 1–16; and Harold Garfinkel, *Studies in Ethnomethodology* (Englewood Cliffs, N.J.: Prentice-Hall, 1967), Chap. 1.

17. Hall, *op. cit.,* and Garfinkel, *op. cit.*

18. Erving Goffman, *Interaction Ritual* (Garden City, N.Y.: Doubleday, 1967), p. 3, and *Behavior in Public Places* (New York: Free Press, 1963).

19. In the past six years I have been present at three major university uprisings, two minor ones, dozens of civil rights demonstrations, and a similar number of antiwar protests. Most descriptions included in this article are found in two of my unpublished documents: "The Sheraton-Palace Sit-In" and "Chicago, A View from the Streets."

20. This concept is borrowed from Jerome Boime, who notes that many classical writers conceive of society as a container.

21. See Hall, *op. cit.*

22. Sheldon Wolin and Seymour M. Lipset (eds.), *The Berkeley Student Revolt* (Garden City, N.Y.: Doubleday, 1965), p. 178; and Heirich, *op. cit.,* pp. 471–475.

23. The use of the term here differs from that in Goffman, *Behavior in Public Places,* p. 24; his use includes the idea of cooperation in sustaining the situation rather than just a common point of attention.

24. *Report of the National Advisory Commission on Civil Disorders* (New York: Bantam, 1968), p. 377; R. D. Smith, *Guidelines for Civil Disorder Mobilization and Planning* (International Association of Chiefs of Police, 1968), pp. 45–46; and Nathanael West, *The Day of the Locust,* in *Complete Works* (New York: Farrar, Straus, and Giroux, 1957).

25. Hal Draper, *Berkeley* (New York: Grove Press, 1965), p. 58; and Heirich, *op. cit.,* p. 316.

26. *Boston Globe,* June 30, 1969, p. 2.

27. Larry Rosenberg used this term in his lectures on Kinematics.

28. Orlando Wilson, *Police Planning* (Springfield, Ill.: Thomas, 1958), p. 427.

29. Hall, *op. cit.;* and H. Jacobs, "How Big Was the Crowd?" (paper presented at the California Journalism Conference, Sacramento, 1967).

30. Both topologically and sociologically, a boundary may bound only one of the adjacent domains. Since social boundaries are created both by expectation and testing, one man's boundary is another's usual domain. The agitator spots plain-clothes policemen where the onlooker sees just a crowd. Similarly, if, say, extensions of topologies from adjacent domains are incompatible, then what are boundaries for one are not for the other. See J. Kelly, *General Topology* (Princeton, N.J.: Van Nostrand, 1963), pp. 50–53; and Andrew H. Wallace, *Introduction to Algebraic Topology* (New York: Pergamon, 1957), p. 114.

31. Raymond M. Momboisse, *Riots, Revolts, and Insurrections* (Springfield, Ill.: Thomas, 1967), Chap. 24.

32. Leon Trotsky, *The Russian Revolution* (Garden City, N.Y.: Doubleday, 1959), p. 101.

33. As is often noted in a crowded subway, one is not allowed to look at the person against whom one is pressed in almost sexual embrace.

34. *Life,* 60 (July–August, 1966).

35. Who takes part in crowds is of much concern, especially to the agents of social control. The Commission on Civil Disorders, *op. cit.,* and Rudé, *op. cit.,* focus mainly on the social classes and criminal records of participants. For the notion of exploiters, see John F. Lofland, *Doomsday Cult* (Englewood Cliffs, N.J.: Prentice-Hall, 1965).

36. Egon Bittner, "The Police on Skid Row," *American Sociological Review,* 32 (1967), 699 ff.; James Q. Wilson, *Varieties of Police Behavior* (Cambridge, Mass.: Harvard University Press, 1968); and Arthur Niederhoffer, *Behind the Shield* (Garden City, N.Y.: Anchor Books, 1969).

37. The failure of the baby buggy technique to work indicates either the extent of rigid social control or the extent of the breakdown of order. See, for instance, the famous "Odessa Steps" sequence in Sergei Eisenstein's movie *Potempkin;* and Arthur Knight, *The Liveliest Art* (New York: Macmillan, 1959).

38. Daniel Walker *et al., Rights in Conflict,* report to the National Commission on the Causes and Prevention of Violence (Washington, D.C., 1968), especially pp. A-77–A-88; and *The New York Times,* April 30, 1968.

39. Hippies quickly learn that their mere presence is a form of aggression. Paul Kecskemeti has observed that because hippies are cognizant of the governing cultural values, the aggression they seem to precipitate is not unprovoked. In fact, he claims there is no unprovoked aggression. Hall, *op. cit.,* notes that nonroutine social and physical patterns not governable by a person are regarded by her as insidious conspiracies against herself.

40. J. B. Calhoun, "A Behavioral Sink," in E. L. Bliss, *Roots of Behavior* (New York: Harper & Row, 1962); and H. Shoemaker, "Social Hierarchy in Flocks of the Canary," *The Auk,* 56, 381–406.

41. Heirich, *op. cit.,* pp. 129–131, tries to account for Blumer's circular reaction by imagining a quite unestablished physiological feedback among neighboring coparticipants.

42. For the logic of this apparently backward method of reasoning, see S. Cavell's comments on Kant in "The Availability of Later Wittgenstein," *Philosophical Review,* 71 (1961), 67–93. Similar reasoning is found in Alfred Schutz, "The Well-Informed Citizen," in Alfred Schutz, *Collected Papers, Vol. II: Studies in Social Theory*, ed. Arvid Brodersen (The Hague:

Nijhoff, 1964). The rationalist tradition of Weber and Parsons takes crowding as the independent variable; see Smelser, *op. cit.*

43. *The New York Times,* April 30, 1968; and the film *Columbia* (Berkeley: Newsreel). See also Note 39, above.
44. See the photo in Walker, *op. cit.,* p. A-55. Of course, there are differences in individual tolerances to stressful situations. Like the woman who, although in no personal danger, became hysterical when a brick was thrown through a window, some people flood out when normal order breaks down.
45. For the ways in which news media create objectivity by framing, see G. Tuchman, "News, the Newsman's Reality" (unpublished doctoral dissertation, Brandeis University, 1969).
46. On the subjectivity of any and every report much has been written. Although at the epistemological level this is what is really at issue, here I stick to the superficial problems that arise from the particular difficulties of describing crowds. See also Alfred Schutz, "Multiple Realities," Schutz, *op. cit.* The notion of remedy is derived from Garfinkel, *op. cit.*
47. Rue Bucher and Anselm Strauss, "Professions in Progress," *American Journal of Sociology,* 66 (1961), 325–334.
48. Sharing depends, among other things, upon the amount of time persons spend together within the crowd and their ability to meaningfully exchange observations.
49. Imagine the testimony given by an officer who makes an arrest for the reasons cited by Bittner, *op. cit.* See also John Hersey, *The Algiers Motel Incident* (New York: Bantam, 1968).
50. Walker, *op. cit.* Or, as a slogan from a Boston University crisis put it, "We are creating a situation in which society is forced to finance, publicize, and broadcast a revolutionary critique of itself and furthermore to confirm this critique by its reaction to it."
51. Harold Garfinkel and H. Sacks, "Setting" (paper presented at the San Francisco meetings of the American Sociological Association, 1967).
52. K. Lang and G. Lang, "The Unique Perspective of Television," *American Sociological Review,* 18 (1953), pp. 3–12; and N. Stoller *et al.,* "Reports and Realities" (paper presented at the meetings of the Society for the Study of Social Problems, 1964).
53. H. Cramer, *Mathematical Methods of Statistics* (Princeton, N.J.: Princeton University Press, 1945), p. 332.
54. Marvin Scott, *The Racing Game* (Chicago: Aldine, 1968), p. 154.
55. Attempts to take large samples often have the effect of overkill. Too many observers spoil the crowd. A well-known example of this is Leon Festinger, Henry W. Riecken, and Stanley Schacter, *When Prophecy Fails* (New York: Harper & Row, 1956).
56. See Herman Kahn, *On Thermonuclear Warfare* (Princeton, N.J.: Princeton University Press, 1961); and Thomas C. Schelling, *The Strategy of Conflict* (Cambridge, Mass.: Harvard University Press, 1960).
57. See, for example, Momboisse, *op. cit.;* and the hearing of the United States Senate Subcommittee on Internal Security, *A Communist Plot Against the Free World Police, An Exposé of Crowd Handling Methods* (Washington, D.C.: Government Printing Office, 1961).
58. See Walker, *op. cit.,* pp. 4–30; and Abbie Hoffman, *Revolution for the Hell of It* (New York: Dial, 1968), pp. 99–144.
59. See the film *People's Park* (Berkeley: Newsreel, 1969).

Observing the Police: Deviants, Respectables, and the Law

Peter K. Manning

You have been told to go grubbing in the library, thereby accumulating a mass of notes and a liberal coating of grime. You have been told to choose problems wherever you can find musty stacks of routine records based on trivial schedules prepared by tired bureaucrats and filled out by reluctant applicants for aid or fussy do-gooders or indifferent clerks. This is called "getting your hands dirty in real research." Those who thus counsel you are wise and honorable; the reasons they offer are of great value. But one thing more is needful: first-hand observation. Go and sit in the lounges of the luxury hotels and on the doorsteps of the flophouses; sit on the Gold Coast settees and on the slum shakedowns; sit in Orchestra Hall and in the Star and Garter Burlesk. In short, gentlemen, go get the seat of your pants dirty in *real* research.

> "Unpublished statement made by Robert E. Park and recorded by Howard Becker while a graduate student at Chicago in the Twenties," in John C. McKinney, *Constructive Typology and Social Theory* (New York: Appleton-Century-Crofts, 1966), p. 71.

Sociology begins with observation of social action in social situations. Fundamentally, it begins with the premise that sociology is possible for the same reasons that society is possible—that is, they are both possible *only* insofar as people establish meanings for each other through and by interaction. Meanings, in their turn, are most accurately studied and understood by sensitive observers. If the quest of the sociologist is to understand social meanings in social situations, then he must do so primarily by means of observation.

Sociologists were initially *moral observers*, reading moral meanings into their interpretations of events. They later became experimenters, *interviewers*, and tabulators, choosing to "observe" through reports by interviewers on the reports of the interviewed. There is lately a renewed interest in firsthand observation that attempts to avoid the moralizing of earlier observers, while seeking to develop a more systematic set of techniques and analytic procedures. In this article, I argue for the centrality of observation in sociology, especially in those areas most concerned with social control and agencies of control, for example, criminology. After tracing some of the historic patterns of concern with "deviance," I argue that in order to sociologically explicate the system of social control, we need to observe the operation of the police as an organization and as an occupation. To that end, the major portion of this article, based on a review of several observational studies of the police, deals with the problems of structuring a research relationship with police organizations and the interpersonal or tactical problems of carrying out such research. The final section explores some of the ethical problems of police studies.

Mapping Society

If society is constituted by a series of paths through a maze, deviance, as Matza suggests, may be seen as recognized wandering away from the standard pathways of the majority.[1] (The transparencies often used in class presentations, if projected together in one multifaceted, multi-layered "super lightshow," might suggest the complexity of societal paths or social organization.) Although we recognize that there are different maps for different categories of persons—for example, the young, males and females, adults, priests, criminals—drawn with different pathways, we are also aware that in everyday life there is a *standard map* for members.

The difference between a standard and the variant maps is illustrated by Alfred Schutz's comparison of the cartographer's map-making objective view of a city and the view of the citizen who must make his way through the city as a practical matter.

The man brought up in the town will find his way in its streets by following the habits he has acquired in his daily occupation. He may not have a consistent conception of the organization of the city, and, if he uses the underground railway to go to his office, a large part of the city may remain unknown to him. Nevertheless he will have a proper sense of the distance between different places and of the directions in which the different points are situated relatively to whatever he regards as the center. The center will usually be his home, and it may be sufficient for him to know that he will find nearby an underground line or bus leading to certain other points to bring them all within his reach. He can, therefore, say that he knows his town, and, though his knowledge is of a very incoherent kind it is sufficient for all his practical needs. . . .

Entirely different means of orientation must be used by the cartographer who has to draw a map of the city. There are several ways open to him. He can start with a photograph taken from an airplane; he can place a theodolite at a known point, measure a certain distance and calculate trigonometrical functions, etc. The science of cartography has developed a standard for such operations, elements the cartographer must know before he begins to draw his map, and rules he must observe if he is to draw his map correctly.[2]

Although the city is physically the "same" for the native and the cartographer, it also has special meaning for each of them. For the native, it is his hometown, a place with sentimental meanings, paths, and memories. For the cartographer, on the other hand, the city is a mere object of scientific interest, of import only because of the demands of map-making. A city, like other socially defined objects, has multiple realities depending on the system of relevancies in which it is located from the point of view of the observer. The distinction made later between the point of view of the observer and that of the person observed is central to the difference between these two perspectives.

Much of modern sociology, even that which studies deviant behavior, adopts a position similar to the cartographer's and deals with the creation of standard maps sanctioned by the conventional morality and legal definitions of society. The deviant is seen as a problem for society and not vice versa.[3] There have always been exceptions to this generalization—men and women who engaged in describing the social worlds of those who had wandered from the pathway of righteousness, deviants who constructed their own morality and planted their own signposts by which to mark their virtue. These observational activities plunged some very respectable people into contact with strange and unusual social worlds. *They became enmeshed in the respectable study of evil.*[4]

Map-making involves a *perspective*, a way of looking at something—via a camera, with the naked eye, through the microscope, and so on—and a *location*—above, as in Schutz's airplane example, below, on the ground, or measuring outward. The resulting map reflects the location and perspective of the observer. Think of the differences between a globe, a city map, a mercator projection, and instructions for locating a party. Social map-making also involves perspective and location, and shifts in these two factors create the major tensions in the sociology of deviance. For example, in order to obtain information needed to sketch alternative maps of society, the map maker, or observer, may be required to take a perspective from below and may thus be plunged into a relationship with the underworld. A relationship is a bond or tie joining two or more individuals or groups, and this bond is qualitatively quite different if the observer locates himself comfortably within the bounds of conventional morality and sentiment and looks *down upon those below* than if he takes on the values of the deviant for the purpose of study and *looks up at the arbitrary nature of the society* above him. Alternatively, he could study the nature of the system of control that maintains the hierarchical arrangements.

Social maps and social mapping are problematic and should not be taken for granted if we wish to understand the relationship between good and evil, between crime and control or the law. To understand how social order is made problematic by its study, we will examine the development of criminology, the systematic study of illegal evil.[5]

Antecedents of Modern Criminology

The problem, as we define it, was not recognized by the early students of society. The moral statisticians of the eighteenth and nineteenth centuries closely linked good and evil and the means for their measurement in a way that now appears strange. As Jack D. Douglas carefully explicates, the discovery of a pattern or consistency in the rate of suicide, murder, and crime—violations of the moral order—were initially taken as a sign of the pervasiveness of that order itself.[6] How else could order in such evil things arise except as a product of the divine will? Even in their deviations from the normal Christian pattern of life, as revealed in the statistics gathered on their failings, men were tied together in a powerful, divinely ordered system. The *statistical order* was taken as a representation of the *moral order*.

Although the statistical study of social phenomena never abated as the primary mode of studying crime, several interpretive schemes gained popularity and provided new theoretical justifications. The wedding of social conservatism and Darwinian theories of evolution in the Social Darwinist position took place toward the end of the nineteenth century and explicitly linked class position, criminal activities, and evolutionary competition. According to Lombroso, the Italian criminologist, human nature was determined by the vicissitudes of birth. The social placement of a person reflected the evolutionary-competitive struggle in which the morally and biologically superior emerged at the top of the class ladder and the incompetent fell to the depths. The social strata reflected the biological endowments of the people who were members of them. Lombroso carried his argument further and pointed out that, logically, if the social strata also represented the levels of morality of their members (he defined the lower classes as the criminal classes) and if their moral levels, in turn, were the same as their biological levels, biological inferiority could be documented among the morally inferior—that is, criminals. Lombroso felt that the inferiority of the criminal, a product of birth or nature, would be visibly distinguishable. Such things as head size, deformities, and atavistic qualities (those reminiscent of the lower species, especially the great apes) were seen as signs of less than human status. By comparing control ("normal") groups from the non-criminal population with criminals, Lombroso found that criminals possessed more of these qualities than noncriminals. He concluded that the primary cause of crime was biological inferiority as indicated by these visible signs. Criminals were seen as a less than human class of refuse, lost to society, and worthy only of incarceration.

In this scheme, the ties between the respectable and the deviant are those between a superordinate—a biologically and socially superior person—and a subordinate—a biologically and socially inferior person. However, as Anthony Platt illustrates in *The Child Savers*, the drives of social reformers, social workers, penologists, and the like for professional status promoted a shift in social ideology.[7] Those concerned with fashioning careers based on the process of socially reforming youth, the poor, the criminal, and the disadvantaged classes in general were important figures in the development of a modified view of the "dangerous classes" in America. Platt writes of this change:

American criminology in the 19th century was pragmatic, cautious and somewhat distrustful of theoretical schemes. The most influential organizations concerning penology and the administration of criminal justice were the National Prison Association and the Congress of Charities and Correction. The delegates to these organizations were for the most part practitioners and technicians who worked from day to day with the "dependent classes." Their annual conferences were generally devoted to practical affairs, and they were not particularly concerned with intellectual creeds or philosophical justifications for their work.

The organization of correctional workers through their national representatives and their identification with the established professions, such as law and medicine, operated to neutralize the pessimistic implications of social darwinism, because hereditary and fatalistic theories of crime inevitably frustrated the professional aspirations of correctional functionaries. At the same time, even though the job of guard requires minimal training, skill and intelligence, crime workers did not wish to regard themselves as merely the custodians of a pariah class.[8]

This represented the forging of a new tie between the dependent and dangerous classes and the reformers. The latter were defined as the secular salvation of the former. The role of the reformer was that of volunteer, stooping to aid the less fortunate from a securely middle-class position. The involvement was one of symbiosis, or mutual dependence, in which each benefited from the mutual bond.

Sociology, caught up in this movement from social determinism to biological determinism, became deeply involved in the social reform activities of America in the early twentieth century. Although a strong European theoretical tradition existed, it was overlooked at this time in favor of a more empirical and pragmatic approach to social problem-solving. The extensive concern of American sociologists with social problems and their Protestant rural backgrounds and religious family ties are well documented.[9]

American criminology at this time shared the same heritage and concern, but it also made use of European sources. It drew upon the work of analysts of the sociology of law, the study of the relation between the development of law and the social structure—Maine, Durkheim, and Weber—and upon the positivist school of criminology then flowering in Italy in the work of Lombroso, Garfaolo, Ferri, and others. The latter influences continued to pattern American criminology, providing a foundation for its strong attention to nonlegal definitions of crime, its social determinism, and its focus on criminals as opposed to criminal law. This emphasis was reinforced in the early work done in America on socialization and disorganization by Cooley, Mead, Thomas and Znaniecki, and Dewey. Jeffery interprets this orientation in terms coinciding with Platt's:

The reason the criminologist is not interested in studying law and society is his reform orientation. There is no way in which knowledge of the law and society can be used to reform the criminal. The criminologist assumes that he must reform the criminal if the science of criminology is to be a success.... Criminology has developed to a great extent as a branch of the penal reform movement in the United States. The major problems of criminology have been derived from needs of parole boards and prison administrators for tools with which to reform or to manage criminals. The interest shown in parole prediction tables and prison research is illustrative of this reform orientation. The development of criminology is limited by this interest in penal reform and prison problems.[10]

It was not until the thirties that a revival of interest in the European sociology of law occurred.[11]

A further extension of this focus was the intertwining of the moral-statistical approach with the development of a system of detection, custody, and treatment of the offender aimed at controlling and manipulating the criminal population. Criminology developed as a result of demands for solutions to practical problems in an industrial society, although, with time, criminological interests came to desire a scientific status and ideology. The point is not so much the origins of the science, but its continued unwillingness to define its concerns outside the practical interests it serves and its willingness to rest with the utterly inadequate official statistics.[12]

There were other forces as well that drove sociologists and criminologists interested in crime or the criminal away from the object of their concern and that made them distant and dependent observers. That is, in spite of the professed interest of American criminologists in criminal behavior and crime, they were satisfied in the main to solve the demands of the established structure for solutions to practical problems and to rely on the figures and concepts generated for this purpose to provide the structure of their own theory and practice. Further, their quest for *respectability* reinforced their willingness to associate with the conventional morality and agencies that dealt with the offender, his reform, and incarceration, rather than to mounting firsthand investigations of crime in natural settings. Their "sociology of crime and the law" was primarily a statistical map from the respectable perspective, looking on crime as a function of certain quasi-incorrigibles. If one uses the conventional data (official statistics) to study unconventional conduct, the result is, as Ball writes:

Such a bag disproportionately represents the technically unskilled and the politically unconnected, and is [not] likely to aid in the constitution of a representative picture of deviant actors, their actions, or the social organization of such phenomena. . . . Though conventionally aggregated data may satisfy the rigid criteria for statistical manipulation, they do so at the cost of a misleading, even an atypical portrait of the deviant actor—what might be called the "unable to make the fix incompetent"—and which furthermore ignores the structural context of such conduct.[13]

In a very real sense, criminologists were now two steps removed from the self-defined object of their attention, the criminal. First, they were taking the conventional and legal definitions of law, crime, and property for granted without either systematic investigation of the distributions of the meanings of these concepts throughout the social structure or analysis of the system of law itself, its evolution, and its function. Second, they were relying on the official statistics of the police, the penal system, probation officers, and welfare agencies to construct a theory of criminal behavior. In doing so, one ignores systematic differences which result from differential reporting, class biases, the impact of resources, variable enforcement policies, differential legal processing of offenders, differential probation and parole policies, and so forth.

The alliance between criminologists and the establishment was reinforced further by their association with members of high status occupation groups, such as lawyers, judges, and lawmakers, whom they had been unwilling to investigate because of the benefits of association and the threats to their position. The higher status, more powerful occupation groups, in their turn, were effectively able to prevent or discourage studies of their behavior by social scientists. Their own conservatism was, and still is, protected in this way.[14] Note here that studies of criminals in the field antedated considerably the first studies of lawyers, judges, and lawmakers by social scientists. The study of other high status professionals, such as physicians, is only beginning. This status differential does not account, however, for the failure of sociologists to study the police. (This is discussed below.)

The questioning of the traditional stance toward the criminal classes began in the 1940s, with the work of Tappan, Sutherland, Van Vechten, and Sellin.[15] Their work documented the suspected differential effect of the judicial system on different social classes, the differential enforcement of laws, such as those involving white-collar offenders, and the relationship of the legal and nonlegal definitions of right and wrong.

This work raised to visibility the question of the focus of criminology itself. American criminological concerns had been positivistic and had tended to reduce the study of crime to the study of deviant behavior, but Jeffery made a clear distinction between the two:

The question why and how people commit crimes is an important one; however, a theory of behavior is not a theory of crime. Behavior is criminal only when judged by some standard of conduct. The term "crime" refers to the act of judging or labeling the behavior, rather than the behavior itself. Why people behave as they do and why the behavior is regarded as criminal are two separate problems requiring different types of explanation. If we wish to include all anti-social behavior within the scope of criminology, we must either state that all deviant behavior is criminal or that criminology is concerned with noncriminal as well as criminal behavior. What we are concerned with is the sociology of deviant behavior, not the sociology of crime. Only in the criminal law do we find the distinction between criminal and non-criminal behavior. People are executed or sent to prison for violating a law; they are not executed or sent to prison for "anti-social" behavior in general. . . .

The removal of crime from the realm of legal fact has blurred the distinction between criminal and non-criminal behavior. [Jeffery here cites the fact that a vast majority of people have committed acts punishable by the law and less than 4% of crimes known to the police result in sentences.] These observations place the criminologist in a *cul-de-sac*. If he is to ignore the legal status of crime, he then must study all deviant behavior. This is an acceptable procedure if one is interested in explaining behavior; it is not too helpful if we wish to understand why individual A is in prison and individual B is not. From these statistical observations of non-criminal populations we must conclude that they differ from criminal populations not in terms of sociological and psychological variables related to the life experiences of the individual offender, but in terms of the process of legal adjudication. The criminal has been caught and convicted in a court of law. The problem shifts from "why and how individuals commit anti-social acts" to "why and how criminal law is administered."[16]

The fact is that the sociology of deviant behavior is the basis for building a criminology and not vice versa.

Recent years manifest a return to the classic concerns of the sociology of law and criminology: the impact of social control and the law on deviant behavior. Modern sociological studies have begun to piece together and revive the important strands of the positivistic view, which emphasizes the *criminal* and *criminal behavior*, and the classical school, which emphasizes the fact that *crime is an entity in the law* and that reactions to the *legal system* are part of the criminal pattern. This concern with social control seen *in utero* in Lemert's *Social Pathology* and in a few recent scholarly works, most particularly Matza's *Delinquency and Drift*, harbingers a movement away from the standard map of official agencies and official morality without losing the perspective of the offender who is in contact with the law. In the next section, we develop some of the ways in which deviance has been observed in this developing framework and then, in the following section, we discuss studies of the police. As we shall see, the police as agencies of social control stand at the gates between evil and good, between criminal and noncriminal labels, and between official and unofficial deviance.

How to Map Society: Observing Deviance

To return momentarily to our initial metaphor of the map, we can see clearly that the standard map of society is drawn up from the definitions of crime provided by certain official and quasi-official agencies, and varies considerably from the maps of criminals, legal theorists, citizens at large, and so forth. We have suggested some of the factors that lead to close association between the social scientist and the establishment: linkages with reform movements, the quest for respectability derived from the statistical approach, the scientific rhetoric, the association with high status professionals, the pragmatism of American criminological theory, and the concern with socialization and social problems.

Why, on the other hand, didn't social scientists attempt to observe the deviant or criminal in his natural habitat? Given that the official stance is comfortable and rewarding, why (until recently) were there not attempts by academic criminologists to reconstitute criminology? From the academic position they were theoretically able to question the social order and critically examine what others had previously uncritically accepted.

Ned Polsky, in the most thoughtful statement to date on observing criminals, attacks social scientists for their failure to study criminals *au naturel*.[17] Polsky claims that recent criminology texts provide easy "cop outs" from this sort of study. Avoidance of fieldwork is based on the distaste sociologists have for criminals, combined with the difficulty the process entails (legal, social, and ethical risks are all high). Some of the most honored studies of criminals and crime are only "half-way houses" according to Polsky. He recommends an alternative strategy:

It is all very well to draw a fuller quantitative picture of the numbers and kinds of criminals or criminal acts. But we cannot use this to dodge what is the ultimate, qualitative task—particularly regarding career criminals, whose importance to any theorist of human behavior, not to mention the rest of society, is so disproportionate to their numbers: providing well-rounded, contemporary, sociological descriptions and analyses of criminal lifestyles, subcultures, and their relations to larger social processes and structures. . . . This means—there is no getting away from it—the study of career criminals *au naturel*, in the field, the study of such criminals as they normally go about their work and play, the study of "uncaught criminals" and the study of others who have in the past been caught but are not caught at the time you study them.[18]

Polsky's point is well taken. The study of the criminal exclusively in the context of the legal system represents a focus that abdicates the sociological task of seeking to understand how society is *really* put together and how it operates, rather than the way our American Government texts say it runs. An adequate understanding of the process of social deviance and control is much too important to be left to the deviants and the controllers.

However, the issue is more complex than Polsky would lead us to believe. It is necessary to ask, first, what one wants *to explain*; then, what sort of *information is needed* and how it is *to be obtained*; and, finally, what *social roles* should be adopted and what techniques should be used to interpret this information. Table 1 outlines these issues.

Table 1. Examples of Research That Examine the Conventional Morality and the Structure and Evolution of Control Agencies

Foci	Substance
A. Conventional Morality: Its Nature and Function	The emergence of legal norms; the evolution of legal systems; the growth of morality; law and social structure; law-making as a political process.
B. Institutions of Social Control: Their Structure and Function	Administration of law: arrest, charge, prosecution, outcomes; the growth and development of official statistics, for example, factors reducing stability in rates, "biases"; growth of social control agencies and control roles, for example, police.
C. Field Observational Studies	The study of the object (deviance) as sociologically defined and described in natural settings from the actor's perspective.

As the table shows, the object of attention need *not* be the behavior of the criminal, nor need criminology be based exclusively on the observation of criminals. As the earlier quote from Jeffery underscores, to explain deviant behavior is not to explain the existence of the law itself, its administration, definition, rise, or change.

The classic tradition attended to the emergence, structure, and function of the conventional morality itself, particularly its abiding concern with the links between society and the legal system.[19] The classic tradition includes the work of Weber, Mannheim, Ranulf, Hall, and some recent work on political sociology, such as Gusfield's *Symbolic Crusade,* Becker's *Outsiders,* and Kirchheimer's *Political Justice.*[20]

A second type of study is, so to speak, at the level of the administration of social control, the background and historical emergence of these roles and processes,[21] and the generalized theme of the growth of control in modern society.[22]

The third type of study that qualified for romantic defense and advocacy is the field, or observational, study of particular social groups, where the object studied is defined sociologically, studied *in situ,* close at hand, usually by means of qualitative techniques, and described with concepts reflecting the perspective of those studied.[23] These studies require special considerations in the areas of sampling and of obtaining the relevant information.[24] In a later section of this article, these and other problems of field observation, along with the scientific and ethical problems of such studies, are addressed.

Deviance and Control

We have attempted to show that the perspective one takes on an object links the observer and the observed, and we have chronicled some of the types of links that have developed between the deviant and the respectable. The tendency has been for observers of deviance and crime to stand at a distance from their interest, a tendency Polsky argues has deleterious effects on the development of sociological theory in criminology.[25] Present interest in the contingencies of social control and the impact of law and law enforcement on the nature of deviance has been paralleled by studies of the major formal instrument for the maintenance of social order: the police. The remainder of the article is concerned with a particular type of field study of social control, which is representative of the tendency to study deviance derivatively. This type of field study accepts society's definitions of who is deviant and makes use of social control organizations for entrée into the deviant world. Such studies provide a rich substrate for understanding and making problematic the nature of social control.

Since 1964 there has been a noticeable increase in the number of published studies of criminals in their natural habitat.[26] Moreover, there has been an increase in the number of police studies. (Polsky does not discuss these field studies of the detection of, initial contact with, and selective enforcement of the law vis-à-vis the potential offender.) The police studies, with Blumberg's, Sudnow's, and Skolnick's studies of criminal lawyers,[27] Green's studies of judges,[28] and Goldman's, Cicourel's, and Briar and Piliavin's studies of the selection of juveniles for file-making and prosecution,[29] permit us to construct a partial picture of the organization of the criminal justice system in the United States. This could not have been accomplished solely by studying the sociology of law itself, but could only have been achieved by studying administrative processes as they are linked with the societal processes of the criminalization of behavior via law-making and the behavior of criminals outside the legal network. Admittedly, the latter is the weakest spot in our present understanding of the system.

The systematic study of criminal justice is intimately linked to the newer conceptions of deviance because the social control system is now seen as having an *independent effect* on the criminal, his role, self, and identity. Erikson makes this summary remark:

It is by now a thoroughly familiar argument that many of the institutions designed to discourage deviant behavior actually operate in such a way to perpetuate it. For one thing, prisons, hospitals and other similar agencies provide aid and shelter to large numbers of deviant persons, sometimes giving them a certain advantage in the competition for social resources. But beyond this, such institutions gather together marginal people into tightly segregated groups, give them an opportunity to teach one another the skills and attitudes of a deviant career, and even provoke them into using these skills by reinforcing their sense of alienation from the rest of society.[30]

Lemert has remarked on this same phenomenon in describing the difference between his concepts of primary and secondary deviation.

The notion of secondary deviation was devised to distinguish between *original* and *effective* causes of deviant attributes and actions which are associated with physical defects and incapacity, crime, prostitution, alcoholism, drug addiction and mental disorders. Primary deviation, as contrasted with secondary, is polygenetic, arising out of a variety of social, cultural, psychological and physiological factors, either in adventitious or recurring combinations. While it may be socially recognized and even defined as undesirable, primary deviation has only marginal implications for the status and psychic structure of the persons concerned. . . .

Secondary deviation refers to a special class of socially defined responses which people make to problems created by the societal reaction to their deviance. These problems are essentially moral problems which revolve around stigmatization, punishments, segregation, and social control. Their general effect is to differentiate the symbolic and interactional environment to which the person responds, so that early or adult socialization is categorically affected. They become central facts of existence for those experiencing them, altering psychic structure, producing specialized organization of social roles and self-regarding attitudes. Actions which have these roles and self-attitudes as their referents make up secondary deviance. The secondary deviant, as opposed to his actions, is a person whose life and identity are organized around the facts of deviance.[31]

Studies of the police are a part of a growing body of studies that will create the basis for understanding the nature of secondary deviation, on the one hand, and the structure and functioning of social control, on the other. The tie with criminals *per se* is a refracted one, but it adds an important dimension to the creation of criminals, since, by dissecting the practices of the police when the police are in contact with the public, one begins to see *in vivo* one aspect of the labeling process, the beginning of the generation of a set of criminals from the pool of people eligible for police attention.

Observing the Police

Scientific problem definition and research is patterned and socially constrained.[32] Recent attention to the police and to social control in general is understandable in fairly obvious, commonsensical terms.[33] Several large-scale social changes are underway.

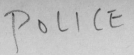

First, there is the growth of the high density, urban proletariat, especially blacks, which, in combination with unemployment, frustration with social services, and inadequate police protection, led to the large-scale "race riots" of 1964, 1965, and 1967. The police faced these large-scale, diffuse, collective phenomena with little or no training and inadequate resources, and they demonstrated the paucity of our collective knowledge of social control under such conditions.

Second, the "liberalization" of procedural law, specifying in greater detail the rights of the alleged criminal with regard to rights to attorney, protection against self-incrimination, and the rights of juveniles, turned legal and social science attention to police practices. Certainly, it made the police more vocal in their own defense and created virulent waves of public support for and condemnation of the police.

Third, the student protest movements against the war placed great demands upon the police for restraint. They failed the test in every significant instance: the Mayday demonstrations in May, 1971, the Democratic National Convention in Chicago in 1968, the Pentagon Peace March, the Oakland Draft resistance movement in 1964–1965 and so on and so forth.

Fourth, the failures of large cities to provide the police with adequate pay, security, and benefits, and the relative decline in police prestige led police to their own forms of protest: slowdowns, "Blue Flu" (conspicuous absence on sick call of large numbers of policemen), selective law enforcement, and a search for political power. This same set of factors underlies the present movement to unionize the police.

Fifth, the police have become symbolic enforcers of scapegoat theories of social decay held by the "middle mass." These people are uneasy and anxious about rapid social change and seize upon the police as their defense against "hippies, radicals, and perverts," whom they see as causing the social decay.

Sixth, the black-white clash has made the policeman a middleman, caught between what Bensman calls the "nutcracker of history"[34]—the demands of a vocal white segment for increased police control and repression of blacks, students, and other protesters, and black demands for community control, claims of harassment, and growing militancy.

Seventh, the police are, by definition, the enforcers of the status quo. When the moral tenor of the times changes rapidly, the laws lag behind, making social movement necessary to change laws. Further, as the morality changes with reference to interpersonal-sexual relations, drugs, and one's control of his own body, the police come into antagonistic contact with middle-class people who are normally their allies and whom they previously confronted primarily in helping roles.

Table 2 lists the major published and unpublished "sociological" studies of the American police. Most of these studies appeared in the second half of the 1960s.

Here, we are concerned only with those studies listed in Table 2 where observation was the primary investigatory technique. Although virtually all the investigators engaged in some observation, a much smaller group relied on it almost exclusively. These observational studies are listed in Table 3 according to the *extent of participation* in the group (active versus passive role) and the degree to which the *observer's role was known* to those studied (known versus unknown role).[35] From this group, we will draw mainly on those observational studies that deal with first-line police work, patrol, and the patrolman's role.[36] Four studies, in particular, contain the bulk of the information available on problems of observation, the strategy and tactics of studying the police, and the actual functioning of police departments: Banton, Buckner, Black and Reiss, and Skolnick. These studies contain important methodological appendices, and the investigators express numerous self-revealing comments. There are frequent, fairly long and detached discussions of the problems they faced in carrying out their studies. It is unfortunate that more studies do not contain similar detailed sections on these problems. Other studies are cited only when relevant to a particular issue. The general treatments of the police by Westley and Wilson are rich sources of ideas.

Table 2. Selected Research Studies of Police:
Published Works, Dissertations, and Works in Progress

Study	Method	Period of Research
Published Works		
Alex, Nicholas. *Black in Blue.* New York: Appleton-Century-Crofts, 1969.	Interviews	1964–1965
Banton, Michael. *The Policeman in the Community.* New York: Basic Books, 1964.	Interviews Observation* Questionnaire	1960–1962
Bayley, David, and Harold Mendelsohn. *Minorities and the Police.* New York: Free Press, 1969.	Interviews (Police and Public)	1966
Bittner, Egon. "The Police on Skid-Row: A Study of Peace-Keeping." *American Sociological Review,* 32 (1967), 699–715.	Interviews Observation	1963–1964(?)
_____. "Police Discretion in Apprehending the Mentally Ill." *Social Problems,* 14 (1967), 278–292.	Interviews Observation Psychiatric Records	1963–1964

* Major data source.

Study	Method	Period of Research
Black, Donald J., and A. J. Reiss. Many studies for President's Crime Commission Report, 1966–1968.	Interviews Observation Questionnaire	Primarily summer of 1966
Cicourel, Aaron. *The Social Organization of Juvenile Justice.* New York: Wiley, 1967.	Observation Police and Probation Reports	4 years
Cumming, Elaine, Ian Cumming, and Laura Edell. "Policeman as Philosopher, Guide and Friend." *Social Problems,* 12 (1965), 276–286.	Police Calls (Incoming)* Interviews Observation	1961
La Fave, Wayne. *Arrest: The Decision to Take a Suspect into Custody.* Boston: Little, Brown, 1965.	Observation Court and Police Records	1956–1957
Niederhoffer, Arthur. *Behind the Shield.* Garden City, N.Y.: Anchor Books, 1967.	Questionnaire Observation	21 years, New York Police Department
Piliavin, Irwin, and Scott Briar. "Police Encounters with Juveniles." *American Journal of Sociology,* 70 (1964), 206–214. See also Piliavin article in Bordua (ed.), cited below.	Observation	9 months
Preiss, Jack, and Howard Ehrlich. *An Examination of Role Theory: The Case of the State Police.* Lincoln: University of Nebraska Press, 1966.	Observation Questionnaires* Interviews	1957–1958
Skolnick, Jerome H. *Justice Without Trial.* New York: Wiley, 1966.	Observation* Interviews Questionnaires	1962–1963
_____, and J. Richard Woodworth. "Bureaucracy, Information and Social Control: A Study of a Morals Detail," in David J. Bordua (ed.), *The Police: Six Sociological Essays.* New York: Wiley, 1967.	Observation Police Records	1962–1963
Westley, William A. *The Police: A Study in Law, Custom and Morality.* Cambridge, Mass.: Massachusetts Institute of Technology Press, 1970.	Observation Interviews	1949
Wilson, James Q. "Generational and Ethnic Differences Among Career Police Officers." *American Journal of Sociology,* 69 (1964), 522–528.	Questionnaires	1960
_____. "Police Morale, Reform, and Citizen Respect: The Chicago Case." in Bordua (ed.), *op. cit.*	Questionnaires	1960–1965

* Major data source.

Study	Method	Period of Research
_____. *Varieties of Police Behavior: The Management of Law and Order in Eight Communities.* Cambridge, Mass.: Harvard University Press, 1968.	Observation (?) Interviews "Visitation"	1964, 1965 1966–1967

Dissertations†

Bacon, Selden, "The Early Development of American Municipal Police." Yale University, 1939.	Historical Study	
Black, Donald J. "Police Encounters and Social Organization: An Observational Study." University of Michigan, 1968.	Observation Police Records	Summer, 1966
Buckner, H. Taylor. "The Police: The Culture of a Social Control Agency." University of California, Berkeley, 1067	Observation	1966–1967
Cummings, Marvin J. "The Frame-Up." University of Colorado, 1967.	Observation	
Guernsey, E. W. "The State Trooper: A Study of an Occupational Self." Florida State University, 1965.		
Guthrie, Charles R. "Law Enforcement and the Juvenile: A Study of Police Interaction with Delinquents." University of Southern California, 1963.		
Harris, James. "Police Disposition: Decisions with Juveniles." University of Ilinois, 1967.		
Levett, A. L. "Organization for Order: The Development of Police Organization in the 19th Century United States." University of Michigan, forthcoming. Cited in Black, *op. cit.*	Historical	
McNamara, John H. "Role Learning for Police Recruits: Some Problems in the Process of Preparation for the Uncertainties of Police Work." University of California, Los Angeles, 1967. See also McNamara article in Bordua (ed.), *op. cit.*	Questionnaires	1960–1963
Petersen, David. "Police Discretion and the Decision to Arrest." University of Kentucky, 1968.		

† Dissertations that were subsequently published, for example, Ehrlich, Niederhoffer, and Alex, are listed above.

Study	Method	Period of Research
Pizzuto, C. L. "The Police Juvenile Unit: A Study of Role Consensus." Brandeis University, 1968.		
Smith, T. S. "Democratic Control and Professionalism in Police Work: The State Police Experience." University of Chicago, 1968.	Questionnaire* Observation Police Records	1967
Trojanowicz, Robert. "A Comparison of the Behavior Styles of Policemen and Social Workers." Michigan State University, 1969.	Questionnaires	1968
Watson, N. "An Application of Social-Psychological Research to Police Work: Police Community Relations." American University, 1967.	Questionnaires Projective Tests Interviews	
Wenninger, Eugene. "Bureaucratization and Career as Determinants of Participation in Police Occupational Groups." University of Illinois, 1966.	Questionnaires	
Works in Progress		
Bordua, David. University of Illinois, Urbana.	Observation Organizational Analysis	
Cummins, Marvin. University of Oregon.	Observation	1967–1969
Savitz, Leonard. Temple University.	Questionnaires	
Walsh, James. Oberlin College.	Interviews* Observation	1969
Ward, David. University of Minnesota.	Observation	

* Major data source.

Police Culture and Organization

Prior to addressing the specific studies that deal with the problematics of police action, an overview of the mandate and the occupational culture of the police as an organization is in order.[37]

Society, as Hughes has written, is organized around sets of people who are allowed or expected to do some things and are forbidden to do

Table 3. Major Observational Police Studies by Type of Participation and Knowledge of the Observed*

Active Role: "Participant"		Passive Role: "Observer"	
Known	*Unknown*	*Known*	*Unknown*
Buckner	Niederhoffer	Banton	
Skolnick		Bittner	
		(both studies)	
		Black and Reiss	
		Bordua	
		Piliavin and Briar	
		Cicourel	
		Cummins	
		La Fave	
		Ward	

* See Table 2 for details on the studies.

others.[38] Hughes calls these rights and prohibitions a *license* and argues that when a group of people become aware of their shared fate in the division of labor, they will claim a *mandate*—the right to define for others appropriate thought and action with regard to their domain. To piece together the fragments of social action that, taken together, form the basis for the police as an occupation, we must begin to formulate the nature of the police's mandate.

Although the police are in violent disagreement with their various audiences on some issues, they share agreement on the impossible nature of their mandate. They are expected both to enforce the law and to keep the peace—two often contradictory activities—doing so in the context of the uncertainties of the law, their departmental regulations, and shifting public expectations. Their inability to accomplish these objectives, especially without major changes in manpower and the allocation of public resources, patterns what James Q. Wilson calls the "police problem."[39]

In their attempts to fulfill their mandate, the police operate within several important constraints of social organization: the problematic nature of the law, the bureaucratic organization of their activities, and their public definition of their role as apolitical. Since these stresses are very real to any investigator, because they characterize his research setting to a greater or lesser degree, they provide a necessary background for understanding police studies.

If crime is an entity in the law, it is a very diffuse and difficult one. Crime has no single shape, location, or characteristic, and it covers a vast range of behaviors. Most behaviors categorized as "crime" are offenses that do not harm anyone; a large portion of them are drunkenness and other crimes without victims: drug use, prostitution, vagrancy, and disorderly conduct. These offenses of the public order are offenses against a normative conception of order within some neighborhood, community, or group; they can have no absolute definitions. Police action in response to citizen complaint typically is the result of community desire for a redress of social balance; the enforcement of the law, or the keeping of order, is the redefinition by legal agents of private social arrangements. The law is problematic because it is called upon to situationally redefine the nature of intentions and responsibilities, and it is a resource for organizing the multiple meanings inherent in any situation. Rarely does the policeman deal with law-breaking; most of the time he deals with problems of public order, where recourse to the law is often not immediately available. Wilson describes the problem in the following quote:

The difference between order maintenance and law enforcement is not simply the difference between "little stuff" and "real crime" or between misdemeanors and felonies. The distinction is fundamental to the police role, for the two functions .involve quite dissimilar police actions and judgments. Order maintenance arises out of a dispute among citizens who accuse each other of being at fault; law enforcement arises out of the victimization of an innocent party by a person whose guilt must be proved. Handling a disorderly situation requires the officer to make a judgment about what constitutes an appropriate standard of behavior; law enforcement requires him only to compare a person's behavior with a clear legal standard. Murder or theft is defined, unambiguously, by statutes; public peace is not. Order maintenance rarely leads to an arrest; law enforcement (if the suspect can be found) typically does. Citizens quarreling usually want the officer to "do something," but they rarely want him to make an arrest (after all, the disputants are usually known or related to each other). Furthermore, whatever law is broken in a quarrel is usually a misdemeanor, and in most states, an officer cannot make a misdemeanor arrest unless one party or the other will swear out a formal complaint (which is even rarer).[40]

The operation of law enforcement is uncertain, providing the patrolman, in particular, with a high degree of discretion in his enforcement patterns. The problematic nature of the law, the degree of danger often involved in intervention in private affairs, and the difficulty in obtaining a "good pinch" (one which will hold up in court) make patrolmen tend to "underenforce" the law or to selectively enforce only those laws that they sense society demands enforcing.

On the other hand, the policeman, reflecting public opinion, tends to see his role as an heroic crime-stopper, engaged in dangerous work; as the enforcer of the law, he pits himself against symbolic assailants. The police department sees its activities as taking place in a hostile, non-supportive, threatening environment. Citizen demand for action and control and prevention of crime coupled with the police definition of their own activities as dangerous has the effect of creating an organization constructed along the lines of a military base, with tight security and secrecy, a paranoid or suspicious style, a hierarchy of command with great arbitrary authority and characteristically a high degree of internal control of discretion. Westley claims that the "secrecy norm" is central to the police organization and occupation:

The maintenance of secrecy is the most important of the norms. It is carefully taught to every rookie policeman; it is observed by all the men, and there are powerful sanctions against its violation. All social and occupational groups probably believe in some degree of secrecy, for the stool pigeon, or squealer, is everywhere an anathema. However, among urban police the rule has the force of life, and the violator is cut off from vital sources of information and the protection of his colleagues in times of emergency.

Secrecy means that policemen must not talk about police work to those outside the department or gossip within the department. Naturally the last is not as stringently observed as the first. Yet it is observed, for some policemen told the researcher that others sometimes planted a juicy item of gossip just to find out whether one did talk. Policemen carry secrecy a long way and with true professional integrity will perjure themselves before revealing secrets. At least this was true of the policemen in the department studied, for when questioned about whether they would first report and then testify against a fellow officer who committed a felony, 75 per cent of the men interviewed declared that they would not.[41]

Since the goals of law enforcement are notably unclear, and the organization defines itself as operating in a hostile environment, the police tendency is to attempt to align action and commitment to the organization by a high degree of punitive regulations applied to lower participants,[42] that is, to the least powerful, to those lowest on the occupational ladder (patrolmen, especially rookies).

The police in a democratic society are, typically, not an arm of the military or the federal government. In the United States, with its over 420,000 law enforcement agencies and high degree of local autonomy, police departments are theoretically only under local control. They have further defined themselves as *apolitical*. The rise of the bureaucratic and proto-professional police style is a means of neutralizing the inherently political nature of policing. The law cannot be defined except as a political phenomenon.[43] It contains the formal rules by which the allocation of power is maintained in the society. By its nature, creation, and

maintenance, the law is inherently political. The stress between existence in a "politically loaded" environment, which the police feel is
increasingly turning against them, and the necessity and mandate to
enforce the law apolitically leaves the police free to attempt to control
their environment in illegal ways, such as through violence, coercion,
political activity, corruption, deals with the other parts of the criminal
justice system, and so forth.[44]

The efficiency themes found in the police rhetoric, the professionalization movement, and the use and display of technology do not obviate
the very simple fact that *it is impossible to detect or know all crime, let
alone to enforce all the laws or to prevent criminal activities. Crime is,
above all, a function of the resources available to know it.*[45] Most police
work deals with problems officially beyond the control of the police—it
is what I have called "symptomatic work."[46] It is also clear that it is
impossible to measure the extent to which the police accomplish their
stated ends, regardless of the efficiency of their means.

The police have come increasingly to define the causes of their problems in terms of a conspiracy. This belief, since it surrounds their everyday practices, impedes any attempt to make them responsible to a range
of citizen demands for sensitivity to social changes. Each new social
change, and the demands it signals to the police, is defined by them as
but another bit of evidence that events are conspiring against them.
Under these conditions, attempts to make the police politically accountable have been highly unsuccessful.[47]

Police organization reflects the contradictory nature of the mandate
itself. However, the ways in which the police attempt to carry out their
mandate, to accomplish it, are filtered through the occupational culture
of policing. The occupational culture provides the assumptions underlying day-to-day police action as seen in their *strategies* and *tactics.*
Strategy is the overall battle plan—the allocation of men, materials, and
resources—and the rhetoric used to describe it; tactics are the specifics
of strategy—the ways in which the plan is implemented in the field.

The American police act in accord with their assumptions about the
nature of social life, their own role in it, the need to control their work,
and the need to maintain self-esteem while satisfying superiors and
other significant figures. The meaning of their actions is filtered through
the screen of the *occupational culture.*[48] Occupational culture refers to
all the norms, values, attitudes, and material paraphernalia that are
shared by and are typical of the practitioners of a named set of work
tasks. Among other things, it provides a set of strategies, based on
these assumptions, for meeting the problems faced by the police in
their everyday round of work. It includes an *implicit* and an *explicit*
dimension. The former refers to abstractions that seem to underlie a

multiplicity of themes and that can be inferred from behavior. The latter is constituted by regularities in word and deed that can be generalized directly from sense data. It is possible to further formulate the nature of the implicit culture, but that task must await a more elaborate systematic description and analysis. Our *focus* will be on one aspect of the implicit culture, *cultural postulates,* verbally expressed clichés, assumptions and rationalizations. The following cultural postulates of the police orient our analysis of the devised strategies that are based upon them directly or indirectly:[49]

1. People cannot be trusted; they are dangerous.
2. Experience is better than abstract rules.
3. You must make people respect you.
4. Everyone hates a cop.
5. The legal system is untrustworthy; policemen make the best decisions about guilt or innocence.
6. People who are not controlled will break laws.
7. Policemen must appear respectable and be efficient.
8. Policemen can deter crime.
9. The major job of the policeman is to prevent crime and to enforce the laws.
10. Stronger punishment will deter criminals from repeating their errors.[50]

With this background we can now turn to problems of access and research in this milieu.

Negotiating Access to Police Organizations

Police research is alternatively dangerous and boring, frustrating and exciting, sympathy-producing and a source of antagonism, tense and funny, the source of several superior sociological studies and the demise of probably three times that number. It shares some of the problems of social research in general that are entailed by a shift from a "craft model" of social research to an *organizational model.*[51] This shift in the size and organizational complexity of research parallels changes in larger social structures to a more bureaucratically patterned mode of life. The craft model of social research involves the researcher and perhaps an apprentice in the research process from problem definition, research design, data gathering, and analysis through to publication. The typical relationships are dyadic, at both the level of research and training for research. The major research tools are the interview, the questionnaire, and observation. Form characterizes methods texts as "manuals on how the craftsman and his apprentice should gather data on personal or interpersonal behavior." In contrast, considerable recent work (since World War II) has been done by large-scale research bureaus or institutes sharing mutually financed large staffs of service people and facilities. Supporting agencies that provide grants often take an implicit or explicit hand in guiding the nature and type of research done. The organizational model is epitomized by the Institute for Survey Research at the University of Michigan, The National Opinion Research Center at the University of Chicago, and the Bureau of Applied Social Research at Columbia.

Police studies reflect this change in the relationship between research and the researched. The larger research operation encounters more problems regarding *sponsorship* and *legitimation, access* and *role definition.* Parenthetically, it is clear that the model for understanding these problems is the industrial research of the 1930s, but none of the writers mentioned in this article refers to the parallel problems experienced by men seeking access to factories during the period of labor strife and class conflict, which in every way was as tense and potentially explosive as the current era of status-race-age divisions.

The nature of the *sponsorship* obtained by researchers doubtless has an effect on the course of their studies. There are two aspects of sponsorship: the source of *funding,* and the source of *legitimation* within the organization. Most of the studies I have reviewed were connected with large, highly respected universities (M.I.T., University of California at Berkeley, University of Chicago, University of Michigan) and often with research units within them, for example, the Center for the Study of Law and Society at Berkeley, the Center for Research on Social Organization at the University of Michigan. Of the observational studies we are considering here, only two did *not* cite support money from grants: Banton and Buckner. Unfortunately, most of the studies do not provide information on the process of negotiating access to the supporting organization. Those that do imply that the development of the researcher-host organization relationship is almost aleatory.

Skolnick describes the way in which he almost drifted into his research role as a plain-clothes detective in the Westville department:

The study commenced with observation of the work of the public defender in the fall of 1962. . . . Approximately two hundred hours were spent in the office of the public defender.

After several months of such observations, I felt that I had not adequately experienced the law enforcement side of the criminal courts system. It became evident that interactions between the defense attorney and the accused, as individuals, were necessarily more infrequent than those between defense attorney and prosecutor. Thus, an appropriate vision of the system of processing of criminal cases places the prosecutor and the defense attorney at the top as spokesmen and interpreters for the real adversaries who are, on the one hand, the complainant, and on the other, the accused. Given this conception, it seemed necessary to see the system of criminal law processing from the law enforcement side.

By this time, I was fairly well known to several of the deputy district attorneys who had met me while I was looking over the shoulders of men on the public defender's staff. I suggested to the head of the public defender's office that I would like to see how "the other half" lived. Through his recommendation, plus an extended interview with the district attorney, I was permitted to become a participant-observer in that office. After several weeks of observation in the office of the Westville district attorney, it seemed important to know more about the work of the police. . . . I asked my "contacts" in the prosecutor's office if it would be possible to arrange observation of the police carrying out their duties.

The Chief of Police was willing to entertain the idea. It is again important to emphasize that this police department regarded itself as exemplary. . . .

The Chief assigned his aide, Lieutenant Doyle, to make introductions within the department. The Lieutenant was a genial man who had been on the force for almost twenty years, knew everybody, and was personally liked, as I later learned, throughout the department. We decided that the best place to begin the study was with the patrol division which, in Westville, has one-man vehicles and three ranks: supervising detective, sergeant, and patrolman.

I spent eight nights with these patrolmen, mostly on weekends, on the shift running from 7 p.m. to 3 a.m. All of this time was spent interviewing and observing, talking about the life of the policeman, and the work of the policeman. I understood my job was to gain some insight and understanding of the way the policeman views the world. I found that the most informative method was not to ask predetermined questions, but rather to question actions the policeman had just taken or failed to take, about events or objects just encountered, such as certain categories of people or places of the city. . . .

With the realization that law enforcement is not to be found in its most significant and interesting forms on the streets [italics added], I again consulted with Lieutenant Doyle (who was most helpful and considerate throughout the study). I felt that I ought to begin to study detective work, especially the work of the vice squad, but I also felt that I wanted to learn more about the policeman's use of legal authority in mundane and routine matters. . . .

. . . I decided to attempt to study that portion of it which seemed to me central to an understanding of the police as legal men, and perhaps also the most difficult to study: the working of the vice control squad.[52]

Skolnick apparently presented himself as a single researcher investigating a problem. His own legal interests probably assisted the ingratiation process, as did his willingness to participate in a wide range of police activities, for example, shooting on the pistol range, driving vans in raids, listening in on phone calls, and signing as a witness to a confession. The impact of Skolnick's observation on the behavior of the policemen he observed, like that of other unknown observers, was probably negligible, at least it is unmentioned in Skolnick's published works.

Large-scale studies, such as the one conducted by Reiss and reported in numerous publications by Black and Reiss, doubtless create more complex problems than did Skolnick's research. The impact of a study as large and systematic as Reiss's presents a threat not only to the patrolmen observed, but to the organization itself. Reiss wrote:

During the summer of 1966 I conducted a study of crime and law enforcement in major metropolitan areas. Among other things, we investigated police and citizen transactions in eight high crime rate areas of three major metropolitan areas of the United States.

Twelve observers and a supervisor were assigned to each of the cities. Each observer was assigned to an eight-hour watch in a police district six days a week for six to seven weeks. Within each district the watches and beats were sampled and observers rotated across beats. Within this period of time, 92 Negro and 608 white officers were observed at least once. There was a total of 212 eight-hour observation periods of Negro officers and 1,137 observation periods of white officers. The police were mobilized in 5,360 situations; in 3,826 of them they had an encounter with one or more citizens. Some information was gathered on 11,244 citizens who participated in the encounters.

The observers recorded only a minimum of information during the eight-hour period, merely keeping a log of encounters. Following the period of observation, an observation booklet was completed for each encounter of two or more minutes duration. There were four types of booklets depending on whether the mobilization situation was a dispatch, a mobilization by a citizen in a field setting, a police mobilization in a field setting (on-view), or a citizen mobilization in a precinct station. The observer was asked to answer 48 questions about the encounter (if applicable) either by checking a response or writing a descriptive account. They completed 5,360 booklets during the period of the study. In addition, they responded to 23 questions about the observation period itself and the general behavior and attitudes of the officer as they learned it through observation and interviewing during the watch period. There are 1,349 such reports.[53]

This study was sponsored and legitimated by the President's Crime Commission and Office of Law Enforcement Administration. It is unlikely that this study could have been accomplished without "high-powered" support and outside political influence.

The importance of the police norm of secrecy can hardly be exaggerated at this point. For even with access, there are often problems in obtaining data. Westley says, "The time consumed in just getting to the data is enormous." He continues:

The degree of rapport obtained had much to do with whether or not a question was pressed. This was of strategic importance because policemen are under explicit orders not to talk about police work with anyone outside the department; there is much in the nature of a secret society about the police; and past experience has indicated to policemen that to talk is to invite trouble from the press, the public, the administration and their colleagues. The result is that when they got the slightest suspicion that everything was not on an innocuous level they became exceedingly uncooperative and the rest of the men caught on in a hurry. As a matter of fact the principal obstacle in the research was to avoid being defined as a spy. This was more difficult than it seems since it sometimes required that one walk up to a policeman, amidst a hostile group, seeing fear in his eyes, and shake his hand (which he tries not to offer) and at the same time maintain an appearance of joviality and unconcern. The research required a continuous campaign of personal propaganda in order to meet repeated waves of suspicion and consequent lack of cooperation. This meant a constant search for ways to define oneself which would be acceptable. Some of the most successful were that of the man in trouble and the policeman's friend. Each definition seems to wear out in time, however, and a fresh one has to be constructed.[54]

Ironically, the paramilitary structure of the organization can be an asset to data gathering, particularly if it is of the standard questionnaire variety. As soon as administrative permission is granted, orders are issued to report and fill out the materials. The response rates of these studies tend to be very high. Police studies of this sort take on the zero-sum two-person game quality: one is either in possession of an almost complete population of a precinct or post, or one has nothing. The former was the case in a project where a student was able, through his father, a state patrolman, to obtain permission to survey a post and headquarters of a Midwestern state police headquarters.[55]

Bordua and Reiss discuss the research implications of the increasing centralization and bureaucratization of police operations:

For the first time in American History the emergence of a self-consciously professional police elite coupled with increasing its (though far from complete) success in tightening internal control over departmental operations provides the organizational conditions whereby not only public demands for efficiency and productivity, but also judicial demands for legality can be translated into operations. Developing professionalization of the police provides the necessary base for the application of sociology of law enforcement concerns. Perhaps even more appropriately put, it provides the base for carrying out the necessary sociological research which in the near future will be translatable into application.[56]

The introduction of professionally oriented, educated, and thoughtful police administrators was a necessary condition for the recent growth of sociological research.[57] The majority of studies we now possess were done in departments that policemen view as "professional": Oakland, San Francisco, Chicago, New York City, and Atlanta.[58]

Police studies demonstrate that police organizations are increasingly ribbed with conflict between blacks and whites, the staff and the line, between the younger and the older policemen, and between those at any level who are professionally oriented and those who are not. The Skolnick Report documents the extent of discontent within the ranks of the patrolmen. He notes that they see themselves as victims not only of social forces, which they view as a conspiracy, but also of the judiciary, lawyers, and the higher administrators, if they work in large departments.[59]

Research in an organization creates new knowledge of the organization itself, particularly of its various levels, and it soon becomes clear that the researcher (or the person in the organization who controls or deals with him) has potential power over other members of the organization. Secrecy and ignorance play an important part in a punishment-centered bureaucracy, while research raises threats to its power equilibrium. Consequently, the association of research with, and legitimization by, the professional segment of an organization is both an asset and a debit.

The police are involved intimately with many aspects of the criminal justice system, and their actions are, in a sense, publicly reviewed by lawyers and the courts. Bordua and Reiss comment on this fact:

Law enforcement is likewise intricately linked with a larger organizational system of criminal justice such that its output is an input into the criminal justice system where it is evaluated. Furthermore, it is directly linked to a municipal, county, or state organizational system that controls at least its budget, and also maintains a host of transactions with other municipal and community organizations in providing "police service." A police system thus engages in transactions not only with clients who are *citizens* demanding a service and with victims and their violators, but with a multiplicity of organizations where problems of service, its assessment, resource allocation, and jurisdiction are paramount.[60]

Buckner illustrates the extent to which the police are tied into reciprocal transactions with such community institutions as local businesses (especially restaurants), newspapers, sports arenas, and influential people.[61] As a general proposition, police research is threatening to the police organization in an environment of exchange and negotiation, an organization that provides one of the few points of loyalty and solidarity for the policeman:

In some cities in the Northern parts of the United States the police departments have been demoralized by political control, poor leadership, and low rates of pay. The life of many districts seems competitive and raw; individuals pursue their own ends with little regard for public morality, and the policemen see the ugly underside of outwardly respectable households and businesses. Small wonder, then, that many American policemen are cynics. . . . Couple this experience with the policeman's feeling that in his social life he is a pariah, scorned by the citizens who are more respectable but no more honest, and need it surprise no one that the patrolman's loyalties to his department and his colleagues are often stronger than those to the wider society.[62]

All these aspects of police organizations—secrecy, threat, paramilitary organization, morale problems; internal schisms, and politicalization— have created a police research situation in which the researcher is often best characterized as a "pussyfoot"—that is, he avoids telling the full aims of his research, avoids certain questions and persons, and constantly renegotiates roles.[63]

The more one probes the questions of power and the allocation of resources, issues that threaten the organization as a whole, the greater the problems of negotiating and maintaining access. It is to the credit of sociologists that they have attempted to study very central issues in police action: brutality, response to citizens' calls, budgetary processes, citizens' complaints, and the enforcement of morality.[64]

These questions of access also bear on the role definition the researcher offers at the initiation of his research. It is fundamental to distinguish the initial role definitions, or roles sent and roles received. Roles sent and received by the host organization need not be stable over time and, as a general rule, are not. Some of the more interesting research chronicles trace the emergence and demise of role relationships of the researcher and the researched.[65]

The placement of the observer within the social system he is observing is an important aspect of role definition vis-à-vis segments of the organization, the data he obtains, and his own view of the world. Buckner felt he began to see the world as a "cop," and apparently this concerned him, although his reasons are not articulated:

I began to perceive the world from a police point of view, seeing vehicle code violations while driving, watching for accidents and setting out flares when in my private car, knowing certain sections of the city only from their geography of crime and violence, immediately going to a call box when I heard a burglar alarm or saw a traffic hazard while in civilian clothes, noticing suspicious people who seemed out of place, noticing prostitutes and pimps, and thinking of the solution to many problems in police terms.[66]

Westley argues that the secretive nature of police organizations makes the role of outside observer very difficult to play.[67] Buckner, on the other hand, felt constrained by the limited view he was able to gather of the higher levels of the organization.[68] Skolnick thought that "law enforcement is not to be found in its most significant and interesting forms on the streets" and focused his attention on the enforcement of morals in the detective division.[69]

In summary, the more "craftlike" the research, the more the focus is on the procedural and the practical (as opposed to the moral and the ethical) aspects of the system operation, the greater the likelihood of gaining access to police organizations. This focus, practically speaking, is to the advantage of the professionalizing segment of the organization and increases the probability of lasting legitimation. These considerations, however, are *not* to be taken as a recipe for the necessary foci of research.

The Management of Research Inside Police Organizations

...researchers who study complex organizations become conscious of their behavior, conscious of their dependency on others, and conscious of how others define them. They must therefore carefully consider what tactics to adopt....[70]

The *tactical aspects of fieldwork* involve interpersonal relationships encountered in the course of the research. A large body of literature on the tactical aspects of managing field roles and interpersonal relationships exists, but, as Form points out, there is relatively little written on matters of politics, interorganizational relationships in which the researcher must move, and large-scale bureaucratic models of social research. Having considered some of the political and power issues above, we turn, in this section, to the interpersonal and interactional "problems" revealed in our studies.

Unfortunately for sociological research, fieldwork (or qualitative analysis) is often taken as synonymous with "soft" or "imprecise" work. In some respects, the "how to do it" aspects of fieldwork are much more carefully developed than the mechanics of large-scale social research— the manipulation of data from large projects, the use of statistical tables to create an argument, and so on.[71] The anthropological tradition provides carefully developed and sensitive orientation to fieldwork, which is otherwise unavailable to students of other modes of research.

There is a tendency for survey techniques and for observational techniques to be defined as polar opposites. It is true that as some researchers use the interview it is insensitive to phenomenological matters, but we have, in fact, little research that systematically compares interview and other sorts of data. However, we have even less on the impact of observers, differences in results and interpretation as a function of role definition, modes of access, sponsorship, and so on. Matters of personal style, class differences, values of observers, simply have not been systematically tested.[72]

A contributing factor to polemics concerning the relative merit of different research techniques is the hesitancy of fieldworkers to develop precise measures and models, as sociologists Becker and Geer have attempted to do.[73] This leads to a continued caveat, or warning, prefacing virtually every field study that claims that the study is only exploratory, the conclusions are only tentative and are based on one case, and so forth. These statements are found in the studies at issue, as shown in the following randomly selected apologia.

In an exploratory study such as this, it is rarely possible to collect precise, numerical data sufficient to permit rigorous analysis. To answer the question of *what* is to be measured, or whether anything *can* be measured, is one reason for doing an exploratory study in the first place. The problem of evidence is not, however, solved by offering such excuses. Much of what is said in this book is asserted, or illustrated, or suggested, but not proved.[74]

Caveats grace the introductory remarks of all but a few of the police studies discussed in this article. Yet, as the bibliography shows, the number and types of these studies are rapidly reaching the state of a "critical mass," where such statements will be indefensible in light of the available information. In short, we have reached a position where more systematic and rigorous studies are needed, and this does not mean more or less quantitative, larger scale, or resembling to a greater degree the natural science–hypothesis-testing type of research. It means research that deals in depth with the social worlds of the participants in their own language and terms. Firsthand immersion in situations that are characteristic of the subjects' lives should result in systematic descriptions that integrate both the categories of social order and the situated management of meanings and are therefore recognizable to the participants. This can be accomplished through a variety of means, but our most fruitful model is that of observer(s), either active or passive, in day-to-day interaction with the empirical world studied. Since the nature of the empirical social world is built up, recognized, modified, constructed, and consistently indicated by people meeting the contingencies of everyday life, I can but suggest the most fruitful general principle of social research articulated by Herbert Blumer: *"Respect the nature of the empirical world and organize a methodological stance to reflect that respect"*[75] (italics added).

The tactical problems of police studies present us with actual attempts on the part of social researchers to understand the nature of the social reality that the police externalize, objectify, and internalize.[76] The tactical problems of these studies can be organized into three broad areas: *value confrontation,* which results from the interaction of social scientists and policemen; how to deal with the typical problematic scenes characteristic of the occupation to which the researcher must respond by *creating and maintaining a series of viable roles and identities;* and the impact on the researcher of *exposure to the dangerous aspects of police life* and the ideology that surrounds it.

The value system of the police has attracted considerable attention in the mass media. As suggested by the outline of police cultural postulates (above), the themes of life as dangerous and threatening, low self-esteem, men as evil, dishonest, cruel, and unfeeling, and themselves as victims of social conspiracy are very strong among the police and tend to increase with time.[77] The police, having been delegated the task of law enforcement, tend to dwell on those aspects of human life that undermine respect for the law and its enforcers. The police are, however, dependent for their existence on the thing they claim to wish to eliminate: crime and immorality. They come, consequently, to invest a part of themselves in the law. Law-breaking is no longer viewed as the result of random processes or mere ignorance but is taken to represent a thrust at the self of the enforcer. The policeman's respectability and honor are involved in the respect and honor the public confers on the law, and the policeman all too easily finds it operationally difficult to separate the two.

The role seems to attract men who are apparently deeply ambivalent about the law, politically conservative, perhaps reactionary, and persons of lower- or lower-middle-class origins with a high school or less education. The police attributes suggested by the brief listing of the postulates of the police culture—suspiciousness, fear, low self-esteem, and distrust of others—are almost diametrically opposed to the usual conception of the desirable democratic man. The exposure to danger, the social background of the policeman, the constant exposure to "life as a pornographic movie," low pay, low morale, and vulnerability to a repressive bureaucracy all combine to make the policeman susceptible to the appeals of political groups and to act in accordance with political beliefs in carrying out the wide range of tasks that depend upon discretion.[78] The social scientist, on the other hand, tends to be politically liberal, of middle-class origins, highly educated, and intellectual as contrasted to "action-oriented."

Although sociology has historically been involved in opening up cross-class communication,[79] the kinds of problems encountered by researchers in police studies are only paralleled by problems of studying right-wing groups, end-of-the-world religionists, and so on. That is, the degree of value discrepancy is wide enough to be almost ever-constant, and both parties are aware of it to a considerable degree.

To the police, the social scientist doubtless represents the critical, carping public and the liberal fringe. Many of the recent protest and reform movements are identified with social science and adopt a social science rhetoric ("power structure," "the system," "the elite," "alienation"), which the police see as threatening to their own security and well-being. The tendency for the policeman is to look for extraordinary dress, demeanor, location, or appearance and to interpret them as signs of moral and legal differentiation—in a sense, all minorities are perceived as potential law breakers, and many are ideologically defined as "anti-cop," such as blacks, peace protesters, hippies, and radicals.[80]

Buckner perceived the extent of his own tension when confronting these differences in personal style, values, and ideology:

. . . becoming a participant and going along with whatever is done, as I feel is necessary to truly experience what is going on, will provide the observer with a massive, and extremely difficult to counter, value confrontation. It is very hard to stick to some abstract value conception in the face of firsthand, disconfirming reality. The observer's personal values and the values of the group he is observing are thus in constant tension until some resolution is reached; he finishes his study or he "goes native" accepting and supporting the values he is living and working with. Unless an observer is prepared to accept value relativism at an emotional level and to treat his own values as just another set of values "appropriate for some situations," long term participation in a group whose values diverge from his own will be an uncomfortable experience.[81]

Sociologist David Ward claims that it was a difficult experience to have his wife call him "Professor Fuzz" when he came home after observing policemen patrol. The police researcher is often caught between the "liberal" values of his occupational group, his family, and his students—his most significant reference points—and the opinions and attitudes of the policemen he is observing. This situation is a classic example of role conflict, and a variation of cognitive dissonance situations in which two sets of facts are in contradiction and a resolution is demanded.

The resolutions of such role dilemmas take interesting and instructive forms. Reiss, writing of the adaptations his observers took, found a pattern that I have detected in talking with and reading the work of sociologists in the police bag: they tend to become sympathetic to the police problem, almost to the extent of becoming police apologists. One sociologist who has become a popular speaker at police training and educational conventions and at sociological seminars and meetings claims he has two speeches: one, an "anti-police" speech that he delivers to policemen, and the other, a "pro-police" speech that he delivers to his sociological colleagues.

This is one resolution of role conflict—the segregation of audiences and messages. In his research, using carefully selected observers from law, police administration, and the social sciences, Reiss found an instructive pattern of adjustment. As we have argued above, observation requires playing not one role, but many roles, and it is simply a truism to state that these performances will in some ways reflect past socialization. Reiss explicates his strategy for selecting observers and training them to take the plain-clothes detective role (without the functions):

The "fit" between observer role and plainclothesman posed problems both for officers and observers in police and citizen transactions. In our study, it was clear that as observers became sophisticated in the problems of the patrol officer, their potential for "going native" or having officers "thrust" the requirements of the role upon them increased. Indeed, situations occurred all too frequently that served to define and solidify the role of the observer as detective. . . .

As in the study of interviewer effects, we discovered that prior socialization does have an effect on some kinds of data but by no means on all observations. Those with legal background reported more fully and seemingly more accurately on legal matters, social scientists more readily judged the social class position of the citizen, and so on. Generally, these are predictable differences. Yet, in the aggregate, these were not differences in kind but differences in the amount of error introduced into the observation.[82]

Describing one of the only systematic attempts to assess differences in observations and the effects of the observational experience, Reiss continues:

What happened to their original perspectives through the experience of being an observer? They all changed and in the same direction, becoming somewhat more "pro-police." But the change according to original perspective is particularly interesting, since they did not become pro-police in the same way.

The social scientists, among them sociologists, had a beautiful sociological resolution of such role conflict as they experienced in becoming pro-police. Who are the police? They are the "poor men caught in the bad system," human beings like everyone else, some good, some bad, but on the whole really reasonable nice human beings. The job makes them what they are. Why? Well, in part because the environment they deal with makes it hard to be otherwise and more so because police departments make them that way. Now that is an obvious sociological argument that makes sense. It says that roles and organizations make people what they are. Incidentally, and very importantly, their experience made the observers what they were then, and I suspect still are. Participant observation can be socialization with a sociological vengeance.

Because of their association with sociologists as supervisors, some of the observers with training in the law also came to see the problem as poor men caught in a bad organizational system. More importantly, they began to see the law and the legal system not only as malfunctioning, but as lacking in relevance for the problems of police and citizens. They probably never will be students of the law in the same way again. Unlike sociologists who were observers, those from the law responded as would-be-reformers.

The police officers changed least of all in their attitudes toward policing but, with one exception, developed a social science perspective. One of our police officers, from a major eastern city, expressed it clearly by saying that he saw all these things from a new perspective—these questions had never occurred to him. He became more objective and began to see things in broader outlines. The role of investigator had changed him into a man who not only saw, but raised questions. He also, by the way, became invaluable in getting information that was hard to get. He played an "undercover role" with less conflict. And why not? He had been socialized to do so.

Interestingly, the graduates of police administration programs became more pro-police. They were less likely to take the textbook view of their more liberal professors and of top police administrators of the modern school, whom they now regarded as too far from the line. They no longer were part of the "empty holster" cadre. They knew.[83]

It is imperative, I think, in situations involving major values clashes that are understood by both parties (for example, studies of criminals, policemen, and "deviant groups," where the observer is known) to differentiate your roles from those of the "normal participant." This makes you a "limbo member" of the group. Polsky, in the essay referred to earlier, makes an important point in regard to this value conflict, and provides several rules for the study of the deviant that are equally valid for police studies:

If you establish acquaintance with a criminal on some basis of common interest, then, just as soon as possible, let him know of the differences between you if he hasn't guessed them already. [This differentiation of roles and interests may lead to some mutual exchanges of pleas for justification, explanations of "why" things are done, and insights into the meanings of the differences in roles. However, Polsky cautions in an oral interpretation: one should not do favors for criminals; they may expect to be repaid. Repayment may implicate the researcher in immoral, illegal acts, which he would otherwise avoid.]

.   .   .

... it is important to realize that he will be studying you, and let him study you. . . . He has got to define you satisfactorily to himself and his colleagues if you are to get anywhere, and answering his questions frankly helps this process along.

. . .

You must draw the line, to yourself and to the criminal. . . . You need to decide beforehand, as much as possible, where you wish to draw the line, because it is wise to make your position on this known to informants rather early in the game. [This is in reference to observing criminal acts, but the police observer has some parallel moral and scientific problems if he wishes to keep his roles straight and if he has strong ethical commitments against assisting the police. This is discussed below.]

. . .

Letting criminals know where you draw the line of course depends on knowing this yourself.

. . .

Although I have insisted that in studying criminals you mustn't be a "spy," mustn't pretend to be "one of them," it is equally important that you don't stick out like a sore thumb in the criminal's natural environment. . . . In other words, you must walk a tightrope between "openness" on the one hand and "disguise" on the other, whose balancing point is determined anew in each investigation. [This is discussed by Reiss and Skolnick above, and is further discussed in the section on ethics.][84]

The marginality and conflict of policemen and their observers introduces the second theme, that of building viable roles. The observer of any social group, if he is known to take the observer role, and it is most assuredly a role, places himself in the unusual position of being a *stranger*. The scientist in general, of course, plays a stranger-role because he suspends his usual system of personal relevances as well as suspending the personal relevances of those he observes or analyzes. Recall the parallels between the scientist and the cartographer in comparison with the attitudes and actions of the native city dweller. The stranger can be objective. Objective rationality is rare in social life and therefore suspect. This suspicion, which accompanies the stranger-role, means that the usual assumptions that people are "like me" and typical of others in this group are questioned: the observer's loyalty and trustworthiness are at issue.[85]

The problems of "strangeness" are most salient in the early stages of fieldwork, where the oddness of the presence of observers is most unlikely to have been integrated, normalized, and accounted for by the system of everyday assumptions. This suggests that observation is a process of *role-building*. Olesen and Whittaker use a framework derived from this insight in their study of nursing students' socialization. Of particular interest are their three final stages of role-making or building: "proffering and inviting," "selecting and modifying," and "stabilizing and sustaining."[86] (The first stage, "surface encounter," is described in Schutz's essay "The Stranger.") These micro-organizational aspects of social research are an outgrowth of the work of Goffman and others, and are nicely captured by Lofland's notion of role management:

Adopting the perspective of someone, some place in particular, behind a role label, the world stretches before him in terms of the immediate present, in terms of the day, and perhaps in terms of weeks and months. First and foremost, reality extends before him in terms of the immediate present and the current day. From behind that label a course of events must be constructed; other persons hiding behind other labels must be dealt with and *managed;* an orderly flow of activity must be negotiated.[87]

The notion of a fragile, processual, social order that is constantly being shaped, definod, and redefined as actors encounter and deal with the intersections of different definitions of social reality lies at the base of such a view of social research. In the stage of proffering and inviting, the system of relevances of the host group, in particular the fit between life roles (age, sex, nonoccupational identities), becomes important. For example, the police culture is essentially a masculine culture with emphasis on virility, toughness, masculinity, and masculine interests such as sexual triumphs, sports, outdoor life, and so forth. (The overlap here with lower-class cultural themes is clear.) The researcher, if known and a male, will doubtless be called upon to pass certain "masculinity tests" in the proffering and inviting stage.

David Bordua, in a public address, humorously recounted his own experiences.[88] While doing observation, Bordua normally rode in the back of the patrol car and followed the patrolmen in to investigate a situation. On one occasion, while investigating a complaint, Bordua found himself leading the two policemen with whom he had been riding up a narrow, winding, and dark staircase. Although the order of march in leaving the car had seen the sociologist at the rear (where he definitely preferred to be), the policemen had arranged it so that Bordua was leading.

Similar testing goes on with rookie policemen. Bordua recounted an incident in a black bar in a lower-class area, where a tall, heavy-set black sergeant had arranged for a rookie to precede him on a "premises check" (a walk through a bar to establish that no gambling or illegal activities were going on and, not unimportantly, to establish the presence of the police in the area). As the rookie moved through a narrow aisle, a "drunk" lurched into his path. Every eye attended the scene, awaiting the outcome of this test. The rookie firmly grabbed the man's arm, moved him in front of himself, and sent him on to rest against the bar. As Bordua describes it, it was an act of skill and grace and established the young man as a potentially "good cop," able to handle himself in a spot without the use of violence or threats. These are risk-taking situations, and most middle-class people prefer to encounter such situations water-skiing or playing cards, where the personal risk is relatively low. They are part of police observation and an intimate part of police life.

This suggests that roles are offered and responded to constantly, and that situations always have definitive properties for members. The question of motives may arise as a result. Why are you doing this anyway? Polsky[89] recounts that criminals assumed he was a "crime buff" or that he had a vicarious interest in crime; other investigators have found that their interest in homosexuality led to imputations by informants that they were "really queer," or "closet queers," unwilling to admit to their true motives. The identity question is always salient in fieldwork (Who am I? Who are they? Why am I here?), and the observed recognize this as well. (I have wondered at my own interest in questions that always seem to involve authority figures and power questions—my research on physicians' political ideology, the police, and deviance in general.) The proffered role may be useful as a fictive device for establishing rapport. Reiss found that his observers were continually being forced into the role of plain-clothes man, as did Skolnick, who *became* a detective, for all practical purposes. Skolnick writes:

I spent six weeks, however, directly observing the vice control squad. In addition, four weeks were spent with the burglary squad and two with robbery and homicide to compare the detective's work where there is typically a citizen complainant. Weeks of intensive observation were spaced over a period of fifteen months, during which time I would drop in at least one or two afternoons a week to keep up acquaintances. I also spent one month in the summer of 1963 studying the La Loma district attorney's office. This is the office to which felony defendants are bound over after a preliminary hearing in Westville. Thus, during three months as participant-observer in the local and county offices of the prosecutor, I frequently came into contact with police.

Under direct observation, detectives were cooperative. They soon gave permission to listen in to telephone calls, allowed me to join in conversations with informants, and to observe interrogations. In addition, they called me at home when an important development in a case was anticipated. Whenever we went out on a raid, I was a detective so far as any outsider could see. Although my appearance does not conform to the stereotype of the policeman, this proved to be an advantage since I could sometimes aid the police in carrying out some of their duties. For example, I could walk into a bar looking for a dangerous armed robber who was reportedly there without undergoing much danger myself, since I would not be recognized as a policeman. Similarly, I could drive a disguised truck up to a building, with a couple of policemen hidden in the rear, without the lookout recognizing me.

At the same time, I looked enough like a policeman when among a group of detectives in a raid for suspects to take me for a detective. (It twice happened that policemen from other local departments, who recognized that I was not a member of the Westville force, assumed I was a federal agent.) Even though I posed as a detective, however, I never carried a gun, although I did take pistol training on the police range. As a matter of achieving rapport with the police, I felt that such participation was required. Since I was not interested in getting standard answers to standard questions, I needed to be on the scene to observe their behavior and attitudes expressed on actual assignments.[90]

Skolnick apparently was able to select and modify his roles to fit his interests and those of the observed. This led to stability in the role system. Very little else is written about these interpersonal negotiations in fieldwork on police. It is needed.

The power relationship in fieldwork places the worker in a dependent position vis-à-vis his informants, and he must attempt to exchange valuables to retain interest, sympathy and cooperation. One of these valuables is simple self-esteem, which flows from being interviewed or observed. The ways in which the observer justifies his use and invasion of the lives of his informants tend to take the form of "rhetorics of justification." Science and scientific work are a very useful rhetoric these days, as is the claim to present an objective account of the police problem to the citizens.

It is important to keep in mind that any stability in a role relationship is in a sense "bought" through continual exchange and reciprocity between the observer and the observed.[91] This is speaking both generally and specifically. For example, several investigators have reported that the police asked them to assist in arrests, for example, putting on handcuffs, monitoring a radio message, holding a suspect with a nightstick, or verifying a description of field encounters as an "objective observer." (These are further discussed below.) A special class of reciprocity is involved in the observation of police "errors."[92] At times, police observers are placed in a quandary as a result of their observations of violations of departmental regulations or of statutes. One observer in a large Midwestern police department observed such violations (brutality) and was uncertain, since he knew the patrolman knew he had observed the incident, whether to turn the man in and thereby possibly destroy the study or "clam up" and gain the trust of those he observed. Given the possibility that other events might raise questions about his presence, the sociologist also thought that this bit of information might give him leverage later. His decision was not to report the incident to headquarters. On the other hand, a student in this same project who observed policemen harassing blacks in an inner city area and indignantly reported the event was banned from further observation. (The policemen were temporarily suspended.) These are clearly moral decisions for the observer. This is a salient problem, given the uncertainty of police work and the great discretion allowed the patrolman. According to Buckner, even recording information in the small field diary he carried raised the hackles of his partner:

The sole feedback of a negative sort which I had was that one officer mentioned that some of the men were worried about me because I was over-educated and wrote down everything in my notebook, unlike many Reserve Officers. I handed him my notebook to let him see that all I wrote down were the details of each incident, which officers are required to do by department policy anyway. I told him to tell anybody who was worried that they could look at anything I wrote at any time they wanted, I had nothing to hide. This was literally true as I kept any private notes at home and did not carry them with me.[93]

A more important question than whether there is a reaction to the presence of the observer (the "reactivity effect") is whether there is an effect on the scene itself—Is a "watched cop" the same as one operating only with a partner? Or put another way, what stabilizes a role relationship? None of the observers mention specifically any effect of their presence, nor do they speculate about the question—that is, ask what might have been. Skolnick, however, felt his presence was normalized by those he observed, once the observer-observed role relationship had stabilized sufficiently:

One problem that this sort of research approach raises is whether an observer's presence alters the normal behavior of the police. There is no certain control for this problem, but I believe the following assumptions are reasonable. First, the more time the observer spends with subjects, the more used to his presence they become. Second, participant-observation offers the subject less opportunity to dissimulate than he would have in answering a questionnaire, even if he were consciously telling the truth in response to standardized questions. Third, in many situations involving police, they are hardly free to alter behavior, as, for example, when a policeman kicks in a door on a narcotics raid.

Finally, if an observer's presence does alter police behavior, I believe it can be assumed that it does so only in one direction. I can see no reason why police would, for example, behave *more* harshly to a prisoner in the presence of an observer than in his absence. Nor can I imagine why police would attempt to deceive a prisoner in an interrogation to a greater degree than customary. Thus, a conservative interpretation of the materials that follow would hold that these are based upon observations of a top police department behaving at its best. However, I personally believe that while I was not exposed to the "worst," whatever that may mean, most of what I saw was necessarily typical of the ordinary behavior of patrolmen and detectives, necessarily, because over a long period of time, organizational controls are far more pertinent to policemen than the vague presence of an observer whom they have come to know, and who frequently exercises "drop-in" privileges.

If a sociologist rides with police for a day or two he may be given what they call the "whitewash tour." As he becomes part of the scene, however, he comes to be seen less as an agent of control than as an accomplice.[94]

There seems to be some consensus in the work reviewed for this article that the process of role negotiation can lead to a satisfactory research relationship.

Danger is a part of a fair number of occupations, but only in a few does it occupy a significant part of the occupational "line" or public ideology.[95] Being a policeman is one of these occupations. The police possess what might be called a "threat-danger-hero" notion of their everyday lives.[96] The structure of rewards within police departments is very conducive to this ideology. Violent or dramatic public action— either in solving or preventing a crime, shooting a man, or aggressively patrolling traffic—is a source of promotion to the Detective Bureau, a way to "get out of the bag."[97] In fact, much of police work is boring or involves frustrating, contentious hassles with citizens. The dangerous activities represent considerably less than 10 percent of police patrol time, and less than 1 percent of citizen-initiated complaints concern violent or dramatic crime (rape, murder, assault).[98] This may only be another way of saying that the highly unpredictable, but potentially possible, dangerous scene is always a part of police patrol operations.[99]

There are, nevertheless, considerations of personal safety for field-workers. Donald Roy, in the preface to an article on union-organizing tactics in the South in a volume dedicated to Everett C. Hughes, makes the ironic observation that fieldwork can be "both fun and safe."

I do not think it too farfetched to claim that Everett Hughes must share responsibility for my inquiry on Southern labor union matters, of which this offering represents a portion. Many years ago, in a course on methods of field research, he taught us that it was fun to sally forth with pencil and notebooks, like newspaper reporters, to observe and to question. I assisted with this course for a time, and learned along with those who took the adventure for credit. We infiltrated an area surrounding the University of Chicago, in team pairs and by task assignments, for reconnoitering, interviewing, and question-nairing. In last-minute reassurance, before his neophytes hit the streets and alleys, our smiling mentor would advise, "My phone number is in the book. If you run into trouble, and need bail, give me a ring—day or night." Thus we learned that field investigation was both fun and safe.

Just the other night, perched on a retaining wall across the street from an entrance to a textile mill, I watched a moving oval of picketing workers and college students attempt to dissuade nonstriking employees from entering the plant grounds to work the graveyard shift. At intervals carloads of incoming millhands would approach the picket line. As they drew up, indicating intent to cross, an otherwise impassive cordon of policemen would quickly form human chains to clear passageway. While a car nosed slowly through the reluctantly yielding mass, the picketers would cry "Scab! Scab! Scab!" in rhythmic uni-son; and often one of them would manage to advance upon an open car win-dow, before the driver could gun his motor for a fast breakaway, to hiss a parting epithet: "Dirty scab!" "Rotten scab!" or "Dirty, rotten scab!" It was a balmy spring night, with a Carolina moon glowing through the pines to give me enough light to pencil a few lines and to note that police cars and an oversize paddy wagon were parked nearby. Additional police cars and a spare paddy wagon cruised up and down the street to give me a secure, comforted feeling as I jotted down my observations. Field work was fun, indeed, and safe, too, as we had learned from Everett Hughes, so long ago.[100]

Accompanying the police in the role of observer places one on the "right side of the law," minimizing some of the dangers of which Roy speaks, but other risks are involved. Buckner once observed an in-credible high-speed chase. It began with a car running a stop sign, which activated the police to give chase. The police pursued the stop sign vio-lator through the city, breaking speed laws, ignoring stop signs, and end-ing with a crash that totaled the police car in which Buckner was riding. The chase was continued, it was later reported, by other police cars. The chased car was finally run off the road by police cars and smashed against a bridge abutment by one of the police cars. The driver was charged, after a brief fight, with: "Two counts of reckless driving, two counts of assault and battery with an automobile, six counts of run-ning a stop sign, and separate counts of trying to elude police, destroy-ing public property, speeding and drunken driving."[101] A police officer who read Buckner's thesis and made comments added:

I thoroughly enjoy that kind of challenge. In a way, it is right out of the old West. During such an event you are pressed to your limit. The exhilaration is unmatched. Such events are thoroughly discussed among officers. Exceptional police "hot chase" drivers are known in the department as "wheelmen."[102]

Other sociologists have described similar chases in tones of mixed feelings of fear and excitement.

There are other, perhaps less common, kinds of dangerous situations that are encountered in a day's work: what are euphemistically called "civil disturbances," but that may involve danger from wild shots (most of them from police guns), fights, crowds, and small collective outbursts at rock concerts or high schools. As mundane as it may seem, one of the most dangerous of police activities from the perspective of injury or death is "domestic disputes," or family brawls, for these often involve knives, hand guns, rifles, and other handy missiles.[103]

In summary, then, observing the police involves one in a secrecy-conscious, tightly organized bureaucracy, peopled by men who see the world as dangerous, isolating, and untrustworthy, and who see themselves as the last barrier between the citizen and total social decay. Police research presents some special problems of value conflict, role management, and danger. The structure of the tactics to be used in this type of research is affected by problems of access, research style, sponsorship, location, and perspective on the action.

The Ethics of Observation

A good study, therefore, will make somebody angry.[104]

This section is not a general discussion of the ethical issues in observational research. Several discussions are already available.[105] Rather, it is meant as an overview of certain persistent issues in social observation.

All social research is an enterprise that raises *moral* issues because it involves probing the collective paths along which people organize their lives. Since this probing also involves questions of power and authority, especially within social systems, field research raises *political* issues. Observing the law involves, at times, not observing it. Finally, since one of the obligations of social research is to reveal to other sociologists the ways in which people make their lives accountable to each other, this research raises *scientific* questions.

Intertwined with the initial question of how one constructs a scientific account are questions of *validity*—how accurate is the picture that one reports—and *reliability*—how well does the picture represent what others might find in other times, places, and settings.[106] The validity question has been suggested in the methodological comments of Skolnick and Buckner and is raised by most of the other sociologists whose work is discussed in this article. In any occupation, the problem of dissembling is encountered by the outside observer—that is, how do you know what and whom to believe? Police organizations are *secretive*, and other occupational studies tell us that people stand ready with various "team efforts" to avoid revealing too much of what is private and "backstage"[107] behavior and information.

Front management, dramatization, and concealing and revealing roles will occur even if rapport is established at the legitimation stage of the research. Others have asked about the "reactivity effect" (mentioned above), since it bears on validity. There are no simple answers or recipes for solving the validity problem in any situation involving a known observer.[108] Since the observer himself serves as a "measuring instrument," he defines himself situationally largely in terms of the demands of the interpersonal process. In the same way that the policeman has a part of himself lodged in the law, the observer has a considerable portion of himself invested in his data; his data are a part of himself. Writing up a field report is cathartic. It is like viewing a home movie in which one is the principal actor. Separating "data" from "self" becomes a matter of determining analytically the nature of the games in which the researcher and other participants are involved.[109]

Useful formulation of the criteria for establishing validity is suggested by Bittner. His article was based on a year's fieldwork in two large cities, eleven weeks of it in "skid-row work," and approximately a hundred interviews with policemen of all ranks. Bittner proposes a "recognizability" rule "borrowed" from anthropologists.

The formulations that will be proposed were discussed in these interviews. They were recognized by the respondents as elements of standard practice. The respondents' recognition was often accompanied by remarks indicating that they had never thought about things in this way and that they were not aware of how standardized police work was.[110]

Questions of reliability have seldom reared their threatening heads in police research. The caveat of "exploratory" is raised against such inquiries. It is perhaps weak to claim that there is substantial agreement among sociologists concerning the major points made in this review. Given the nature and scope of the studies discussed here— mostly careful ethnographies or descriptions of single types of organizations or problems—the usual reliability questions have little relevance. The information necessary for verification by others is often limited because sociologists conceal the names of the cities, policemen, and citizens involved in their studies. Wilson's *Varieties of Police Behavior* is one of the few studies in which the names of the cities involved are revealed. On the other hand, the cities are generally known by social researchers, and investigators are usually very willing to communicate privately with any other serious researcher about procedures and findings.

Some ethical issues are involved with these questions of scientific procedure. In order to protect their informants, sociologists often have to conceal the information necessary to ascertain usual notions of validity and reliability. A quick scan of other articles in this book will make the problems clear. These problems are most salient for students of criminal behavior, as Polsky and Yablonsky show; witnessing or knowing about a crime is a part of almost any deviant scene, and the sociologist has no legal protection. Some sociologists, Becker, Denzin, and Polsky,[111] have argued for a "philosophic calculus" in which the value of the scientific knowledge gained is weighed against the impact of the information on those studied. Who is benefited by such information? Any information on social life has potential discrediting effects; the functions of ignorance and secrecy in social life are well known.

The issue of overt (or known) versus covert (or unknown) observation further affects the shape of the moral questions. Whose privacy is invaded in what settings when playing what roles? What disruptive effects will the information have if it is gathered under conditions unknown to the observed? What information can ethically be concealed from those studied? For example, when one participates under the guise of science as a legitimating force, is it ever ethical to use the information for political purposes to discredit the organization and people whom you studied?[112] Under what conditions is it ethical?

Yablonsky feels that associations with deviants tend to encourage their deviancy by playing up their deviant roles, roles that, he claims, one should, in fact, be trying to reform.[113] Although I reject any association of reform or therapy with a scientific role in the same research project, Yablonsky's reasoning might have important implications. Does studying the police provide information, a basis for creating more efficient social control? Does improving the practice and theory of police departments serve a meta-scientific end—providing "the greatest good for the greatest number of people"?

There are at least two levels at which political issues can be explored: the *micro* and the *macro* levels. At the micro level, there are questions of legal liability in witnessing crimes (perhaps being asked to appear in court as an expert witness), and assisting the police in dangerous situations such as those discussed above—holding prisoners, handcuffing them, passing on radio messages, assisting officers in fights where their lives are in danger, and so forth. What guilty knowledge gained as a result of observation should be reported to superiors in the police department, to the public at large in "muckraking articles," or to colleagues only in professional meetings? Police expect help in these kinds of situations. They do not define you in a lasting fashion as an "outsider" (and help in time of stress may be a fairly universal human expectation). You may become friendly with many policemen. Again, the study of deviants supplies a parallel. Does one participate in their activities—drug use, minor theft, abortion, and so forth—in order to legitimate one's own role? There is no simple answer. An a priori decision about where to "draw the line" is urged by many people who are "involved" in dangerous or illegal activities as a result of their research. Not only would this assist the researcher in striking an "honest" research bargain, it would assist him in drawing "identity lines" limning his own social placement, expectations, and obligations.

The political issues at the macro level are almost patently obvious in these days of questioning the establishment and those who enforce the laws of the establishment. Most of the research listed here was sponsored by foundations or by the federal government through the National Institutes of Mental Health. However, the Omnibus Crime Control Bill and the legislation issuing from the President's Crime Control Commission's recommendations contain provisions for funding research in such areas as police handling of juveniles, riot control, and police training. Future investigators may consider taking money to study the police equivalent to taking money from the defense department for bolstering the war machine.

If research is undertaken on the police, regardless of sponsorship, political issues still remain. Does the observation, if it occurs, of brutality, harassment, incompetence, or malfeasance *obligate* the researcher to reveal it immediately to the policeman's superiors, or should he overlook them and pussyfoot in the interest of completing the study? Will a complete study have an even greater cumulative impact on the organization than revelation of instances of wrongdoing?

Radicals have argued, with their usual tendency to dichotomize the world, that any involvement with "the pigs" is prima facie evidence of one's loyalty to the establishment. However, attempts to reorganize police departments in the areas of police-community relations and interpersonal civility, to alter the reward structure and training and recruitment procedures, and to introduce social science knowledge are contributions to a more decent, democratic society.

Two further cautions. First, moral decisions about the focus and scope of research should distinguish between two broad types of research: the first type are those studies that might have an impact in creating more humane, civil police work, that protect the legal rights of the accused, or that assist municipal governments to construct systems of civil accountability for the police; the second type are studies that deal with improving or inventing ineffectual, but perhaps dehumanizing and tyrannizing, systems of scientific surveillance, wire-tapping, or computerized criminal banks or files on "suspects" (which include demonstrators protected by the First Amendment, juveniles who are suspicious, radicals, politically outspoken people, mentally ill people). Second, I see the police problem as more complex than a question of contradictory mandate or of inadequate resources or training. I hold little hope for the "professionalization" rhetoric. Ultimately, it is a political question *of reformulating the law* and bringing police organizations under democratic political control.[114]

Notes

I wish to thank H. Taylor Buckner, Nanette J. Davis, and Ned Polsky for their comments.

1. David Matza, *Becoming Deviant* (Englewood Cliffs, N.J.: Prentice-Hall, 1969).
2. Alfred Schutz, *Collected Papers, Vol. II: Studies in Social Theory,* ed. Arvid Brodersen (The Hague: Nijhoff, 1964), p. 66.
3. See, on this perspective, Howard S. Becker, "Whose Side Are We On?" *Social Problems,* 14 (Winter 1967), 239–247; and Ned Polsky, "Research Method, Morality, and Criminology," *Hustlers, Beats and Others* (paper ed.; New York: Anchor Books, 1968), pp. 109–143.
4. I have chronicled this plunge into deviance and its relationship to respectability in Peter K. Manning, *Theories and Research in Social Deviance* (forthcoming).
5. The place of evil in the sociology of deviance is treated in Peter K. Manning, *Explaining Deviance* (New York: Random House, forthcoming).
6. Jack D. Douglas, *The Social Meanings of Suicide* (Princeton, N.J.: Princeton University Press, 1967), and *American Social Order* (New York: Free Press, 1971), especially Chaps. 3 and 4.
7. Anthony Platt, *The Child Savers: The Invention of Delinquency* (Chicago: University of Chicago Press, 1969).
8. *Ibid.,* pp. 28–29.
9. See, for example, C. Wright Mills, "The Professional Ideology of Social Pathologists," in I. L. Horowitz (ed.), *Power, Politics and People: The Collected Writings of C. Wright Mills* (New York: Ballantine Books, 1963); and Roscoe Hinkle and Gisela Hinkle, *The Development of Modern Sociology* (New York: Random House, 1954).
10. C. Ray Jeffery, "The Historical Development of Criminology," in Hermann Mannheim (ed.), *Pioneers in Criminology* (Chicago: Quadrangle Books, 1966), p. 373.
11. *Ibid.,* pp. 364–394.

12. Donald Cressey, in his Foreword to Edwin H. Sutherland, *White Collar Crime* (paper ed.; New York: Holt, Rinehart and Winston, 1965), describes the need for an evaluation of official statistics:

> What is needed in effect, is a "sociology of crime reporting" which will explain, among other things, why we compile the statistics we do. The kinds and amounts of statistics compiled on crime are, in a very real sense, an index of social concern about crime. Why does a society report the crimes it reports, why does it overlook what it overlooks, and how does it go about deciding that it has, in fact, overlooked something?

13. Donald W. Ball, "Conventional Data and Unconventional Conduct" (unpublished paper presented to the Pacific Sociological Association, 1967), pp. 1 and 7.

14. Vilhelm Aubert, "White Collar Crime and Social Structure," *American Journal of Sociology,* 58 (November 1952), 263–271.

15. See Paul Tappan, "Who is the Criminal?" *American Sociological Review,* 12 (February 1947), 96–102; Sutherland, *op. cit.;* Torstein Sellin, *Cultural Conflict and Crime,* Social Science Research Council Bulletin 44 (1938); and Courtland Van Vechten, "Differential Case Mortality in Selected Jurisdictions," *American Sociological Review,* 7 (December 1942), 833–839. This general issue is discussed in every criminology text.

16. Jeffery, *op. cit.,* pp. 370–371.

17. Polsky, *op. cit.*

18. *Ibid.,* pp. 114–115.

19. A useful review is Leon Radzinowicz, *Ideology and Crime* (London: Heinmann, 1966).

20. See Howard S. Becker, *Outsiders* (New York: Free Press, 1963); Joseph Gusfield, *Symbolic Crusade* (Urbana: University of Illinois Press, 1963); Jerome Hall, *Theft, Law and Society,* 2nd ed. (Indianapolis: Bobbs-Merrill, 1952); Otto Kirchheimer, *Political Justice* (Princeton, N.J.: Princeton University Press, 1961); Swen Ranulf, *Moral Indignation and Middle Class Psychology* (New York: Schocken Books, 1964); and Max Reinstein (ed.), *Max Weber on Law in Economy and Society* (paper ed.; New York: Simon & Schuster, 1967).

21. See Selden Bacon, "The Early Development of the American Municipal Police" (unpublished Ph.D. dissertation, Yale University, 1939); Samuel Chapman, *The Police Heritage in England and America* (East Lansing: Michigan State University Press, 1963); Platt, *op. cit.;* Roy Lubove, *The Professional Altruist* (Cambridge, Mass.: Harvard University Press, 1965); and Charles Reith, *The Blind Eye of History* (Edinburgh: Oliver and Boyd, 1956) and *The Police Idea* (London: Oxford University Press, 1967).

22. Robert Boguslaw, *The New Utopians* (Englewood Cliffs, N.J.: Prentice-Hall, 1965); Jack D. Douglas (ed.), *Social Problems of Freedom and Tyranny in Modern Society* (New York: Random House, 1970); Jacques Ellul, *The Technological Society* (New York: Knopf, 1964); John K. Galbraith, *The New Industrial State* (Boston: Houghton Mifflin, 1967); and Herbert Marcuse, *One Dimensional Man* (Boston: Beacon Press, 1967).

23. Some of the better treatments of this approach are S. F. Nadel, *Foundations of Social Anthropology* (New York: Free Press, 1951); Buford Junker (ed.), *Fieldwork* (Chicago: University of Chicago Press, 1960); Hortense Powdermaker, *Stranger and Friend* (New York: Norton, 1966); John Lofland, *Analyzing Social Settings* (San Francisco: 1971); and Matza, *op. cit.*

24. The best treatment of problems of sampling and access in field studies of deviance is Howard S. Becker, "Practitioners of Vice and Crime," in R. W. Habenstein (ed.), *Pathways to Data* (Chicago: Aldine, 1970).

25. Polsky, *op. cit.*

26. Some notable examples are Polsky's unpublished work on criminals; Donald W. Ball, "An Abortion Clinic Ethnography," *Social Problems,* 14 (Winter 1967), 293–301; James M. Henslin, "Craps and Magic," *American Journal of Sociology,* 73 (November 1967), 316–330; Laud Humphreys, *The Tearoom Trade: Impersonal Sex in Public Places* (Chicago: Aldine, 1970); and the articles in this book, as well as other works by their authors.

27. Abraham Blumberg, *Criminal Justice* (Chicago: Quadrangle Books, 1967); David Sudnow, "Normal Crimes: Sociological Features of the Penal Code in a Public Defender's Office," *Social Problems,* 12 (Winter 1965), 255–276; and Jerome H. Skolnick, "Social Control in the Adversary System," *Journal of Conflict Resolution,* 40 (March 1967), 52–70.

28. Edward Green, *Judicial Attitudes in Sentencing* (New York: St. Martin's, 1961) and *Sentencing Practices* (London: MacMillan, 1963).

29. Nathan Goldman, "The Differential Selection of Juveniles for Court Appearance," National Council on Crime and Delinquency (New York, 1963); Aaron Cicourel, *The Social Organization of Juvenile Justice* (New York: Wiley, 1968); and Irving Piliavin and Scott Briar, "Police Encounters with Juveniles," *American Journal of Sociology,* 70 (September 1964), 206–214.

30. Kai T. Erikson, *Wayward Puritans* (New York: Wiley, 1066), pp. 14 ff.

31. E. M. Lemert, *Human Deviation: Social Problems and Social Control* (Englewood Cliffs, N.J.: Prentice-Hall, 1967), pp. 40–41.

32. See Thomas Kuhn, *The Structure of Scientific Revolutions* (Chicago: University of Chicago Press, 1962); and Warren Hagstrom, *The Scientific Community* (New York: Basic Books, 1965).

33. Several of these themes are developed in the Skolnick Report to the National Commission on the Causes and Prevention of Violence, published as: Jerome H. Skolnick (ed.), *The Politics of Protest* (paper ed., New York: Ballantine Books, 1969), especially Chap. VII, "The Police in Protest," pp. 241–292. See also the *Kerner Commission Report,* National Advisory Commission on Civil Disorders (Washington, D.C.: Government Printing Office, 1968).

34. See the Foreword to Nicholas Alex, *Black in Blue* (New York: Appleton-Century-Crofts, 1969). This is an interesting and unique study of the black police officer.

35. These ideas are based on concepts developed by Sherri Cavan in a forthcoming book on field methods, and Raymond Gold, "Roles in Sociological Field Observations," *Social Forces,* 36 (March 1958), 217–223.

36. Works on special kinds of policemen (the cynical policeman [Neiderhoffer] or the black policeman [Alex]), or special sorts of police problems (dealing with juveniles [Cicourel, Briar and Piliavin], or the mentally ill of slum dwellers [Bittner]), unpublished works (Bordua, Cummins, Ward), and legalistic studies (La Fave) are eliminated from detailed consideration.

37. The following section is based on Peter K. Manning, "The Police: Mandate, Strategy and Appearances," in Jack D. Douglas (ed.), *Crime and Justice in American Society* (Indianapolis: Bobbs-Merrill, 1971). The "basic"

262 PETER K. MANNING

literature in the area of police studies is cited therein, including a broader
range of materials than those cited in Table 2.

38. Everett C. Hughes, *Men and Their Work* (New York: Free Press, 1958),
especially Chap. 6, "License and Mandate," pp. 78–87.
39. James Q. Wilson, "The Police and Their Problems: A Theory," *Public
Policy*, 12 (1963), 189–216. While William A. Westley, "The Police: Law,
Custom and Morality," in Peter I. Rose (ed.), *The Study of Society* (New
York: Random House, 1967), p. 774, is the essential empirical examination
of the police, in my opinion Wilson's article is the essential theoretic
statement.
40. James Q. Wilson, "What Makes a Better Policeman?" quoted in *The
Police and the Rest of Us*, special issue of *Atlantic*, 223 (March 1969),
p. 131.
41. Westley, *op. cit.*
42. See John H. MacNamara's fine article on this problem "Uncertainties in
Police Work: The Relevance of Police Recruits' Backgrounds and Training,"
in David J. Bordua (ed.), *The Police: Six Sociological Essays* (New York:
Wiley, 1967), pp. 163–252.
43. See Kirchheimer, *op. cit.*; and George Vold, *Theoretical Criminology* (New
York: Oxford University Press, 1968); Manning, *Explaining Deviance;* and
Turk's excellent *Criminality and the Legal Order* (Chicago: Rand McNally,
1969). Richard Quinney, "Crime in Political Perspective," *The American
Behavioral Scientist*, 8 (December 1964), 21–22, develops this thesis very
well.
44. See Manning, "The Police . . ."
45. See A. J. Reiss and David J. Bordua, "Environment and Organization:
A Perspective on the Police," in Bordua (ed.), *op. cit.*, pp. 47 ff.
46. Manning, "The Police . . ."
47. Skolnick (ed.), *op. cit.*, establishes the discrepancy between the police
and their "clientele" on the causes of civil disorders, crime, and demon-
trations.
48. The notion of occupational culture is taken from the work of Hughes,
op. cit. In the following paragraphs, I have also drawn on the conceptual
distinctions of Clyde Kluckhohn, "The Study of Culture," in Rose (ed.),
op. cit., pp. 74–93. A full ethnography of the police has yet to be done.
Each of the recent works (see Note 50, below) has a rather specific
focus overlooking many of the interesting social psychological adjustments made both interpersonally and organizationally by the policeman.
Particularly absent are detailed proximal descriptions of the tactics used
by policemen in interaction with "suspects" and in their everyday round
of work. Marvin Cummins, of the University of Oregon, alerted me to the
importance of this dimension of the occupational life of policemen.
49. Some qualifications are needed. These tenets apply primarily to the
American policeman, to the patrolman in particular, and to the noncollege-
educated patrolman most specifically. They probably do not apply as well
to nonurban, state, and federal policemen, nor to administrative policemen, nor to minority members of police departments. They do typify the
most important symbolic police role, the man on the beat, the patrolman.
The homogeneity of these attitudes is as yet unknown (see Neiderhoffer,
op. cit.). But it is likely that most of them are shared by police administrators. It is only recently that some policemen have begun their police

work at the policy-making level rather than working their way up through the ranks.

50. These postulates have been derived from the work of Michael Banton, *The Policeman in the Community* (New York: Basic Books, 1964); the essays in Bordua (ed.), *op. cit.*, especially those by Reiss and Bordua, and MacNamara; Arthur Neiderhoffer, *Behind the Shield* (Garden City, N.Y.: Anchor Books, 1967); Skolnick; William A. Westley, "Violence and the Police," *American Journal of Sociology,* 59 (July 1953), 34–41; "Secrecy and the Police," *Social Forces,* 34 (March 1956), 254–257; and "The Police," in Rose (ed.), *op. cit.;* and James Q. Wilson, "The Police and Their Problems"; "Generational and Ethnic Differences Among Career Police Officers," *American Journal of Sociology,* 69 (March 1964), 522–528; and *Varieties of Police Behavior: The Management of Law and Order in Eight Communities* (Cambridge, Mass.: Harvard University Press, 1968). These references are, for the most part, not studies that focus on organizational or historical aspects of the police. Bordua (ed.), *op. cit.*, contains a useful bibliography, as does William Chambliss (ed.), *Crime and the Legal Process* (New York: McGraw-Hill, 1969), and Arthur Neiderhoffer and Abraham Blumberg (eds.), *The Ambivalent Force* (Waltham, Mass.: Ginn, 1970).

51. William H. Form, "The Sociology of Social Research," in Richard O'Toole (ed.), *The Organization and Management of Research* (Boston: Schenkman, 1970).

52. Jerome H. Skolnick, *Justice Without Trial* (New York: Wiley, 1966), pp. 31–34. This is a very important statement of methodological problems written with candor and insight. See also H. Taylor Buckner, "The Police: A Culture of a Social Control Agency" (unpublished Ph.D. dissertation, University of California, Berkeley, 1967), "Appendix: Methodology," pp. 465–488.

53. A. J. Reiss, "Stuff and Nonsense About Social Surveys and Observation," in Howard S. Becker *et al.* (eds.), *Institutions and the Person* (Chicago: Aldine, 1968), pp. 355–356. Reiss deals with many important similarities between surveys and observation and quite rightly minimizes the *intrinsic* differences between them.

54. William A. Westley, "The Police: A Study of Law, Custom and Morality" (unpublished Ph.D. dissertation, University of Chicago, 1951), pp. 30–31.

55. Robert Trojanowicz was thus able to gather data for "A Comparison of the Behavior Styles of Policemen and Social Workers" (unpublished Ph.D. dissertation, Michigan State University, 1969).

56. David J. Bordua and A. J. Reiss, "Law Enforcement," in P. Lazarsfeld, W. J. Sewell, and H. L. Wilensky (eds.), *The Uses of Sociology* (New York: Basic Books, 1967), p. 287. The implications of professionalization of the police for sociological research are not as clear to me as this statement implies. As the authors point out in detail, the barriers to professionalization are major and not likely to be rapidly dissolved; see especially pp. 289–290.

57. *Ibid.*, p. 275.

58. The exact meaning of "professional" in the context of the police has not satisfactorily been worked out. In "The Police" I conclude that it is not a useful concept. See Wilson, *Varieties of Police Behavior, op. cit.*, and "Police and Their Problems," *op. cit.;* Bordua and Reiss, *op. cit.;* and

David J. Bordua, "Police," *International Encyclopedia of Social Science*, pp. 174–181. *The Challenge of Crime,* Report of the President's Crime Commission (Washington, D.C.: Government Printing Office, 1967), chap. on the police; and *The Police,* Task Force Report (Washington, D.C.: Government Printing Office, 1967) also deal with the issue. The authors of *The Challenge of Crime* are more optimistic than the social scientists cited above, even though there is a considerable overlap between the authors of the report and the writers cited above. The Douglas volume *Crime and Justice* is a criticism of *The Challenge of Crime.*

59. Skolnick (ed.), *op. cit.,* pp. 258–268.

60. Bordua and Reiss, *op. cit.,* p. 291.

61. Buckner, *op. cit.,* pp. 117–127. This is not to say that there is a moral consensus as a result; cf. Banton, *op. cit.,* and John P. Clark, "The Isolation of the Police: A Comparison of the British and American Situations," in J. Scanzoni (ed.), *Readings in Social Problems* (Boston: Allyn and Bacon, 1967), pp. 384–410. See Niederhoffer, *op. cit.,* on the cynicism of American policemen.

62. Banton, *op. cit.,* pp. 169–170.

63. One police researcher told me he had developed a severe psychosomatic problem in the course of his study of a police department while trying to manage the complex grant monies, the various sponsors, federal and local, and avoiding being thrown out of the department for his research probing. He has since been thrown out. This pattern of avoidance led him to avoid any involvement in one of the major demonstrations in the city, hoping not to be caught in the middle of internal political forces in the department, particularly the scape-goating which followed the events.

64. This is contrary to Form's assertion that sociologists tend to deal with peripheral issues to avoid conflict with the power structure and legitimating members of host organizations. See Form, *op. cit.*

65. See the articles in Richard N. Adams and Jack Preiss (eds.), *Human Organization Research* (Homewood, Ill.: Dorsey Press, 1960); Phillip E. Hammond (ed.), *Sociologists at Work* (New York: Basic Books, 1964); Gideon Sjoberg (ed.), *Ethics, Politics, and Social Research* (Boston: Schenkman, 1967); and Arthur J. Vidich, Joseph Bensman, and Maurice R. Stein (eds.), *Reflections on Community Studies* (New York: Wiley, 1964). Form, *op. cit.,* suggests several role sets possible: social photographer or ethnographer, public relations expert, social engineer, teacher, scientist, and others. Given the paucity of information on the development and self-definition of police researchers, such a typology would be of little value.

66. Buckner, *op. cit.,* pp. 471–472.

67. Westley, "Violence," *op. cit.*

68. Buckner, *op. cit.,* pp. 480–483. Buckner reflects, I think, the feeling of the lower-level patrolman quite accurately.

69. Skolnick, *Justice Without Trial, op. cit.,* p. 33.

70. Form, *op. cit.*

71. See Reiss, in Becker *et al., op. cit.*

72. *Ibid.*

73. See Howard S. Becker, "Inference and Proof in Participant Observation," *American Sociological Review,* 23 (December 1958), 652–660; Howard S. Becker and Blanche Geer, "Participant Observation and Interviewing:

A Comparison," *Human Organization,* 16 (Fall 1957), 28–32; and Blanche Geer, "First Days in the Field," in Hammond (ed.), *op. cit.* These studies are reviewed in Peter K. Manning, "Problems in Interpreting Interview Data," *Sociology and Social Research,* 51 (April 1967), 203–216.

74. Wilson, *Varieties of Police Behavior,* p. 14. This is not an accusation leveled specifically at Wilson—the same statement could have been drawn from any of fifteen studies.

75. Herbert Blumer, *Symbolic Interactionism* (Englewood Cliffs, N.J.: Prentice-Hall, 1969), p. 60. This book is strongly recommended to students who wish to develop an understanding of the theoretical position that underlies most sociological field studies.

76. These terms are borrowed from Peter Berger, *The Sacred Canopy* (Garden City, N.Y.: Anchor Books, 1969), Chap. 1 and *passim.*

77. See the Appendix to Neiderhoffer, *op. cit.,* "The Study of Police Cynicism."

78. This paragraph is taken from Manning, "Police Trouble."

79. See David Riesman and Mark Benney, "The Sociology of the Interview," in David Riesman (ed.), *Abundance for What?* (Garden City, N.Y.: Anchor Books, 1964), pp. 492–513; and Manning, "Problems . . . ," *op. cit.*

80. This theme is developed in Skolnick, *op. cit.;* Piliavin and Briar, *op. cit.;* Carl Werthman and Irving Piliavin, in Bordua (ed.), *op. cit.,* and Paul Chevigny, *Police Power* (New York: Pantheon, 1969).

81. Buckner, *op. cit.,* p. 480.

82. Reiss, in Buckner *et al., op. cit.,* p. 362.

83. *Ibid.,* pp. 364–365.

84. Polsky, *op. cit.,* pp. 125–128.

85. Alfred Schutz summarizes this observational problem in his essay "The Stranger," in Schutz, *op. cit.,* pp. 91–105.

86. Virginia Olesen and E. Whittaker, "Role-Making in Participant Observation: Processes in the Researcher-Actor Relationship," *Human Organization,* 26 (Winter 1967), 273–281.

87. John Lofland, "Role Management: A Programmatic Statement," Working paper 30, Center for Research in Social Organization (University of Michigan, June 1967), p. 11.

88. David J. Bordua, in an address to the National Institute for Police-Community Relations (Michigan State University, May 20, 1969).

89. Polsky, *op. cit.* Also in paper presented to American Sociological Association, September 1969.

90. Skolnick, *Justice Without Trial, op. cit.,* pp. 35–36.

91. This is not an argument for the generality of the exchange notions of social organization. It is relevant where the basis for establishing the role relationship is labeled instrumental by both parties and where the observer is directly asking rights of intrusion.

92. This is a general problem, as Hughes, *op. cit.,* points out in the chapter "Mistakes at Work." It is made more difficult when the observer is also trained in the same occupation. Dorothy Douglas, an RN-sociologist, faced an extremely difficult moral problem whenever she observed "errors" in an emergency room (personal communication). John MacNamara (personal communication) also comments that the existence of secrets is always a part of the power structure of police organizations. People are likely to "save up" incidents, violations, and errors for strategic use against other parts of the organization or persons.

93. Buckner, *op. cit.*, pp. 477–478. See also, Skolnick, *Justice Without Trial, op. cit.*, p. 48.
94. Skolnick, *op. cit.*, pp. 36–37.
95. On the concept of an occupational "line," or ideology, see Manning, "Problems . . ."; and Oswald Hall, "The Informal Organization of Medical Practice" (unpublished Ph.D. dissertation, University of Chicago, 1944), quoted in Junker (ed.), *op. cit.*, p. 95.
96. To the policeman, these are considered the "core skills" of the occupation and the "characteristic professional acts." These concepts are found, respectively, in Harvey L. Smith, "Contingencies of Professional Differentiation," *American Journal of Sociology,* 63 (January 1958), 410–414; and Rue Bucher and Anselm Strauss, "Professions in Process," *American Journal of Sociology,* 66 (January 1961), 325–334. For an application of these concepts to medicine, especially in regard to associated political attitudes, see Peter K. Manning, "Occupational Types and Organized Medicine: Physicians' Attitudes Toward the American Medical Association" (unpublished Ph.D. dissertation, Duke University, 1966), especially Chap. 3. Although the image of the police and their own self-definition coincide on the danger involved in being a policeman, at least one study found that many other occupations are more dangerous. Policemen kill six times as many people as policemen are killed in the line of duty. In 1955, Gerald D. Robin, "Justifiable Homicide by Police Officers," *Journal of Criminal Law, Criminology and Police Science,* 54 (1963), 228–229, found that the rate of police fatalities on duty, including accidents, was 33 per 100,000, less than the rate for mining (94), agriculture (55), construction (76), and transportation (44). Between 1950 and 1960, an average of 240 persons were killed by "criminals." (Summary from Task Force Report, *op. cit.*, p. 189).
97. See MacNamara, in Bordua (ed.), *op. cit.*
98. Donald J. Black, "Police Encounters and Social Organization: An Observational Study" (unpublished Ph.D. dissertation, University of Michigan, 1968). See especially Tables 2 and 18 and discussion thereof. This is a report based on the same project that is discussed by Reiss, in Becker *et al., op. cit.*
99. The dangerous view of life may have become a self-fulfilling prophecy. Buckner, *op. cit.*, pp. 230–231, lists the astounding weapons he was required to carry:

> The authority of the uniform alone is not sufficient to control many situations which the police encounter, so the police officer is fitted out as a weapons system with a variety of weapons useful in various situations. An officer will routinely carry a .38 caliber revolver and spare ammunition, a 12 to 14 inch truncheon, club, or baton, a flashlight, handcuffs and key, call box key and a whistle, a notebook and pen, a citation book, an arrest book, possibly a two-way radio. In addition, he may carry a spare gun, a "come-along" or "bear's claw," brass knuckles, a blackjack, a confiscated switchblade knife, a palm sap, a canister of tear gas or a more potent chemical agent depending on his own preferences and the rule of his department. . . . My uniform, which does not include a radio or any additional weapons, weighs almost twenty pounds.
> In addition to these weapons which are carried on his person, his patrol car may well contain a shotgun loaded with four rounds of "00" buckshot (9 .32 caliber pellets per round), additional ammunition, a 26″ baton, a riot helmet, a small law library, copies of the department's regulations, forty to

fifty types of report forms, flares, blankets, first aid equipment, chalk, measuring tape, a two-way radio, red light and siren, and a "hot sheet" of stolen cars and license plates.

100. Donald Roy, "The Union-Organizing Campaign as a Problem of Social Distance: Three Crucial Dimensions of Affiliation-Disaffiliation," in Becker *et al., op. cit.,* pp. 49–50.

101. Buckner, *op. cit.,* pp. 208–209.

102. *Ibid.,* p. 210. Buckner comments on his admission that he enjoyed the chase and notes that ". . . every officer within range customarily joins in any high speed chase."

103. Morton Bard, speech delivered at Michigan State University (Spring 1968). This is generally acknowledged among police officers. They view family intervention as "dirty work."

104. Howard S. Becker, "Problems of Publication in Field Studies," in Vidich, Bensman, and Stein (eds.), *op. cit.,* p. 276.

105. See *ibid.,* pp. 267–284, for a general statement and useful bibliography; Lewis Yablonsky, "Experiences with the Criminal Community," A. W. Gouldner and S. M. Miller (eds.), *Applied Sociology* (New York: Free Press, 1965), pp. 55–73; Polsky, *op. cit.;* and the articles by Lee Rainwater, Theodore Mills, and John Seeley in *Social Problems,* 14 (Spring 1967). See also Norman K. Denzin, "On the Ethics of Disguised Observation," 502–504, and Kai T. Erikson's reply, 505–506, both in *Social Problems,* 15 (Spring 1968); Becker, in Habenstein, *op. cit.;* and Lewis Yablonsky, "On Crime, Violence, LSD and Legal Immunity for Social Scientists," *American Sociologist,* 3 (May 1968), 148–149.

106. See Ball, *op. cit.;* Becker, "Problems of Publication . . . ," *op. cit.;* and Polsky, *op. cit.*

107. These concepts are taken from Erving Goffman, *The Presentation of Self in Everyday Life* (Garden City, N.Y.: Anchor Books, 1959). This is a "field manual" for students embarking on observational research.

108. In many participant-observation studies, this reactivity effect has reached hilarious proportions. Leon Festinger, Henry W. Riecken, and Stanley Schacter's *When Prophecy Fails* (paper ed.; New York: Harper Torch Books, 1964) is based on a study of a group of people predicting the world's end. The group was essentially a construction of those who studied it, and during the course of the research, observers probably outnumbered participants at critical points. John F. Lofland, in his study *Doomsday Cult* (Englewood Cliffs, N.J.: Prentice-Hall, 1966), found one of the only converts to the cult that he was doing as a study of conversion. A fascinating fictional treatment that spoofs sociology and sociologists is Alison Lurie's *Imaginary Friends* (New York: Avon, 1968), which insightfully explores the tendency for sociologists to confuse their scientific reality with other people's reality and to confuse both with fantasy. Miss Lurie's books are "sociological" in the best sense of that word; that is, she artistically penetrates the complexity of social experience and reveals the relativity of reality, perspective, feeling, and meaning.

109. See Manning, "Problems . . . ," *op. cit.*

110. Egon Bittner, "The Police on Skid-Row: A Study in Peace-Keeping," *American Sociological Review,* 32 (October 1967), 699–715. This criterion is suggested by anthropologists; see Ward Goodenough, "Cultural Anthropology and Linguistics," in Dell Hymes (ed.), *Language in Culture and Society* (New York: Harper & Row, 1964).

111. Becker, "Problems of Publication . . . ," *op. cit.;* Denzin, *op. cit.;* and Polsky, *op. cit.*

112. One of the police observers cited in this chapter recently wrote an "exposé" of the department he observed in a popular men's magazine. Rumor has it that the department now refuses access to any social researchers. I do not think popular exposés are ethical in light of the usual "scientific research contracts" that legitimate sociologists' access for most of their studies of organizations.

113. Yablonsky, in Gouldner and Miller (eds.), *op. cit.* Polsky, *op. cit.,* attacks this assertion.

114. This issue is addressed in Manning, in Douglas (ed.), *op. cit.*

About the Authors

James T. Carey (Ph.D., University of Chicago) is an associate professor of sociology at the University of Illinois. He is the author of several articles on drugs, several on popular culture, and a book entitled *The College Drug Scene.*

Dorothy J. Douglas (Ph.D., University of California, Davis) is an assistant professor in the department of clinical medicine and health care at the University of Connecticut Health Center, with joint appointment in the department of sociology. Among the research reports she has co-authored are: "Who Will Treat the Poor?" and "Behind the Front: One Aspect of Data Validity."

Jack D. Douglas (Ph.D., Princeton University) is an associate professor of sociology at the University of California, San Diego. He is the author of *The Social Meanings of Suicide, American Social Order, Youth in Turmoil, The Sociology of Social Problems* and the editor of *Observations of Deviance, Freedom and Tyranny: Social Problems in a Technological Society, Deviance and Respectability, Crime and Justice in American Society,* and other books.

Charles S. Fisher (Ph.D., University of California, Berkeley) is an assistant professor of sociology at Brandeis University. He has written several articles on the sociology of science.

James M. Henslin (Ph.D., Washington University) is an assistant professor of sociology at Southern Illinois University. His books include *The Sociology of Sex: A Book of Original Studies* and *Down to Earth Sociology: Introductory Readings.*

John Irwin (Ph.D., University of California, Berkeley) is an associate professor of sociology at Sonoma State College. He is the author of the book *The Felon* and articles in various journals.

Peter K. Manning (Ph.D., Duke University) is an associate professor of sociology and psychiatry at Michigan State University. He is the editor of *Collective Behavior and Change* and author of the forthcoming book, *Explaining Deviance.*

Carol A. B. Warren (M.A., San Diego State College) is a research assistant at the University of California, San Diego. Her articles "Social Problems in a Changing Society" and "A Phenomenological Critique of Labeling Theory" will appear in forthcoming anthologies.

Martin S. Weinberg (Ph.D., Northwestern University) is an associate professor of sociology at Indiana University and senior sociologist at the Institute for Sex Research, Indiana University. He has co-authored (with Earl Rubington) *The Study of Social Problems* and (with Colin Williams) *Homosexuals and the Military: A Study of Less Than Honorable Discharge.*

Colin J. Williams (Ph.D., Rutgers University) is an assistant professor at Indiana–Purdue University at Indianapolis and research sociologist at the Institute for Sex Research, Indiana University. He has co-authored (with Martin Weinberg) *Homosexuals and the Military: A Study of Less Than Honorable Discharge.*